Form in Tonal Music

Music

AN INTRODUCTION TO ANALYSIS

DOUGLASS M. GREEN

Holt, Rinehart and Winston, Inc.

NEW YORK · CHICAGO · SAN FRANCISCO · TORONTO · LONDON

How all's to one thing wrought!

—*Gerard Manley Hopkins*

ON A PIECE OF MUSIC

Preface

The American college student, upon taking up the study of musical analysis, is often placed under an unnecessary hardship. When attempting to master the disciplines of harmony and counterpoint, he has traditionally been given help of a very specific nature. Before being required to construct phrases in the harmonic style of the nineteenth century, he learns step by step how to fashion chords, how to connect them, how to choose them. Before attempting to reproduce the style of a late sixteenth-century motet, he labors painstakingly through the five species, acquiring bit by bit the requisite skills. But on being led to the field of musical analysis, although much of the technique of the analyst is no less an acquired skill than that of the contrapuntist, he is virtually abandoned. The standard forms are explained, but as he starts to discover for himself the form of a given composition the student generally suffers from inadequate directions as to how to proceed.

From one point of view this book is much like its predecessors in that it attempts to acquaint the student with the standard forms of tonal music. More important, however, it begins to equip him with the necessary technique for achieving the real aim of the study of form and analysis: the ability to approach a piece of music unencumbered by *a priori* notions as to what characteristics it should or should not have, and to discover, it might be said in *innocence*, the structure of the music.

For the purpose of developing such a technique, many exercises have been devised and placed at frequent intervals throughout each chapter. The exercises have been arranged according to two plans, the instructor electing at the outset which of them the class is to follow. Plan A calls for the following scores, most of them easily and inexpensively obtainable in pocket editions:

1. Bach: *Four-part Chorales* (Nos. 1–131). Optional.
2. Bach: *Violin Concerto in E Major* (abbreviation: *VC*).
3. Bach: *Well-Tempered Clavier,* Vol. 1 (abbreviation: *WTC*).
4. Beethoven: *Piano Sonatas Nos. 1–12* (referred to by opus number).
5. Chopin: *Preludes, Op. 28* (abbreviation: *Prelude*).
6. Mozart: *The Magic Flute,* vocal score (abbreviation: *MF*).
7. Schubert: *The Winter Journey* (abbreviation: *WJ*).
8. Mozart: any late piano concerto (*K. 450* and upwards, except *K. 453* and *K. 482*).
9. Davison and Apel: *Historical Anthology of Music,* Vol. 2 (abbreviation: *HAM*). Optional.

If a broader scope of musical styles is desired, Plan B should be chosen. This calls for Charles Burkhart's *Anthology of Musical Forms* (New York: Holt, Rinehart, and Winston, 1964). Occasionally an exercise requires access to music not included in either Plan A or B. In this case a choice of a number of different compositions is given so that the student can work with music he already owns or in which he has a special interest.

In the Appendix will be found two suggested assignment schedules, Schedule I for courses meeting three times a week for one term, Schedule II for those meeting twice a week over a full school year. Due to the limited time allowed to Schedule I, it has been necessary to omit portions of Chapter 12 and all of Chapter 14. As most college music curricula include the study of fugue, invention, and chorale-prelude as part of the discipline of counterpoint, the student will not be totally lacking in acquaintance with these composition types. In addition, the instructor may have to exclude certain of the exercises. Schedule II covers the entire text and all the exercises. Should even more time be available than Schedule II assumes, additional projects in analysis can be devised by the instructor.

Among the many works to which I am indebted, specific mention should be made of the detailed treatises, now classics of the field, by Percy Goetschius, and of Felix Salzer's *Structural Hearing*. From the former I have borrowed much terminology and from the latter several important concepts. Although applied in a different way and, indeed, to different ends, the view of form as an interaction of *tonal structure* and *design* owes its origin to Dr. Salzer's book.

I should like to express my thanks to Leo Kraft of the music faculty of Queens College of the City University of New York for welcome criticism and helpful advice.

D. M. G.

August 1964

Contents

Form in Tonal Music

AN INTRODUCTION TO ANALYSIS

1

Introduction:
Form, Shape, and Genre

In discussing and writing about music, the word "form" is used quite frequently. The student must soon realize, however, that this word has more than one meaning. Before we can proceed to analyze a piece of music, we must distinguish between these meanings. Let us begin by considering three basic terms: genre, shape, and form.

1-1. MUSICAL GENRE

The collection of *Encyclopedia Britannica* articles by D. F. Tovey describing the aria, cantata, suite, symphonic poem, and so on, is entitled "The Forms of Music."[1] Bukofzer writes, ". . . the forms of the renaissance, such as the madrigal, the motet, the canzona, ricercar, the dance . . ."[2] Such categories of musical composition may be referred to as genres. Beethoven's *Op. 61* and Mendelssohn's *Op. 64* are identical in genre—both are violin concertos—but different in form. Mozart's *Rondo for Piano, K. 511,* and the *Agnus Dei* from his *Mass, K. 317,* are quite different in genre but happen to be similar in form. Example 1-1 illustrates a composition which is in genre an orchestral dance of the minuet type, and which constitutes part of an opera, another genre.

[1] New York: Meridian, 1956.
[2] *Music of the Baroque Era.* New York: Norton, 1947, p. 351.

1

Ex. 1-1. MOZART: *Don Giovanni*, Act I, Minuet

1-2. MUSICAL SHAPE

Listen to the Minuet from Mozart's *Don Giovanni* (Ex. 1-1). A melody with accompaniment is heard which gathers tension [measure (m.) 5], rises to a climax (m. 7), then comes to a close (m. 8). After a repetition of this passage, the melody continues at a somewhat higher pitch and is accompanied by a new figure in sixteenth notes. In m. 13 begins a rise toward a new melodic climax (m. 15) higher than that of the previous passage (m. 7). In the following bar, the second passage comes to a close. It is then repeated.

We have here a composition in which each of two adjacent passages is built on the principle of a curve, increasing in tension and rising in pitch to a point of climax, then quickly subsiding. The increased activity in the accompaniment of the second passage and the more highly placed melodic zenith combine to give the second passage a more intense quality than the first. The general impression that is made on the listener can be approximated in diagram by a pair of curving lines.

The Prelude to Wagner's *Lohengrin* begins with high, barely audible, sounds in the flutes and strings. Other instruments enter and the music becomes louder, fuller, and more complex until it reaches a great climax. It tapers off to a low point, then grows higher, softer, and simpler until it disappears in silence.

From the beginning of the prelude to its climax, tension is gradually increased in spite of a general descent in pitch from high to low. Crescendo, increased complexity of texture, fuller instrumentation, and greater rhythmic activity are the elements that have been used to bring about the climax in this case. The shape of the prelude might be graphically represented in this way:

The term "shape," when applied to music, refers to the surface contour of a piece and depends on the action and interaction of the qualities of tension and relaxation. These qualities can be influenced by any of a number of factors:

1. Rise and fall of melodic lines, particularly in outer voices
2. Rhythmic activity
3. Dynamics
4. Texture
5. Instrumentation
6. Relative amount and degree of consonance and dissonance

1-3. MUSICAL FORM

The two aspects of musical form are design and tonal structure.

Design

Let us turn our attention once more to Ex. 1-1. The composition is clearly in two parts due to the divisive nature of mm. 7 and 8. The repetition sign at the end of m. 8 is a clue to the location of the division, but does not determine it: The division would be equally strong without it.

Although they contain important differences, the melodies of the two parts run roughly parallel to each other. Rhythmically, they are almost identical and they each rise to a melodic zenith in corresponding places (mm. 7 and 15) and return to their starting points. Caesuras—light breaks in the flow of the music—are found in corresponding places (after every two bars) and each part comes to an emphatic close, or *cadence* (mm. 7–8; 15–16). Yet, the two halves are different. The melodic line itself, though almost similar rhythmically, follows a different contour during its first five bars, and the quarter- and eighth-note accompaniment of the first part is replaced in the second by sixteenth notes.

We have observed certain rhythmic similarities and differences, both in the melodic line and in the accompaniment. We have located parallelisms in the placement of the caesuras and cadences and in the location of melodic zeniths. The organization of these melodic and rhythmic factors makes up what is called the design of a composition. The design of other pieces may include such factors as changes of tempo, texture, and even of instrumentation.

> Design is the organization of those elements of music called melody, rhythm, cadences, timbre, texture, and tempo.

Tonal structure

> The harmonic organization of a piece is referred to as its tonal structure.

In the Minuet from *Don Giovanni* (Ex. 1-1) the harmony moves from a tonic chord (I) in m. 1 and cadences in m. 8 on the dominant (V). This V has been approached through a secondary dominant (mm. 5 and 7) and has thus been given prominence as a secondary tonic. Measure 9 begins with V_7 and cadences in the final bar on I.

$$\| : I \rightarrow V : \| \ \| : V_7 \rightarrow I : \|$$

At the first cadence (m. 8), there is a break in the flow of music. In spite of this cadence, however, the listener is not satisfied that the end of the piece has been reached. Surely there is more to come. Repetition of the eight bars does nothing to dispel the incomplete feeling they produce, but with the playing of the remaining eight bars the listener is satisfied. The final cadence (mm. 15–16) is completely conclusive, even though comparison shows that, except for a change in pitch, it is almost identical to the previous one. Why should the same cadence be conclusive at one pitch and not at another? Clearly because the first cadence, unlike the last, was not on the tonic chord. The harmony moves from I to V but returns in a cadence on I only at the end of the minuet. We have here, then, a single journey—a removal from home to a different point and return. We say that the tonal structure involves a single harmonic movement.

1-4. DESIGNATIONS AND CATEGORIES OF FORM

Form is an inclusive term which refers both to the design of a composition and to its tonal structure. In arriving at the form of Mozart's minuet, we must consider that the design is, as we have seen, in two parts while its tonal structure involves a single harmonic movement.

Since the tonal structure has not completed itself when the design has rounded off the first part, the listener expects a continuation. The second part fulfills this expectation, continuing and concluding the piece. The form, then, is one continuous movement divided into two parts. It is called a *continuous binary form*.

The designation "continuous binary" has meaning because it reveals something about both the tonal structure and the design of this minuet. Although it leaves much unsaid, it indicates enough to show that the piece is constructed, in some important respects, like a number of others. It belongs to a general category of musical forms, members of which appear often enough in music literature to warrant recognition as a group. Within the general category of continuous binary forms there are a number of distinct types, of which Mozart's minuet represents one.

Other forms appear often enough to be grouped into other formal categories. Frequently, however, disclosure of the tonal structure and design of a composition results in the discovery that the form is unlike that of other known compositions. Such pieces are said to have free, or more aptly, unique forms.

Our approach will be to consider those forms that occur frequently before directing our attention to the unique ones. But first it will be necessary to consider the smaller unit of music: the phrase, its parts, its development, and its combination with other phrases into larger units.

2

Harmonic Structure
of the Phrase

2-1. THE NATURE OF THE PHRASE

Although the phrase is the basic unit of music it almost eludes precise definition. Yet writers on music seem to agree that the phrase (1) exhibits some degree of completeness, and (2) comes to a point of relative repose.

Usually there is no problem in defining the phrase structure of folk songs, hymns, and other music of a popular nature, for each phrase comes but once to a point of repose (for example, *The Bluebells of Scotland*). If we listen again, however, to Mozart's Minuet from *Don Giovanni* (Ex. 1-1), we may note a number of pauses in the melodic line (mm. 2 and 4), a slight one in m. 6, and a very distinct one in m. 8. While all of these may be considered points of relative repose, only those in mm. 4 and 8 seem to appear as the completion of a musical thought. We might feel that mm. 1–4 comprise one phrase and mm. 5–8 another.

To pinpoint the exact reasons for this impression is difficult for it is likely that a variety of factors are at work here. Measures 1–2 may seem to be incomplete because of their shortness. Undoubtedly, brevity does play a part, but occasionally one does find two-measure phrases in other music, even when the tempo is faster than that of this minuet (for instance, Ex. 6-10). A more likely reason is to be found in the uneventful harmony of mm. 1–2, expressing only a tonic chord. Measures 3–4, introducing V_7 and a return to I, produce harmonic action, however simple. Measures 5–6 are harmonically active, it is true, but the caesura in the melodic line is too slight to halt its

6

steady upward rise before it reaches its climax in m. 7. Measures 5–8 comprise, then, a single phrase.

With these considerations in mind, we can approximate a definition of the phrase in the following terms:

> A phrase is the shortest passage of music which, having reached a point of relative repose, has expressed a more or less complete musical thought.

Each of the two essential characteristics of the phrase—its measure of completeness and its arrival at a point of repose—carries with it a further implication that can be of aid in phrase recognition.

Harmonic action

We have maintained that in all likelihood the chief reason for the incomplete impression given by mm. 1–2 of Ex. 1-1 is their harmonic inactivity. Examination of a large number of phrases reveals that the great majority exhibit a definite harmonic movement. It would seem, then, that harmonic action is a normal characteristic and is certainly responsible in part for the impression that in the phrase a musical event has taken place. Exceptional phrases dwelling on a single harmony are, of course, not lacking in music literature. In Chopin's *Preludes*, for instance, are several remarkable cases (*No. 3*, mm. 1–6; *No. 21*, mm. 17–24 and 25–32; *No. 24*, mm. 1–7 and 19–25). Here the rise and fall in the melodic line and its clear caesuras are enough to express the musical thought.

Relationship of consonance and dissonance

A dissonant chord strikes the ear as more active, more restless, than a consonant chord. It might be expected, then, that the final chord of a phrase—the point at which there is a certain feeling of rest—will be consonant. Examination of many phrases reveals that the great majority do end with a consonant triad. Nevertheless, phrases closing with a dissonant chord, especially a primary or secondary V_7, are not rare and occur in certain musical styles, such as the Wagnerian, rather frequently. Yet even here a feeling of relative repose can be present if there is a definite caesura. In addition, the final chord, though dissonant, is often noticeably less so than the chords immediately preceding it. (See Ex. 2-1.)

Ex. 2-1. WAGNER: *Tristan und Isolde,* Prelude

There is no infallible guide by which every phrase can with certainty be recognized. Much depends on the listener's own insight, and even experienced analysts may hold differing opinions. Occasionally passages occur that might be construed as part of a phrase, as one phrase, or as more than a phrase. Different theorists would almost certainly disagree, and it is doubtful if the composer himself would be able to decide, even if he cared. Such a case is Bach's exquisite *Come, Sweet Death,* in which several possibilities present themselves. The student need not be concerned, however, if he should come across certain passages that defy all attempts at division into a definite succession of phrases. Great writers of poetry and prose do not always follow the rules of grammar if by ignoring the rules they can express an idea more clearly or with greater power. Nor need great composers follow rules. If the student has learned to recognize and appreciate music which is systematic and precise, he will be in a better position to recognize and appreciate that which is not.

2-2. THE CADENCE

The immediate goal of the phrase is its cadence, the chords that bring it to a close. An important characteristic of any cadence is its degree of finality, expressed in terms of relative strength. The greater the conviction of conclusiveness exhibited by a cadence, the stronger that cadence is considered to be. There are a number of factors involved here.

Basic fifth relationship

If the roots are a fifth apart, the cadence is stronger when this interval is made apparent to the ear by placing both roots in the bass. In other words, a cadence will be strengthened if the final pair of chords, roots lying a fifth apart, are both used in fundamental position.

Position of root in final tonic

Root in top

If the phrase concludes with a tonic chord, it will be stronger if the root, rather than the third or fifth, appears in the uppermost voice of this chord.

Conclusion on a tonic chord

A cadence that ends on a tonic chord is stronger than one that does not. This is true even when this final tonic is a secondary tonic.

Presence of leading tone

The chief key-defining tendency note is the leading tone. If a phrase is to conclude on a tonic chord, the cadence in which a leading tone appears in the penultimate chord is stronger than one which lacks it. Therefore, the authentic cadence (V–I) is stronger than the plagal cadence (IV–I).

Masculine ending *– strong beat*

The masculine ending is a stronger form of cadence than the feminine ending; that is, if the final chord of the cadence falls on a stronger beat of the measure than does the penultimate chord, the cadence is stronger than when the reverse situation obtains.

2-3. CADENTIAL FORMULAS

Conclusive cadences   The various cadences, while exerting enough conviction of finality to bring a composition to a satisfactory close, are of very different relative strengths, and, of course, they appear as phrase endings throughout a composition, not only at its close. Any of the penultimate chords may be either a triad or seventh chord. Not infrequently, the composer mixes the major and minor modes within a single passage with the result that various alterations may occur (Ex. 2-2c and e). Example 2-2f is the result of a vestige of the Phrygian mode.

With Leading Tone	*Without Leading Tone*
(Authentic and related)	(Plagal and related)
V–I	IV–I
VII–I	(♭)VI–I
III–I	(♭)II–I

Ex. 2-2. Illustrations of some conclusive cadences

Example 2-3a shows a cadence that is often to be found in nineteenth-century music. Although on paper the penultimate chord appears to be III₆, the ear easily recognizes it as a variant of V (see Ex. 2-2b).

Ex. 2-3. Authentic cadence with substituted 6th

Composers of the twentieth century have regularly avoided the pure authentic or plagal cadence. The chief cadential practices of recent composers of tonal music can be grouped by procedure.

1. Addition or substitution of tones in the cadential chords

Ex. 2-4. PROKOFIEV: *Peter and the Wolf,* Triumphal March

2. Omission of tones in the cadential chords

Ex. 2-5. BARTÓK: *Quartet No. 2*, Finale

a: (IV$_6$?) I   ? (IV$_6$?)

    II$_4^6$ II$_4^6$ I

3. Contrivance of new penultimate chord made up of notes that resolve stepwise into the final tonic

Ex. 2-6. SCHOENBERG: *Variations on a Recitative for Organ*

4. Approach to final tonic by systematic descent or ascent of seconds, thirds, or fourths

Ex. 2-7.   HINDEMITH: *Das Marienleben* (revised), *No. 15*

Perfect and imperfect authentic cadences

When the V of the authentic cadence is in fundamental position and the root of the final I appears in both outer voices (as in Ex. 2-2a and Ex. 2-4), the cadence is considered perfect. Otherwise, it is imperfect. The strongest cadence is an authentic perfect cadence with masculine ending.

The full cadence (3 cadence chords)

When the authentic cadence is enlarged by preceding the V with another chord, we speak of a full cadence. The usual choice for the additional chord is II or IV; occasionally VI, III, or ♭II is substituted.

Cadential elaboration

The cadences in m. 7 and m. 15 of Ex. 1-1 are full cadences using the formula II_6–V–I. The student may note that no mention has been made of the I_4^6 which both times precedes the V. The reasoning behind the method of harmonic analysis employed here is that, since the I_4^6 is not heard as a I in its own right but as an ornamentation (two accented passing tones) of the V, only one real harmony, the dominant, has actually sounded. Indeed, the nomenclature I_4^6 is misleading, since it implies a tonic chord whereas the entire harmony is dominant. The I_4^6 merely delays for a moment the unqualified appearance of V. This delaying action is a method of elaborating the cadence.

Another commonly used elaboration of the full cadence involving a delay in the appearance of V is the connection of V with its preceding chord by means of chromatic passing notes (Ex. 2-8a).

Ex. 2-8. Illustrations of cadential elaboration

A delay may occur not in the appearance of V, but in the appearance of I. Example 2-8b shows how a delay by means of nonharmonic tones might take place. On paper the aggregation of tones on the first beat of m. 2 of that example looks like a IV_4^6 chord, but, because of the bass note, the listener hears this as a delayed I. The implication here of an intervening IV can be openly manifested (Ex. 2-8c). It is this elaboration of the authentic cadence that Wagner employs on a large scale in the final bars (m. 25 ff from end) of *Tristan und Isolde*.

From these examples we conclude that a cadential progression is elaborated by delaying one or more of its chords through the introduction of nonharmonic tones which comprise in themselves an intervening chord.

The semicadence

The semicadence is one which can close a phrase within a composition but is not conclusive. It can take various forms, the most common being one in which the chord progression ends with the V. Other types of semicadence occasionally appear, however, such as that which ends with IV or I in first inversion. The *deceptive cadence*, in which the V is followed not by the expected I but by some other chord, often VI, is actually no more than a type of semicadence.[1]

Ex. 2-9. Semicadences

2-4. SPECIAL TREATMENT OF THE CADENCE

The various phrases within a good composition do not give the impression of having been baldly juxtaposed with obvious gaps between them. Rather, the composer treats the cadences in ways designed to create a certain continuity throughout a number of phrases. These means can be grouped into several categories.

Continued rhythmic movement in the accompaniment

A simple and extremely common method of linking two phrases is to provide rhythmic motion in the accompaniment. Example 1-1 illustrates this method (mm. 4 and 12).

---

[1] In this book a chord with a secondary function is represented by a diagonal line: Thus, V_7/IV (read "V_7 of IV") indicates that the chord is a secondary dominant in relation to the subdominant.

Continuation of the melodic line

2. The motion linking the two phrases might take place in the main melodic line itself.

Ex. 2-10.   HINDEMITH: *Quintet, Op. 24 No. 2, Waltz*

© Copyright 1922, B. Schott's Soehne, Mainz. Reprinted by permission of the original copyright owner and Associated Music Publishers, Inc., New York.

Elision of the cadence

Ex. 2-11.   BIZET: *Carmen*, Second Entr'acte

In Ex. 2-11, Bizet achieves a particularly smooth effect by causing the cadence of one phrase to occur simultaneously with the beginning of the next. In such cases, which occur frequently, we speak of elision, or the elided cadence. (See also Beethoven's *Symphony No. 8*, First Movement, mm. 11–12.)

Overlapping

Ex. 2-12. WOLF: *Gebet, Mörike-lieder No. 28*

In Ex. 2-12, the new phrase begins in the piano on the second beat of the second bar while the voice continues the old phrase until the end of that bar. This is an illustration of the overlapping of phrases, a device most frequently found in music with a contrapuntal texture. [See also Bach, *The Well-Tempered Clavier* (WTC), Vol. 2, *Prelude No. 19*, mm. 8–9.]

EXERCISES

1. Terms to define:

Conclusive cadence	Plagal cadence
Semicadence	Deceptive cadence
Authentic cadence	Full cadence

2. Contrast:
a. Masculine and feminine endings
b. Overlapping and elision

3. Answer the questions in reference to each of the passages given (numbering of bars begins with the first *full* bar).[1]

(1) How many phrases does the passage comprise?
(2) Do these phrases exhibit caesuras in the melody?
(3) Identify cadences as to type. Which is stronger? Why?
(4) Are the phrases connected by any special means? If so, what are these means?

[1] See the Preface for an explanation of plans A and B of the exercises.

	A		B
a.	*MF, No. 7*, mm. 3–11	a.	Anon.: *Minuet;* mm. 1–16
b.	*MF, No. 18*, mm. 7–18	b.	Schubert: *Who Is Sylvia?*, mm. 5–10
c.	*WTC, Prelude No. 10*, mm. 1–9	c.	Schumann: *Album, No. 7*, mm. 1–8
d.	*VC*, Third Movement, mm. 1–16	d.	Schumann: *Album, No. 31*, mm. 1–12
e.	*Chorale No. 32*, mm. 1–4	e.	Chopin: *Nocturne*, mm. 2–9
f.	*Chorale No. 26*, mm. 1–6	f.	Wolf: *Das verlassene Mägdlein*, mm. 5–12
g.	*Chorale No. 28*, entire	g.	Bartók: *Mikrokosmos No. 150*, mm. 5–22; and mm. 58–78

2-5. THE HARMONIC ORGANIZATION OF THE PHRASE

The question of the organization of the harmony within a phrase is an exceedingly important one. To a large extent, phrases present in miniature the same basic tonal structures exhibited on a larger scale by entire sections and, indeed, by complete compositions.

How does the composer arrive at the series of harmonies which connects the first chord of his phrase with the cadence? The ensuing discussion should not be taken as implying that the composer is necessarily conscious of the process during the act of composition. It seems likely that the creative artist who has mastered his craft will grasp intuitively what is "right" in a composition without having to plod through the intervening steps.

Ex. 2-13.   Melodic motions

A comparison of the first three melodic motions (Ex. 2-13a, b, c) with the last two (d, e) reveals that the former conclude by returning to the first note, whereas the latter move to a different note. The first three may be described as motions *within* an area, the last two as motion *from* one area *to* another.

In Ex. 2-13a, the middle tone, a neighbor note, provides motion that simply returns to its starting place. Its function is decorative but, more than that, the movement it engenders serves to prolong the main tone. In d, on the other hand, the middle tone is a passing note that serves to fill up the space between the first tone and the third. Its function is to lead from one tone to another. The middle tones of b and c have a function essentially the same as that of a: prolongation of the main tone. The function of the middle tone of e is to divide in half the distance from the first note to the third, thus leading from one to the other.

Example 2-14 illustrates in the harmonic sphere the same types of motion exemplified by the melodic fragments of Ex. 2-13.

Ex. 2-14.   Harmonic motions

Example 2-14a, b, and d show extremely simple harmonic motions within an area, c a more complex one. A series of chords moving within an area is called a *chord succession*. Example 2-14e and f show harmonic motion from one area to another, illustrations of the *chord progression*. Although Ex. 2-14d and e have identical melodies, the former is harmonized as a succession, the latter as a progression. Progression to a chord whose bass lies a fifth away is often accomplished by means of a chord whose bass cuts this distance into two equal parts (Ex. 2-14f).

Ex. 2-15.   **a.** Chord succession   **b.** BACH: *Christmas Oratorio,* Part VI

The opening chord of Ex. 2-15a changes from root position to first inversion. Although the bass seems to "progress" from g to B, the fact that the first and third chords comprise the same harmony results essentially in movement within an area. We have, then, a chord prolongation: a succession, not a progression. The same is true of Ex. 2-15b. In spite of the longer bass movement down a sixth, the end result is a prolongation of the tonic triad followed by the full cadence.

Bearing in mind these distinctions of chord succession and chord progression, the chief ways of organizing a phrase harmonically can be set forth under seven headings.

Harmonic scheme of the phrase equivalent to the cadence

Ex. 2-16. **a.** BEETHOVEN: *Sonata, Op. 31, No. 3,* First Movement
b. SCHOENBERG: *Gurrelieder,* Part One

Copyright 1914 by Universal Edition A. G., Vienna. Reprinted by permission of original copyright owner and Mrs. Arnold Schoenberg.

By means of cadential elaboration it is possible for the harmonic scheme of a phrase to consist of no more than the chords of a cadential formula. Example 2-16a shows cadential elaboration by means of chromatic passing tones (pt) in the manner illustrated by Ex. 2-8a. Example 2-16b allows a IV to intervene between the VII and its resolution on I (see Ex. 2-8c, wherein the penultimate chord was V, not VII).

Cadence preceded by single chord

Ex. 2-17.   VERDI: *La Traviata*, Act I

By permission of G. Ricordi & C., Milan.

Example 2-17 is a ten-bar phrase ending with an authentic cadence. The first six bars consist, harmonically speaking, of nothing more than a tonic chord. (See also Chopin, *Nocturne in D flat Major, Op. 27, No. 2,* and Ex. 1-1, first phrases.)

Chord succession within the cadence

Not infrequently a cadence is preceded by a single chord and, at the same time, the phrase presents an impression of greater harmonic complexity than that of Ex. 2-16. This impression comes about through the use of a chord succession within the cadence, a form of cadential elaboration (see section 2-3).

Ex. 2-18. PURCELL: *Dido and Aeneas*, Act III

Example 2-18 shows a lengthy extension of the penultimate cadential chord by approaching it through a secondary dominant (m. 2) and chord succession (mm. 3–4). Example 2-19 is another example of chord succession used as a means of cadential elaboration, this time applied to the V.

Ex. 2-19. MENDELSSOHN: *Symphony No. 3 in A Minor* ("Scotch"), First Movement

Cadence preceded by chord succession

The harmony of much music of a light character, such as the waltzes of Johann Strauss, often merely alternates between I and V. This back and forth motion extending until the cadence is reached is actually no more than motion within an area. Alternation between I and VII is the characteristic of the chord succession that makes up the first part of the phrase in Ex. 2-20.

Ex. 2-20. D. SCARLATTI: *Sonata, K. 446*

In Ex. 2-21, the cadence is preceded by a series of harmonies overlying a tonic pedal point. The continual sounding of the tonic note in the bass tends to cause these harmonies to be heard as a prolongation of I.

Ex. 2-21. C. P. E. BACH: *Sonata, Wq 57, Second Movement*

In the chord succession in Ex. 2-22, the tonic triad (with added sixth) makes its final appearance at the lower octave, the interval being filled in by a series of seventh chords descending stepwise.

Ex. 2-22. DEBUSSY: *Suite Bergamasque, Clair de lune* (harmonic outline)

Cadence preceded by chord progression

Ex. 2-23.   SCHUBERT: *Ständchen*

The distance from the bass of the first chord of the phrase (m. 1) to the bass of the first chord of the semicadence (m. 3) is a perfect fifth. By using a chord whose bass note falls in the middle of this interval, Schubert divides a large leap into two smaller ones, the same principle we have seen used melodically in Ex. 2-13 and harmonically in 2-14f. We have here, then, a chord progression, for the VI of m. 2 leads from I to II$_5^6$, motion not within an area, but from one area to another.

It is important to note that we concern ourselves here not so much with harmonic roots as with the bass. A listener's orientation comes from the bass line as it is actually sounded rather than from a theoretical knowledge of the root of each chord.

Ex. 2-24.   FAURÉ: *Requiem*, Part VI

The distance from the low note D which opens the phrase to the G with which the bass of the cadence begins (m. 5) is a perfect fourth. Here the progression moves not by two small leaps as in the former example, but stepwise.

Both preceding illustrations have shown bass lines that aimed at their goals and went there directly. Often the progression makes a slight detour. In Ex. 2-25, the bass line in m. 2 passes over its goal, then returns to it in m. 3.

Ex. 2-25.   HANDEL: *Concerto Grosso, Op. 6, No. 6,* First Movement

Not infrequently a series of harmonies will progress by means of descending or, more rarely, ascending fifths.

Ex. 2-26.   VIVALDI: *Concerto for Four Violins, Op. 3, No. 10,* Third Movement

Elaborations of the chord progression

Ex. 2-27. RAVEL: *String Quartet*, Third Movement

Used with the authorization of Durand & Cie, Editeurs-proprietaires, Paris, copyright owners; Elkan-Vogel Co., Inc., Philadelphia, Pa., agents.

Example 2-27 shows a movement from a tonic *g♭*, expressed at the upper octave, downwards to a *c♭* (m. 4). The implied interval of a perfect fifth is cut in half by the note *e♭* of m. 3, much as in Ex. 2-23. The *e♭* itself, however, is prepared by means of the chord at its upper fifth *b♭* (m. 2). Again it must be stressed that analysis of harmonic progression is concerned more with the bass line than with root movements. If we considered only the roots of the chords, we should assume that the progression in Ex. 2-27 was arrived at by means of descending fifths (III–VI–II–V–I), a reading belied by the ear.

Ex. 2-28. ZIPOLI: *Suite No. 4 in D Minor*, Minuet

Example 2-28 is another illustration of a progression which, judged by roots, moves by descending fifths. The ear, on the contrary, hears a progression from the V that closes the preceding phrase (m. 2) to the I (m. 10) via descending stepwise motion (mm. 4, 6, 8), each chord being emphasized by its secondary dominant in first inversion. (The harmony of m. 7 serves as the secondary dominant of m. 8 by analogy.)

Cadence preceded by combination of succession and progression

Perhaps a majority of phrases combine the two methods so far discussed, beginning with a chord succession, then progressing to the cadence. The illustrations in Ex. 2-29 are self-explanatory.

Ex. 2-29. **a.** MENDELSSOHN: *Symphony No. 3 in A Minor* ("Scotch")
         b. BACH: *WTC, Vol. 1, Prelude No. 1*
         c. COUPERIN: *Messe à l'Usage des Couvents, Quoniam Tu Solus*

EXERCISES

4. Terms to define:
   Chord succession   Chord progression
5. Consider the passages for Exercise 3 of this chapter. Studying the harmonic organization with special attention to the bass line, describe the harmonic movement of each phrase.

2-6. SUMMARY

Although the phrase is not always easy to pinpoint, there are certain criteria that can be of aid to the student.

1. A change of chords, harmonic action, helps give the impression of a measure of completeness, a characteristic of the phrase.
2. Common to all phrases is the feeling of comparative repose reached at the end. This is often brought about through either or both of the following:
   a. A pause, or caesura, in the flow of the music accomplished through held notes or rests.
   b. The movement of the harmonies from dissonance to consonance or from greater to lesser dissonance.

An important aspect of the phrase is its cadence, the chords that bring it to a close. Cadences have differing effects and are of varying strengths. A conclusive cadence carries with it a definite conviction of finality lacking to the semicadence. The strongest conclusive cadence is the perfect authentic (V–I, root in soprano of I) in a masculine rhythmic position.

For the sake of continuity, composers have generally made a practice of tying a number of phrases together by one of the following cadential treatments:

1. Filling in the gap between two phrases by continued rhythmic movement in the accompaniment
2. Directing the melodic line over the gap between two phrases
3. Avoiding a gap between two phrases by causing the last moment of one phrase to occur simultaneously with the first moment of the next; that is, elision of the cadence
4. Avoiding a gap between phrases by the process of overlapping, in which the various voices of a contrapuntal or semicontrapuntal texture may cadence at difference times

An understanding of the harmonic organization of the phrase depends upon distinguishing succession and progression in a chordal sequence. The former refers to harmonic movement within the area of a single chord. The latter refers to movement from one chordal area to another.

The phrase, as a rule, is organized harmonically by the use of

1. Chord succession followed by the cadence
2. Chord progression leading to the cadence
3. Chord succession followed by progression leading to the cadence

Sometimes, on the other hand, the phrase consists harmonically of no more than a single cadential formula, such as II–V–I or VII–I, or of a single chord followed by a cadence.

3

Melodic Structure
of the Phrase

3-1. INDIVISIBLE PHRASES

Some musical phrases are not susceptible to subdivision. They consist simply of one steady flow of sound with no break, real or implied. Phrases with melodies of the *perpetuum mobile* type often fall into this category (Ex. 3-1a), but there are a number of other examples as well (Ex. 3-1b).

Ex. 3-1. **a.** BACH: *Cantata 147*, Part One, No. 6
  b. BEETHOVEN: *Symphony No. 4*, Second Movement

3-2. SUBDIVISION OF THE PHRASE

Example 3-2 is the beginning of the famous English horn melody in the second movement of Franck's *Symphony in D Minor*.

29

Ex. 3-2.   FRANCK: *Symphony in D Minor,* Second Movement

The first five notes comprise a short melodic unit that is twice repeated, each time in a different version. Another melodic fragment brings the phrase to a close. Although no actual rests exist in the score, the presence of a caesura after each of these melodic fragments is clearly felt, and the composer has emphasized these caesuras by means of his phrasing. The eight-bar phrase, then, appears divided into four equal parts, called phrase members.

Many phrases are symmetrically subdivided either in the manner of Franck's English horn melody or into two phrase members of equal length. In the latter case, the first phrase member is often further subdivided into two equal parts. Not infrequently, however, a phrase is unevenly subdivided. In the following excerpt, for instance, the first phrase member consists of three bars and the second of five. This division shows a different kind of symmetry, the symmetry of the "golden mean," wherein the smaller portion is (approximately) to the larger as the larger is to the whole ($3:5 \sim 5:8$).

Ex. 3-3.   MOZART: *Quartet, K. 458,* Second Movement

EXERCISE

1. Consider the passages listed for Exercise 3 of Chapter 2. Decide whether each phrase melody is indivisible or whether it consists of several phrase members. In the latter case, mark and number the phrase members. Are the divisions symmetrical?

3-3. THE MOTIVE

Ex. 3-4.   BACH: *Brandenburg Concerto No. 3,* First Movement

The melody in Ex. 3-4 is built almost entirely from a three-note melodic fragment called a motive. The motive is a short melodic fragment used as a constructional element. However, not every short melodic figure is a motive. In order to act as a constructional element and thus constitute a motive, a melodic fragment must appear at least twice, though reappearances need not be in the original form. A motive can be as short as two notes, as in the opening theme of Brahms' *Symphony No. 4*. It is rarely longer than six or seven notes (Ex. 3-6).

The motive is characterized by its melodic contour, with its harmonic implication, and by its rhythm.

Some melodies, such as Ex. 3-4, are built out of one motive only. More often the melody contains two or even three motives. Example 3-5 is a melody constructed from two motives (marked a and b).

Ex. 3-5.   GOUNOD: *Faust*, Duet, *"Il se fait tard"*

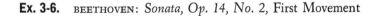

3-4. MOTIVIC CONSTRUCTION OF THE PHRASE MELODY

Repetition and sequence

Ex. 3-6.   BEETHOVEN: *Sonata, Op. 14, No. 2*, First Movement

The phrase excerpt in Ex. 3-6 is built entirely of a single six-note motive, a melodic fragment with a definite harmonic implication: The first, second, fourth, and sixth notes outline a triad, the third and fifth notes embellishing the fourth and sixth respectively. The first appearance of the motive expresses the tonic triad. After an exact repetition the motive again appears, this time at a new pitch level, expressing the supertonic triad. When a motive is thus repeated in the same voice at a new pitch level, we speak of sequence. Repetition and sequence comprise the two simplest ways of using the motive in building a phrase melody.

The fact that the I is a major triad while the II is minor necessitates in Ex. 3-6 slight changes within the motive in the sequence. The interval between the second and third notes is, in the first appearance, a diminished fourth, and that between the fourth and fifth notes a perfect fourth. In the corresponding places of the sequence these intervals are reversed. Such slight changes due to transposition are extremely common in sequences and are not to be considered actual variations of the motive. Motivic variation, as we shall see, involves much more than this.

Motivic variation

An examination of Ex. 3-5 will reveal some of the methods of motivic variation.

VARIATION BY ORNAMENTATION   The first motive of Ex. 3-5, marked a, outlines a tonic triad in the key of Db major. At its second appearance (a′) it is somewhat changed, not due to transposition as in the case of the sequence, but due to the addition of an appoggiatura to its final note. Its third appearance (a″) is similar to the second in that the final note is ornamented by an appoggiatura, but it differs from both preceding versions in that this final note is changed from the fifth degree of the scale to the fourth degree.

VARIATION BY INTERVALLIC CHANGE   A comparison of the second motive of Ex. 3-5, marked b, with the version in which it makes its final appearance (b′) shows an even more radical change of its melodic intervals. In spite of the great difference in melodic contour between b and b′, the motive is recognizable due to its characteristic rhythm. Even though the melodic intervals are altered, if the rhythm is maintained the listener will generally be aware of the presence of the motive. Brahms' *Symphony No. 4* opens with a melody made up of a two-note motive that takes various melodic guises (descending third, ascending sixth, descending octave, ascending third) but persists in the same rhythmic pattern. Example 3-7 is another phrase made up of a motive the intervals of which are constantly altered, while the rhythm is only slightly altered.

Ex. 3-7.   SCHUBERT: *Sonata, Op. 53,* Second Movement

VARIATION BY INVERSION

Ex. 3-8.   STRAVINSKY: *L'Oiseau de feu, Berceuse*

Reprinted by permission of B. Schott's Soehne, Mainz.

Interval changes in the melody sometimes occur by systematic change of direction. In Ex. 3-8, an upward leap of a third becomes a downward leap of a third, a descending fourth becomes an ascending fourth. (See also the beginning of the Second Movement of Brahms' *Symphony No. 4.*)

A motive can be freely, rather than strictly, inverted. A general upward movement becomes a general downward movement, and vice versa, with no attempt to retain the precise intervals involved.

Ex. 3-9.   BRAHMS: *Symphony No. 3,* Third Movement

(See also beginning of Puccini's *La Bohème.*)

VARIATION BY RETROGRESSION   When the notes of the melody recur in reverse order we speak of retrograde motion or retrogression.

Ex. 3-10.   DEBUSSY: *Prelude No. 10* ("The Engulfed Cathedral")

Used with the authorization of Durand & Cie, Editeurs proprietaires, Paris, copyright owners; Elkan Vogel Co., Inc., Philadelphia, Pa., agents.

Although in the past retrograde motion has been used only sporadically, many twentieth-century composers have come to include it among their means of organization.

VARIATION BY AUGMENTATION OR DIMINUTION   Another method of motivic variation involves an alteration in the rhythm while the intervallic structure of the melody is retained. Since a rhythmic change is apt to destroy the identity of the motive, this method is not common. However, if the rhythm is varied systematically, such as by augmentation or diminution, the motive is readily perceived.

By augmentation the rhythmic value of each note is multiplied, usually by two. By diminution it is divided. The change by augmentation or diminu-

Ex. 3-11.   **a.** BEETHOVEN: *Sonata, Op. 90,* First Movement
                b. BRAHMS: *Sonata, Op. 120, No. 2,* First Movement
                c. BRAHMS: *Intermezzo, Op. 118, No. 6*

tion may be general rather than exact. Measures 9–10 of Ex. 3-9 include augmentations of the main motive, and Ex. 3-11 provides further illustrations.

VARIATION BY COMBINATION OF MEANS   Any of the foregoing methods may be used in combination. In illustration let us examine Ex. 3-12. The devices used are intervallic variation and ornamentation. The melody is built up out of a single motive. Example 3-12a represents a conjectural version of the theme before being ornamented. Each pair of bars consists of the original motive with rhythm maintained but melodic intervals varied. Example 3-12b shows the theme as Brahms left it, each motive further varied by means of ornamentation.

Ex. 3-12.   BRAHMS: *Sonata, Op. 38,* First Movement

Another possible combination of methods is that of both rhythmic and intervallic variation.

Ex. 3-13.   HAYDN: *Symphony No. 104,* Third Movement

The chief methods of variation can be summarized under three headings:

1. Change of intervals with retention of rhythm (intervallic, inversion)
2. Change of rhythm with retention of intervals (augmentation, diminution)
3. Ornamentation of the motive

3-5.   MOTIVIC CONSTRUCTION IN PHRASE TEXTURE

So far we have limited ourselves to a discussion of motivic construction of the phrase melody only. Example 3-14 illustrates motivic interplay among all the parts of a phrase, not only the uppermost voice.

The motive is presented first as a sequence in the first violin. Immediately the second violin and viola invert it, then turn it right side up again, while the cello enters with the inversion only. The various instruments give out the motive one after another, either at the original pitch level or transposed to a different one.

Ex. 3-14.   MOZART: *Quartet, K. 387,* First Movement

The technique of imitation, as this kind of writing is called, occurs quite commonly in any of its various types.

1. *Real,* or *exact imitation* exists when the motive is unchanged by the imitating voice, except perhaps for transposition to a new pitch level (Ex. 3-11a, left hand imitating right hand).

2. *Imitation by inversion* is illustrated in Ex. 3-14.

3. *Tonal imitation* is present in Ex. 2-29c (mm. 1–3). Here the imitating voice presents the motive in a version corresponding to that of a fugal answer, explained in Chapter 14 (section 14-3).

4. *Imitation by augmentation* or by *diminution* is occasionally found as well. In Ex. 3-15, with one exception, each note of the imitating voice is six times the length of its corresponding note in the original motive. This motive is itself a diminution of the fugue subject that had appeared earlier in the movement.

5. *Free imitation* occurs when the imitating voice changes the motive rhythmically (but not systematically as in augmentation and diminution) or by intervallic change and/or ornamentation.

Ex. 3-15.   BEETHOVEN: *Sonata, Op. 110,* Third Movement

6. *Imitation of rhythm only,* a simple use of imitation, is the appropriation of the motive's rhythm for the accompaniment without any attempt at imitating its melodic contour.

Ex. 3-16.   ROSSINI: *Stabat Mater, No. 2*

EXERCISES

2. Terms to define:

Motive   Diminution
Sequence   Augmentation
Inversion   Real imitation
Retrograde motion   Free imitation

3. Contrast:
a. Imitation and sequence
b. Inversion and retrograde motion

4. Consider the passages for Exercise 3 of Chapter 2. Decide whether each phrase melody is motivically constructed. If it is, mark the various appearances of each motive and point out the relationships among them.

5. Decide whether motivic construction exists within the phrase texture of each of the phrases listed below. If so, mark the various appearances of each motive and point out the type of imitation used.

A	B
a. *MF*, Overture, mm. 1–7 (Adagio)	a. Bach: *Invention IV,* last 9 measures
b. *WJ, No. 8,* mm. 10–20	b. Bach: *WTC, Fugue No. 16,* mm. 1–3
c. *WJ, No. 20,* mm. 5–10	c. Haydn: *Symphony No. 101 in D Major* ("The Clock"), Fourth Movement mm. 1–8
d. Beethoven: *Op 2, No. 3, Scherzo,* mm. 1–16	d. Beethoven: *Quartet, Op. 135,* Fourth Movement, mm. 1–4
e. *WTC, Prelude No. 24,* mm. 1–7	e. Brahms: *Intermezzo, Op. 118, No. 2,* mm. 34–38
f. *WTC, Prelude No. 22,* mm. 13–15	f. Bartók: *Mikrokosmos No. 133,* mm. 1–8
	g. Bartók: *Mikrokosmos No. 150,* mm. 58–62

3-6. SUMMARY

From the melodic point of view, the phrase may exhibit a single unbroken line. More often it subdivides itself into smaller sections, the phrase members. These are often built up of very short melodic fragments called motives. The motive can, by repetition, sequence, and variation, become the primary melodic factor of a phrase, appearing as a constructional element not only in the phrase melody but also, through imitation, in the bass line and inner voices.

4

Development
of the Phrase

A phrase is developed by expanding it at one or more points. Expansion at the beginning of the phrase takes the form of *introduction*, during the phrase it takes the form of *interpolation*, and at the end, of *extension*.

4-1. INTRODUCTION TO THE PHRASE

There are four common methods of introducing a phrase:
1. By a bar or two of the accompaniment

Ex. 4-1. SCHUBERT: *Quartet, Op. 29*, First Movement

(See also Mozart, *Symphony No. 40*, mm. 1–3.)
2. By one or more chords

Ex. 4-2. IVES: *The Greatest Man*

(See also Beethoven, *Symphony No. 3*, mm. 1–4.)

3. By one or more tones without definite melodic character

Ex. 4-3. BEETHOVEN: *Sonata, Op. 106*, Third Movement

(See also Ex. 6-1, first phrase.)

4. By anticipation of the opening motive of the phrase

Ex. 4-4. BARTÓK: *Quartet No. 2*, First Movement

(See also Schubert, *Sonata, Op. 147*, Finale, mm. 1–3.)

While there are additional ways of introducing a phrase, it would be impractical to attempt to enumerate every possible method which the imagination of a gifted composer might conceive. The student's attention is, nevertheless, directed to the openings of Beethoven's *Symphony No. 5* and Brahms' *Symphony No. 2.*

4-2. INTERPOLATION DURING THE PHRASE

Motivic interpolation

Ex. 4-5.   BEETHOVEN: *Symphony No. 5*, Third Movement

Example 4-5 shows a phrase and its repetition. While the original phrase is eight bars long, the repetition has been expanded to a length of ten bars, accomplished by means of a two-bar interpolation. This interpolation begins with a sequence of the final motive of the first phrase member (m. 11). The method employed here is called, then, phrase expansion by motivic interpolation.

Prolongation of a note or chord

Ex. 4-6.   BEETHOVEN: *Sonata, Op. 57*

In Ex. 4-6, the second phrase expands the first by a prolongation of a chord. Asterisks in the original phrase mark the points that are prolonged in the second.

Unless the phrase with the interpolation has appeared previously in its original form, one cannot speak confidently of an interpolation. Lacking the original phrase for comparison, there is no certainty whether the assumed interpolation is really such, or is an integral part of the phrase.

Ex. 4-7.   HAYDN: *Quartet, Op. 76, No. 5*

In Ex. 4-7, the two phrases begin in an identical manner. Since they are so similar the listener might well expect them to be of the same length, and hence he might interpret the rising scale fragment in mm. 7–8 as an interpolation. However, similar phrases are under no compulsion to be the same length. It is at least as valid to consider the scale fragment an integral part of the phrase as to deem it an interpolation.

4-3. EXTENSION OF THE PHRASE

There are two chief ways of extending a phrase at its end. The first is to add to it after the cadence; the second is to evade a conclusive cadence until after the extension has been made.

Extension added after the cadence

PROLONGATION OF FINAL NOTE OR CHORD   A frequent method of lengthening a phrase by adding to it after the cadence consists in repeating the final chord or chords, or in prolonging the final chord by means of succession. Many compositions end with such extensions of the final phrase. Phrases within the piece may also be extended in the same manner.

Ex. 4-8.   BRAHMS: *Rhapsody, Op. 119, No. 4*

REPETITION OF FINAL PHRASE MEMBER

Ex. 4-9.   SCHUBERT: *Ständchen*

Often the phrase is extended by a simple repetition of the final phrase member. In vocal music and music for a solo instrument with accompaniment, such extensions frequently take the form of interludes, as in Ex. 4-9. Still, one must not assume that each time the soloist is silent and the accompaniment becomes prominent, the resulting interlude is an extension of the phrase. A regular phrase member or motive may be taken up by the accompaniment while the soloist rests.

Schumann, in Ex. 4-10, has given the first phrase member to the voice, and the second (the cadence) to the piano. There is no question here of an

Ex. 4-10.   SCHUMANN: *Der Nussbaum*

interlude formed by any device of phrase expansion. Only if the interlude is clearly an addition to the phrase, considering the whole complex of sound and not only the soloist's part, should it be attributed to phrase development.

SEQUENCE OF FINAL PHRASE MEMBER

Ex. 4-11.   HAYDN: *Symphony No. 88*

In the excerpt in Ex. 4-11 the phrase cadences regularly on the tonic, the subsequent extension, a modified sequence, establishing V as a secondary tonic.

Extension by evaded cadence

Ex. 4-12.   SCHUBERT: *Winterreise, Wasserfluth* (*No. 6*)

The original phrase of Ex. 4-12 closes with a deceptive cadence. The extension is derived by free inversion from the preceding phrase member. At other times the extension is a repetition or sequence of a previous phrase member, or it may be entirely new.

4-4. PHRASE DEVELOPMENT BY A COMBINATION OF METHODS

The methods of phrase expansion used in combination with themselves and also with those of motivic construction may result in phrases of considerable length.

Ex. 4-13.   SCHUBERT: *Trio, Op. 99,* Third Movement

In Ex. 4-13 a two-and-one-half-bar phrase member is greatly expanded by sequences, repetitions, and imitations before coming to a cadence. In addition, the phrase is introduced by two appearances of the initial motive and is closed with two extensions following the cadence. What could have been a four-bar phrase has thus been worked up into a length of twenty-one bars.

EXERCISE

1. Locate, identify, and describe all phrase developments to be found in the following passages

<table>
<tr><td align="center">A</td><td align="center">B</td></tr>
</table>

a. *MF, No. 3,* mm. 1–15

b. Beethoven: *Op. 2, No. 3,* First Movement, mm. 1–13

c. Beethoven: *Op. 2, No. 3,* Second Movement, mm. 5–11

d. *WJ, No. 2,* mm. 25–46

e. *WJ, No. 3,* mm. 8–20

a. Beethoven: Quartet, *Op. 135,* Third Movement, mm. 1–6; and mm. 7–12

b. Schumann: *Album No. 31,* mm. 21–28   340

c. Chopin: *Mazurka No. 5,* mm. 1–12   371

d. Wagner: *Tristan,* mm. 1–17   385

e. Brahms: *Intermezzo, Op. 119, No. 2,* mm. 3–6 (compare mm. 1–2)   407

f. Wolf: *Das verlassene Mägdlein,* mm. 38–47 (compare mm. 5–12)   416

g. Bartók: *Mikrokosmos No. 133,* mm. 18–24 (compare mm. 3–4)   466

5

Phrases in Combination

Just as motives may combine to become a phrase member and phrase members become a phrase, so may a number of phrases combine to become a larger unit. When we hear two or more phrases as a larger unit, we may describe the result in one of three ways. These are the *period*, the *phrase group*, and *phrase chain*. For the composer, the challenge is to use these seemingly limited resources in such a way as to give the listener the impression of unlimited richness and variety. For the student, the challenge is to learn the methods by which he can discover for himself just what it is that the composer has done.

Before considering the structure of the larger unit, we must be prepared to distinguish between a phrase that is a varied repetition of a previous phrase and one that is a different phrase although similar to a previous one.

5-1. VARIED AND SIMILAR PHRASES

Cadences differing radically

Ex. 5-1. SCHUBERT: **a.** *Die Nebensonnen* **b.** *Am Meer*

Each excerpt of Ex. 5-1 consists of two phrases greatly resembling each other in melody. Those of *Am Meer* carry out this resemblance in the harmony as well, while the second phrase of *Die Nebensonnen* is harmonized quite differently from the first phrase. But in the cadences the situation is reversed. In spite of the difference in harmonies of the two phrases of Ex. 5-1a, the cadences are identical. Although the phrase melody is supported in the second phrase by a new harmonization, the difference between the two phrases is superficial, for the goal of both harmonic sequences is the same: V_7–I. The second phrase is a varied repetition of the first.

In Ex. 5-1b the cadences are radically different, the first being a semi-cadence ending on V, the second a perfect cadence, V_7–I. Regardless of the fact that the two phrases, up to the cadences, exhibit identical harmonies, the second is not a repetition but a different phrase similar to the first, for the two harmonic sequences have different goals.

The plan of a house is altered if a wall is moved, but not if the wall is only painted. Phrases are varied if unessential, but not essential, changes have been made between them. Altered harmony, transfer of the melody to a higher or lower octave, melodic embellishment—these are decorative changes, not structural ones.

The crux of the question of whether an essential or an unessential change has been made lies in the cadence.

> If the harmonic movement of the two phrases leads to the same goal, the second is a varied phrase. If the cadences are radically different, then an essential change has been made, and the second is a similar phrase.

A wall can be both moved and painted. It need hardly be pointed out that if both decorative and structural changes have been made in the second of two phrases, from the point of view of the study of form it is the structural change which is the more noteworthy.

Cadences differing in strength

The first two phrases of the familiar song, *Believe Me If All Those Endearing Young Charms,* illustrates an important point. Although both phrases close with an authentic cadence, they exhibit very different degrees of strength. The first ("fondly today") is an imperfect cadence, for the third of the tonic triad is in the melody. The second ("fading away") is a perfect cadence, the root of the tonic triad in the melody. Since both use the progression V–I, the two cadences cannot be considered radically different. Nevertheless, the greater strength of the perfect cadence is enough to give the listener the impression of an essential change in the second phrase. In this case, then, and in others which exhibit decided differences in cadential strength, the second phrase is to be considered not a varied repetition of the first, but a different phrase, similar to the first.

Repetition of phrases

It is common for a speaker to make a statement and repeat it at once, either exactly or in different words. This device emphasizes, or clarifies, the original statement but does not cause the argument to progress. Similarly, in music a phrase may be sounded, then immediately repeated, either exactly or with some variation. The repetition does not contribute to the growth of the musical form, but exists, if repeated exactly, for emphasis. It exists as a means of elaboration or clarification if repeated in a variation—the composer is saying, "In other words. . . ." Identification of the larger unit depends upon the distinction between varied and similar phrases. A series of phrases each one of which is no more than a repetition, varied or exact, of the other remains a series of repeated phrases. They do not form a larger unit. The period, phrase group, and phrase chain must each comprise at least two *different* phrases.

EXERCISE

1. Compare the second phrase of the following passages with the first. Is it a similar phrase, a dissimilar one, or a varied repetition? Why?

A	B
a. *MF, No. 10,* mm. 21–28	a. Couperin: *La Bandoline,* mm. 1–8
b. Beethoven: *Op. 13,* Second Movement, mm. 1–16	b. Anon: *March,* mm. 10–17
c. Beethoven: *Op. 13,* Third Movement, mm. 5–12	c. Beethoven: *Sonata, Op. 13,* Third Movement, mm. 5–12
d. Beethoven: *Op. 14, No. 1,* Second Movement, mm. 1–16	d. Schumann: *Album No. 5,* mm. 1–8
e. Beethoven: *Op. 14, No. 2,* Second Movement, mm. 1–8	e. Chopin: *Prelude No. 20,* mm. 1–8
f. Chopin: *Prelude No. 7* (entire)	f. Brahms: *Intermezzo, Op. 118, No. 2,* mm. 1–8; and mm. 57–64
g. Chopin: *Prelude No. 20,* mm. 1–8	g. Wolf: *Das verlassene Mägdlein,* mm. 5–12
h. Chopin: *Prelude No. 21,* mm. 1–16	h. Debussy: *L'après-midi d'un faune,* mm. 55–74
i. Chopin: *Prelude No. 21,* mm. 17–32	i. Bartók: *Mikrokosmos No. 144,* m. 1—first beat of m. 5
j. *WJ, No. 19,* mm. 6–20	

5-2. PHRASE CHAIN

Ex. 5-2. MOZART: *Don Giovanni,* Overture

Example 5-2, found between the principal and secondary themes of Mozart's Overture to *Don Giovanni*, consists of three phrases which do not resemble each other in any definable way. True, they are not completely contrasting for they show singleness of meter and tempo with unity of key and general style. But no definite relationships are readily apparent. Such phrases are spoken of as dissimilar. Several dissimilar phrases sometimes appear consecutively in a composition and may be referred to as a phrase chain.

5-3. PHRASE GROUP

Ex. 5-3. CHOPIN: *Prelude, Op. 28, No. 22*

Example 5-3 consists of two different phrases that are similar. Their similarity links them together in the mind of the listener and we, therefore, speak of them as forming a group rather than a chain of phrases. Some phrase groups contain a number of phrases. To qualify as a group, however, it is necessary for at least two of these phrases to be similar.

Special note should be taken of the fact that neither phrase group nor phrase chain ends with a conclusive cadence.

5-4. PERIOD

From the melodic standpoint, the period may resemble either the phrase chain or the phrase group. It consists of similar phrases, dissimilar phrases, or a combination of both. But it is distinguished from the others in a different way. The period consists of a series of phrases which, aside from the question of resemblances in design, are related by virtue of harmonic organization or *tonal structure* (see section 1-3).

Ex. 5-4. BEETHOVEN: *Symphony No. 7*

Phrase 1 presents a chord succession prolonging the I, then cadences on III, treated as a secondary tonic. Phrase 2 begins with III, progresses to I, prolonged by chord succession, and closes with a perfect authentic cadence. There are two important observations to be made in connection with this harmonic movement.

Singleness of tonal structure

The tonal structures of both phrases can be considered together as comprising a single harmonic movement. Phrase 1 moves from I to III, phrase 2 from III to I, brought to a close with V–I. The first fourteen measures of the example can be understood in the light of the whole passage as an extended chord succession, I–III–I, preceding the final cadence V–I.

The harmonic organization of the phrase was pointed out (section 2-5) as particularly important since it exhibits on a small scale the same type of structures that the larger sections show magnified. We have just witnessed a simple case, still on rather a small scale, of the resemblance between the tonal structure of the phrase and that of a larger unit. As we concern ourselves more and more with forms of greater dimensions, we shall continu⌐ to note this striking phenomenon.

Strength of final cadence

The second observation to be made is concerned with the relative strength of the cadences of Ex. 5-4. The cadence of phrase 2 is stronger than that of phrase 1, for the latter is an imperfect cadence, the former a perfect one.

These two observations combine to point to an essential characteristic of the period:

> The final phrase of the period completes a harmonic movement that the preceding phrase or phrases had left incomplete.

The final cadence, exhibiting greater strength than any previous one, helps to bring about the conclusive quality requisite to the completion of the entire harmonic movement. The total impression of the period is not unlike that of question and answer. Some theorists do speak of the phrases in these terms, but in common usage they are called *antecedent* and *consequent*.

Example 5-4 is a two-phrase period consisting of one antecedent and one consequent. The consequent is, in fact, repeated, this pianissimo echo providing an exquisite conclusion. But a repeated consequent does not change a two-phrase period into one of three phrases. Only when three different phrases are present, as in *Silent Night*, does one speak of a three-phrase period. Occasionally periods consist of even more than three phrases.

5-5. TYPES OF HARMONIC MOVEMENT IN THE PERIOD

Complete harmonic movement

Ex. 5-5. BRAHMS: *Wie Melodien zieht es mir*

The final section of Brahms' song, *Wie Melodien zieht es mir, Op. 105, No. 1,* is made up of three phrases which show such slight motivic resemblances that they must be considered virtually dissimilar. Being dissimilar, they are not to be thought of as a phrase group. An examination of the tonal structure will reveal whether they are a phrase chain or a period. If the final phrase fulfills a harmonic movement left unfulfilled by the previous phrases, the passage is a period.

Phrase 1 moves from I through IV to the imperfect cadence $\flat\text{II}_6$–I. Phrase 2 progresses from I to an imperfect authentic cadence on $\flat\text{VI}$. Phrase 3 leads through $\flat\text{II}$ (prepared by the $\flat\text{II}_6$ in phrase 1) back to I where it closes with a perfect full cadence. The essential harmonic movement of the whole excerpt may be summarized as:

phrase 1	phrase 2	phrase 3
$\text{I} \rightarrow \flat\text{II}_6\text{–I}$	$\text{I} \rightarrow \text{V}_7\text{–I}$	$\text{V}_7\text{–I} \rightarrow \text{II}_6\text{–V}_7\text{–I}$
	of $\flat\text{VI}$	of $\flat\text{II}$

The three phrases of the period embody a series of harmonies which establish I, move to $\flat\text{VI}$ and $\flat\text{II}$, then return to I with a perfect full cadence: A complete harmonic movement, expressed succinctly as $\text{I}\text{–}\flat\text{VI}\text{–}\flat\text{II}\text{–}\text{II}_6\text{–}\text{V}_7\text{–}\text{I}$. It is this completion, this rounding off of the tonal structure, that creates the most significant relationship among the three phrases of this period.

Re-examination of Ex. 5-2 and Ex. 5-3 will reveal no such completion in the final phrase of a harmonic movement begun by the preceding phrases. On the contrary, in each of these examples the final phrase ends with a semicadence.

Interruption of the harmonic movement

Referring back to Ex. 5-1b, we now realize that its two similar phrases form a period, for the authentic cadence that closes the second phrase concludes a harmonic movement that was left inconclusive by the semicadence of phrase 1. Nevertheless, the tonal structure of this period is quite unlike that of the periods illustrated in Ex. 5-4 and Ex. 5-5. These periods consisted of a complete harmonic movement begun by the antecedent, continued (in Ex. 5-5) by the second antecedent, and further continued and concluded by the consequent. In Ex. 5-1b, however, the consequent does not merely continue and conclude a harmonic movement begun by the antecedent—it first repeats this movement from the beginning, both in harmony and in melody, then brings it to a close with the authentic cadence. In other words, the antecedent, initiating the harmonic movement, brings it as far as the cadential V which, instead of going on to a final I, is left unresolved. At this point the harmonic movement is interrupted. The consequent begins the movement again, traverses the same harmonic and melodic path, and this time reaches a conclusion.

Interruption of the harmonic movement will be indicated in this book by two vertical lines. Thus the tonal structure of Ex. 5-1b can be outlined as:

$$\underbrace{I–V–I–IV^6_4–I–V}_{I} \parallel \underbrace{I–V–I–IV^6_4–I–V_7–I}_{I}$$

or, $I \rightarrow V \parallel I \rightarrow V_7–I$.

The harmonic and melodic pattern of the consequent in Ex. 5-1b is, up to the cadence, identical to that of the antecedent. Example 5-6 is an illustration of another possibility.

Ex. 5-6.   BERLIOZ: *The Damnation of Faust,* Part IV, Romance

Both antecedent and consequent precede their respective cadences with chord successions prolonging the tonic chord, first in root position, then in first inversion (see Ex. 2-15). However, the two harmonic sequences of which these successions are comprised are decidedly different, in spite of melodic similarity. The consequent in this case travels from the starting point of the antecedent to its goal, but not via the same route.

Progressive harmonic movement

Ex. 5-7.   SCHUMANN: *Kinderscenen No. 7*

The antecedent of the preceding period ends with a semicadence on V. The consequent, too, ends with V, not as a semicadence, but as a secondary tonic. The harmonic movement here differs from that of the previous examples, for it progresses from the tonic area to that of the dominant. The full cadence at the end of the second phrase closes the movement even though this movement has led away from the starting place without returning to it. Periods making up portions of larger forms often establish such secondary tonics at their close.

Repetition of the harmonic movement

Earlier we had occasion to note that the second phrase of the song *Believe Me If All Those Endearing Young Charms* is different from, though similar to, the first phrase (see section 5-1). In spite of the fact that the harmonic sequences of the two phrases are identical, the second is not a varied repetition of the first. Attention was called to the differing strengths of the two cadences, the first being imperfect, the second perfect. The question now arises as to whether two similar phrases, identical in harmony even to their cadences, can form a period. In spite of the differing strengths of the cadences, both phrases have the same harmonic goal, and hence the second phrase cannot complete a harmonic movement left incomplete by the first phrase. The two phrases of Ex. 5-8 show a parallel situation.

Ex. 5-8.   GOUNOD: *Faust*, Act I

The ear hears phrase 1 as incomplete, phrase 2 as complete. The reason for this phenomenon is that although the harmonic movement completes itself in both antecedent and consequent, the melodic movement is such that at the end of phrase 1 the uppermost voice has not reached the tonic note but the mediant or the dominant note. When, then, in phrase 2 the melody as well as the harmony arrives at the tonic, the listener is given a definite impression that something incomplete has now been completed. This is, however, merely an impression. The imperfect cadence is actually a conclusive cadence, not an inconclusive one, as many compositions ending with the third or fifth of the tonic triad in the soprano testify (for instance, *Chorale No. 74* or Schumann's

Kinderscenen No. 1). It is only after the listener has heard the perfect cadence and compared it ex post facto with the imperfect, that the latter seems inconclusive. This strong, universal impression is the probable cause of the general recognition that two phrases with identical harmonic goals can, under the circumstances just described, form a period.

Summary of Types of Harmonic Movement Found in the Period

1. *Complete harmonic movement* refers to a move away from a tonic with a return to that tonic via a conclusive cadence.

2. *Interrupted harmonic movement* occurs when a passage makes its way as far as the cadential V but does not reach the final I. Instead, it returns immediately to the beginning and repeats both the melodic and harmonic movement, exactly or with variation, altering the ending so that it concludes with a final tonic.

3. *Progressive harmonic movement* refers to a move away from a tonic without an immediate return. Such a move may embody a real modulation or the establishment of only a brief secondary tonic.

4. *Repeated harmonic movement* occurs in a period when the harmonic goal of the consequent is reached by the antecedent (or, in a multiphrase period, by one or more of the antecedents). In this case, it is the melodic goal that remains for the consequent to fulfill, and in so doing the harmonic movement takes place twice.

Complete, interrupted, and progressive are all single harmonic movements. When the harmonic movement is repeated, it is a double harmonic movement.

EXERCISES

2. Terms to define:

Phrase chain	Complete harmonic movement
Phrase group	Interrupted harmonic movement
Period	Progressive harmonic movement
Antecedent	Repeated harmonic movement
Consequent	

3. Consider the passages of Exercise 1 of this chapter. Which type of harmonic movement is represented by each?

5-6. DESIGN OF THE PERIOD

The symmetrical period   A number of two-phrase periods have been illustrated in previous examples (Ex. 4-7, Ex. 5-1b, Ex. 5-4, Ex. 5-6). The two-

don't have to be
Scanned (enger)

phrase period, consisting of a single antecedent balanced by a single consequent, is considered to be a symmetrical period. Whether or not the consequent is of precisely the same length as the antecedent is immaterial here. Usually they are the same, but the consequent of Ex. 4-7 is one bar longer than the antecedent; in Ex. 5-6 it is two bars longer. These "irregularities" do not destroy the basic symmetry created when a single antecedent is answered by a single consequent.

The double period

Ex. 5-9.   MENDELSSOHN: *Song without Words, Op. 85, No. 1*

Example 5-9 illustrates a symmetrical period in which both the antecedent and the consequent have been extended to two phrases. Since each component part of this symmetrical period consists of two phrases, we refer to this type of larger unit as a double period.

A comparison of Ex. 5-9 with Ex. 6-5 (Brahms' *Cradle Song*) will point up the essential difference between a double period and two symmetrical periods of two phrases each. In Ex. 5-9, the second phrase ends with a weaker cadence than that of the fourth phrase. The four phrases comprise one double period because the last two phrases (the consequent) complete a harmonic motion left incomplete by the first two phrases (the antecedent). In Ex. 6-5, on the other hand, the cadence of the second phrase has the same strength as that of the fourth. The harmonic motion completes itself in the first two phrases, the last two phrases constituting a second harmonic motion.

The asymmetrical period

Silent Night and Ex. 5-5 are three-phrase periods. Example 5-10 is one of five phrases.

Ex. 5-10.   BRAHMS: *Intermezzo, Op. 118, No. 6*

In the above cases we have a series of antecedents, an *antecedent group*, followed by a consequent.

Ex. 5-11. MOZART: *Die Zufriedenheit, K. 349*

The melodic resemblance between the last two phrases of the preceding period causes them to be associated together in the mind of the listener. It would be proper, then, to speak here of an antecedent followed by a *consequent group*.

Parallel and contrasting periods

Symmetrical periods consisting of similar phrases are called parallel (represented by the letters AA'), those of dissimilar phrases are called contrasting (AB). Parallel periods are represented by the following examples: 4-7, 5-1b, 5-4, 5-6, 5-7, and 5-8. Example 5-9 is a parallel double period. One cannot always be absolutely certain of the category of some periods. Example 1-1, for instance, is clearly a double period (with repeated antecedent and repeated consequent), but whether it should be considered parallel or contrasting is difficult to decide.

EXERCISE

4. Contrast:

a. Symmetrical and asymmetrical periods
b. Two-phrase symmetrical period and double period
c. Double period and two adjacent symmetrical periods
d. Parallel and contrasting periods

5-7. IDENTIFICATION OF THE LARGER UNIT

The six steps outlined below are offered as an aid to the student. After acquiring a certain amount of practice, he may find it unnecessary to employ these steps methodically. The experienced musician is often able to grasp the essence of a musical form at once without having to resort to a slow, painstaking process. But until the student acquires the requisite experience, he would do well to use consciously and carefully the method presented here.

Step 1. Locate each phrase and note its cadence, discovering whether the phrases are different or merely repetitions of a single phrase.

Step 2. Consider the phrase melodies, taking note of any varied or exact phrase repetitions, and identifying similar and dissimilar phrases.

Step 3. In the light of steps 1 and 2, decide whether the phrase series forms a larger unit or not, and if so, in which general category—period, phrase group, or phrase chain—it belongs. (Remember that the larger unit must consist of at least two *different* phrases and that only the period comes to a conclusive cadence.)

Step 4. Locate the phrase which seems to close the larger unit, then examine the phrases which immediately follow it to make certain they do not belong with those in question. It is possible that a subsequent phrase might conclude with a cadence stronger than that of the presumed final phrase, or it might be a repetition of the final phrase.

Once the ending of the larger unit has been definitely located, one can proceed with confidence. If step 3 has led to the conclusion that what is being dealt with is only a series of repeated phrases, there is no more to be done, for no larger unit is present. If a decision in favor of a phrase group or phrase chain has been reached, the identification is complete at this point. But if a period exists, steps 5 and 6 must be taken.

Step 5. Examine the phrases again for harmonic content, noting whether the period exhibits:

a. A single harmonic movement (as in Ex. 5-4 and Ex. 5-5)
b. Interrupted harmonic movement (as in Ex. 5-1b and Ex. 5-6)

c. Progressive harmonic movement (as in Ex. 5-7)
d. Repetition of harmonic movement (as in Ex. 5-8)

Step 6. Come to a conclusion regarding the symmetry of the period. If symmetrical, is it a single or double period? If asymmetrical, does it exhibit an antecedent group or a consequent group? (In an asymmetrical period, all phrases except the last are antecedents unless the last shows a close and exclusive relationship to the phrase or phrases immediately preceding it.)

5-8. APPLICATION OF THE SIX STEPS

For demonstration purposes we shall consider the beginning of César Franck's *Violin Sonata in A Major* following the six steps (see Ex. 5-12).

Step 1. Measures 1–4 consist of dominant harmony, played by the piano alone, and anticipate the opening two notes of the violin's melody. Clearly these four bars are an introduction to the first phrase. We begin, then, at m. 5, the harmony moving from a succession on V_9 to an imperfect cadence on I (m. 8), the melody dividing itself into two halves of two bars each. This would seem to be a phrase of two phrase members. It ends with a conclusive cadence, but as this is still phrase 1 we can hardly have reached the end of a larger unit. The next melodic caesura is at m. 12, supported by the semicadence on V_7/III. These four bars (mm. 9–12) form phrase 2. Another melodic caesura appears in m. 16 accompanied by the semicadence on V_7/V, and we recognize phrase 3. In m. 20 the melody again shows a clear caesura, indicating the end of phrase 4, although only a very slight harmonic movement has taken place ($V/V \rightarrow VII_5^6$, with no change of bass). Phrase 5 begins with m. 21 and continues like the others for four bars, semicadencing similarly to phrase 4 on VII_5^6/II. Phrase 6, unlike the preceding phrases, is not a four-bar phrase but is extended to seven, cadencing with an imperfect authentic cadence on V. Although this is not the strongest possible cadence with which a period can end, the different character of the music taken up at this point by the piano gives us a hint that we should, at least for the time being, stop here. Whether we have really reached the end of a period remains to be seen. Meanwhile, we go on to step 2.

Step 2. It is a universal practice in formal analysis to employ symbols that stand for the various members of a composition. A phrase, for example, could be symbolized by the letter A. Its repetition, whether varied or exact, would also be dubbed A, while a similar phrase would be represented by A′ (A prime). Should there be a third phrase similar to the others it would be called A″ (A double prime). When dissimilar phrases appear they are labeled B, C, D, and so on, and each of these might carry with it a similar phrase of its own: B′, C′, D′, and so on.

Ex. 5-12.   FRANCK: *Violin Sonata in A Major*

In applying step 2 to Ex. 5-12, then, the pattern of similar and dissimilar phrases could be represented by the symbols ABB'CC'A'.

Step 3. Step 1 has shown that the cadences of the six phrases are all radically different. We are, therefore, dealing with six different phrases combined into a larger unit. Since phrase 6 ends with a conclusive cadence the general category of this larger unit is the period.

Step 4. The phrase that follows phrase 6 ends with a semicadence and therefore cannot act as a final phrase to the previous six, for to do so it would have to be stronger than the cadence of phrase 6. Phrase 6 is therefore the end of the period. A number of other factors combine to separate the seventh phrase from the previous six, factors having to do with design:

a. The cadence of phrase 6 carried the direction *molto ritard.*, the first *ritardando* so far and indicative of a conclusion
b. Phrase 7 is for piano alone, an important change in timbre
c. Phrase 7 shows a new figure in the accompaniment
d. Phrase 7 carries with it a different dynamic and emotional quality

These additional factors can do no more than confirm what the cadential relationships have already established.

Step 5. It frequently happens that step 5 can be much simplified by making an outline of the essential harmonic movement of each phrase, for an outline readily shows the cadential relationships.

Ex. 5-13. FRANCK: *Violin Sonata in A Major* (harmonic outline)

In the harmonic outline (Ex. 5-13a), we perceive at once that the period closes with V treated as a secondary tonic. The seventh chord on B which acts as V_7/V had already made its appearance at the close of phrase 3 and was retained throughout most of phrase 4. The harmonies, then, which intervene between the V_7/V in phrase 3 and the V_7/V in the cadence of phrase 6 are part of a chord succession prolonging this V_7/V. These harmonies themselves point to II (that is, V/V) as a secondary tonic and throughout phrases 5 and 6 proceed by descending fifths.

Another interpretation of the harmonic events of this period is equally plausible. The bass outline (Ex. 5-13b) is self-explanatory.

By either reading, this period is based on a single harmonic movement of the progressive type, moving from I through III to V (Ex. 5-13c).

Step 6. The design, as symbolically represented in step 2, is clearly not an ordinary symmetrical period. Yet it shows a certain symmetry in that the first phrase is balanced by a similar phrase acting as a consequent.

The application of the six steps has led to the conclusion that Franck's *Violin Sonata* opens with a six-phrase period (a five-phrase antecedent group, a single phrase consequent) based on a progressive harmonic movement that passes from I through III to V. The phrases in the antecedent group are of a uniform length of four bars, while the consequent is extended to seven. Phrase 1 is preceded by four bars of introduction. The design of the period (ABB′CC′A′) is symmetrical to the extent that the first antecedent is balanced by a consequent which is similar.

EXERCISES

5. Consider the passages of Exercise 1 of this chapter. Following the six-step method, identify those which comprise a larger unit and the type (period,

phrase group, phrase chain). Give further identifying labels to all the periods.
6. Do the same for the following passages, some of which comprise more than
   two phrases.

	A		B
a.	*WJ*, No. 11, mm. 27–42	a.	Haydn: "Clock Symphony," Finale, mm. 1–8
b.	*WJ*, No. 12, mm. 6–34	b.	Schumann: *Album No. 17*, mm. 1–8
c.	VC, First Movement, mm. 1–11	c.	Chopin: *Mazurka No. 24*, mm. 1–16; and 17–32
d.	*VC*, Third Movement, mm. 1–16	d.	Wagner: *Tristan*, mm. 1–24
e.	Beethoven: *Op. 26*, Second Movement, mm. 1–16	e.	Brahms: *Intermezzo, Op. 119, No. 2*, mm. 1–12
f.	Beethoven: *Op. 14, No. 1*, First Movement, mm. 1–12		

In learning to recognize the phrase and its component parts and in considering the larger unit created by combining several phrases, we have completed the preliminary work of this study. For the most part we shall no longer be dealing with bits and pieces but with whole compositions or with complete movements of multimovement works.

6

The Analytical Method

6-1. FORM AND ANALYSIS

Analysis is the separation of a whole into its parts and the exploration of the relationship of these parts to the whole and to each other. In this study we have so far done the opposite: We have begun with the basic unit of music, the phrase, and concerned ourselves with the various methods of developing it and combining it with other phrases to form phrase chains, phrase groups, and periods. We have been dealing with recognition and identification, which are preliminary to analysis.

We are now prepared to begin the process of analysis, either of complete one-movement compositions or of isolated movements from larger works, such as symphonies, concertos, quartets, sonatas, operas, oratorios, and so forth.

The works of the great composers rarely seem to have been created by pouring musical ideas into a preconceived mold. On the contrary, great music shapes itself into whatever form is most fitting to make explicit the particular concept in the mind of the composer. Consequently, it is a mistake to think of the study of form as a process by which we familiarize ourselves with a certain number of standard "blueprints," then proceed to label each composition accordingly. To approach a composition with an open mind, ready to discover what the composer has in store for us, is a safer procedure than to assume in advance that any particular pattern will be in evidence.

This does not mean that we cannot attempt a systematization of form. A perusal of the great musical literature of the past shows that most compositions can in fact be grouped into certain broad formal categories. Thus we speak of "standard forms" and give them names. Such an undertaking is

70

advantageous only if at the same time it is clearly realized that these names are applied by theorists to the music. The composer does not adapt his music to the form. Indeed, if it were otherwise, two compositions with precisely the same form would not be such a rarity.

6-2. DIVISION INTO PARTS

Most compositions divide themselves into two or more parts, and the first goal of analysis is the discovery of the number of these parts. We have seen that Ex. 1-1 is a continuous binary form (section 1-4). We have also seen that it is a double period (section 5-6). These labels do not conflict with each other for they move in different spheres. The former is an analytic term indicating that the piece divides itself into two parts. The latter is a descriptive term indicating the particular relationships exhibited by its various phrases. In the case of Ex. 1-1, part one of the composition is made up of a pair of phrases in a periodic relationship; part two is similarly disposed and these two pairs combine to form a double period. In other binary compositions, part one may be a single phrase, a phrase group, a series of repeated phrases, several periods, or anything else, and part two may show similar or entirely different constructions.

A part may be further divided into sections, and a section into subsections. Lengthy works usually exhibit these subdivisions but many short compositions do not.

Occasionally compositions are found that show none of the characteristics of division. These are the *one-part forms*.

6-3. NAMING THE FORMS

Binary and ternary   Some standard forms have names which are, and which have been for many years, in common use. We shall retain many of these names. "Binary" and "ternary," for instance, standing for forms in two and three parts respectively, are compact and useful. They are somewhat imprecise, however, in that they give no indication as to which of the several types of two- and three-part forms they refer. In this book we shall attempt to convey some idea of the tonal structure of the piece by employing in addition either the word "continuous" or the word "sectional."

Continuous and sectional

An "open" part of a composition is harmonically incomplete. The listener expects a continuation. A "closed" part contains within itself a complete harmonic movement. A tonal structure that causes the listener to expect a continuation after the first part gives rise to a continuous form. Thus, any form with an "open" first part is continuous. A form with a "closed" first part grows by the addition of sections and hence is called a sectional form. Additional words of definition added to the names of some forms will be introduced later.

Unique

Forms to be observed in only one composition scarcely need to be given names. They can be considered unique or nonstandard forms (see Chapter 15). At the same time, it is important to remember that the so-called "standard forms" are standard only in their broad outlines, almost never in details.

EXERCISE

1. Terms to define:
   Binary   Continuous forms _— open_
   Ternary   _open to go on_   Sectional forms _— closed_
   "Open" part   _— open to go_   Standard forms
   "Closed" part   Unique forms

6-4. TWO-PART FORMS

The continuous binary form: division by design   Continuous forms in two parts are referred to as continuous binary forms. There are three standard types: (1) simple, (2) rounded, and (3) balanced.

SIMPLE CONTINUOUS BINARY

Ex. 6-1.   HANDEL: *Suite No. 5 in E Major*, Air ("The Harmonious Blacksmith")

The Air from Handel's *Suite in E Major* for harpsichord consists of a three-phrase period. The first phrase moves from I to a strongly conclusive (masculine perfect authentic) cadence on V. The second phrase ends with a semicadence on V, while the third returns to I with another strong conclusive cadence. The basic tonal structure, then, comprises a single harmonic movement: I–V–I. Nevertheless, the listener feels a definite division take place at the close of the first phrase due to the strength of the masculine perfect authentic cadence on V. Only the final cadence approaches its strength. Further, in comparing the cadence at the end of the first phrase with that which concludes the second, we observe that the eighth-note motion stops with the first B major chord, increasing the feeling of strong punctuation, while the less conclusive ending of the second phrase is partly due to the continuing rhythmic movement in the bass. The piece, then, is in two parts: Part one consists of the first phrase, part two of the two remaining phrases.

The repetition of each part is a by-product, not a cause, of the division. Nor is the tonal structure responsible for the separation into two parts. Example 6-1 illustrates the fact that a composition with a single harmonic movement can divide itself into two parts by means of an emphatic conclusive cadence on a nontonic chord, that is, by an aspect of design. It is the design of the piece as manifested in the relative strength of the cadences that has brought about the division. Division into two results in a binary form. The first part is harmonically "open": It is, therefore, continuous. Its form is referred to as continuous binary and the design symbolized by the letters AB, or, as in Ex. 1-1, AA'.

ROUNDED CONTINUOUS BINARY In the description of the technique of interruption in the preceding chapter, the examples of this technique showed the harmonic movement returning to the beginning immediately upon reaching the cadential V (Ex. 5-1b and Ex. 5-6). It often happens, however, that this V is prolonged by means of chord succession before the actual interruption takes place. In Ex. 6-2, for instance, the V is reached in m. 2, then prolonged by succession (IV_6–V–IV_6–V) before the interruption occurs in m. 3.

Ex. 6-2.   PERGOLESI: *Lo Frate 'Nnamorato,* Act I

Used by permission of Gli Amici Della Musica Da Camera, Rome.

The prolongation of V in Ex. 6-2 took the form of a short extension, repeated, to the phrase. Example 6-3 is a piece in which the chord succession prolonging V becomes a phrase of its own.

Ex. 6-3.   MOZART: *Symphony, K. 183 ("Little G Minor"),* Third Movement

Let us examine Ex. 6-3 first from the point of view of its tonal structure. Phrases 1 and 2 (mm. 1–8) comprise a progressive harmonic movement from I to V. The ensuing chord succession making up phrase 3 (mm. 9–12) prolongs this V. Interruption now occurs. The harmonic and melodic movement returns to the beginning, this time cadencing on the tonic. The tonal structure can be summarized as follows:

$$I \rightarrow \underset{\text{of V}}{\underbrace{\text{V–I}}} \dots V_7 \parallel I \rightarrow \text{V–I}$$

Special notice should be taken of the fact that the interrupting V which is prolonged by means of the chord succession plays a different role at the beginning of the succession than at the end. The succession begins with this dominant chord acting as a secondary tonic; it closes with the same chord acting as V (more often V_7) of the home key.

Regarding its design, Ex. 6-3 exemplifies the principle of statement, digression, restatement. Part one is a two-phrase period. Phrase 3, though based on the first two bars of phrase 1, is somewhat contrasting by virtue of the change from homophonic to an almost contrapuntal texture. Phrase 4 is a literal restatement of phrase 1; phrase 5 is a variation (transposed from V to I) of phrase 2, expanded by interpolation. The design of the piece, then, can be symbolically expressed by the letters AB ‖ A′, and the form called a rounded continuous binary, or simply rounded binary.

In the rounded binary the cadential and the melodic aspects of design are in conflict. The two conclusive cadences mark the ends of the two parts into which the listener senses the music to be divided. Nonetheless, melodically there are three sections. This explains how a two-part form can have the design AB || A'.

BALANCED BINARY Very often the cadences that end each part of a simple binary movement are identical except in pitch. The first is usually on III or V while the second is on I.

Ex. 6-4.   HANDEL: *Suite in E Minor for Harpsichord, Allemande*

Sometimes the similarity in the endings of each part goes further than the final bar or two. For instance, in the *Courante* of Handel's *Suite in E Minor* (from which Ex. 6-4 was taken), the last eight bars of the first part, in the dominant key, appear in an almost exact transposition to the tonic as the last eight bars of the second part. Since the closing section of part one reappears as the close of part two, a piece so constructed is called a balanced binary. A parallel case is the well-known *Invention No. 8 in F Major* of J. S. Bach.

Historical Note   Neither Bach nor Handel wrote balanced binary forms so often as they did simple binaries. Domenico Scarlatti, on the other hand, made very frequent use of the form. While his hundreds of sonatas show much variety in other ways, the great majority of them conclude part two with a transposed restatement of the final bars of part one. Scarlatti, however, did not care much for exact transpositions. Instead, he liked to end the two halves with a somewhat varied form of the same material.[1]

EXERCISES

2. Contrast:

a. Simple continuous binary and rounded binary
b. Simple continuous binary and balanced binary
c. Rounded binary and balanced binary

[1] See No. 274 in Davidson and Apel, *Historical Anthology of Music.* Cambridge, Mass.: Harvard University Press, 1956. For a detailed study of form in Scarlatti's sonatas, see R. Kirkpatrick's *Domenico Scarlatti.* Princeton, N. J.: Princeton University Press, 1953, Chapter XI.

3. Examine the compositions in continuous binary form listed below, answering the following questions:

(1) Which measure marks the end of part one?
(2) How is division into two brought about in each case?
(3) What is the design of the composition?
(4) Which type of continuous binary (simple, rounded, balanced) is represented by each piece?

<table>
<tr><td colspan="2" align="center">A</td><td colspan="2" align="center">B</td></tr>
</table>

A	B
a. Beethoven: *Op. 2, No. 1,* Third Movement (omit Trio)	a. Anon.: *Minuet*
b. Beethoven: *Op. 2, No. 1,* Third Movement (Trio only)	b. Anon.: *March*
c. Chopin: *Prelude No. 10*	c. Schumann: *Album No. 1*
d. MF, No. 2 (omit orchestral prelude)	d. Schumann: *Album No. 7*
e. MF, No. 7 (first stanza only)	e. Chopin: *Prelude No. 20*
f. WJ, No. 10, mm. 6–31	f. Beethoven: *Sonata, Op. 28, Scherzo* (omit Trio)
g. *Chorale No. 44*	
h. *Chorale No. 57*	

333

The sectional binary form: division by double harmonic movement

Sectional forms in two parts are referred to as sectional binary forms. There are three standard types: (a) simple, (b) rounded, and (c) barform.

SIMPLE SECTIONAL BINARY

Ex. 6-5. BRAHMS: *Wiegenlied*

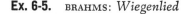

Phrases 1 and 2 form a symmetrical period ending with the strongly conclusive perfect authentic cadence on I. The harmonic movement can in no sense be considered incomplete. Phrases 3 and 4 form another symmetrical period ending with a cadence as strong as the former. We have here, then, two periods (not a double period), each manifesting a complete harmonic movement. On the basis of this tonal structure the piece divides into two parts. The design follows suit: Each period consists of two similar phrases, but the periods contrast with each other. Brahms' *Cradle Song* is a two-part form because of the double harmonic movement. The song's design, two symmetrical, parallel periods which contrast with each other, reinforces and confirms the division brought about by the tonal structure. The design is represented by the letters A-B, the hyphen indicating that A comprises a complete harmonic movement.

Ex. 6-6.   Folk song

The nursery tune in Ex. 6-6 implies a harmonization of alternating V_7 and I, resulting in an authentic cadence on I at the end of each of its two phrases. The melodic line is directed at the end of phrase 1 to the fifth of the tonic chord, and at the end of phrase 2 to the root. We have here, then, a situation similar to that described in section 5-5, wherein the second of two phrases with identical harmonic movements is not a varied repetition of the first. Due to the greater strength of the perfect cadence that closes it, phrase 2 is different from, though similar to, phrase 1. The two phrases form a period with the design A-A' (see Ex. 5-8). Because of the repetition of harmonic movement displayed by the two phrases, the composition falls into two parts.

Examples 6-5 and 6-6 illustrate the fact that

> a composition may divide itself into two parts by means of a tonal structure which consists of two complete harmonic movements.

Division into two results in a binary form. The first part is harmonically "closed": It is therefore sectional. Its form is referred to as sectional binary and the design symbolized by the letters A-B (Ex. 6-5) or A-A' (Ex. 5-8 and Ex. 6-6).

ROUNDED SECTIONAL BINARY   Example 6-7 illustrates a design frequently found in the sectional binary form. This design will be recognized as the counterpart of the rounded continuous binary. It differs from that form only in that its first part completes a harmonic movement. It may be spoken of as the rounded sectional binary.

Ex. 6-7. HAYDN: *Symphony No. 100* ("Military"), Third Movement

BARFORM

Ex. 6-8. BACH: *Schmücke dich, o liebe Seele, Chorale No. 22*

The chorale (Ex. 6-8) consists of five phrases, the third of which is repeated in a variation. Phrases 1 and 2 comprise a symmetrical period which, concluding with a divisive perfect authentic cadence on the tonic, is readily recognized as part one, the remaining phrases forming part two. The tonal structure, like that of all sectional binaries, consists of two complete harmonic movements. The feature that distinguishes the form of this piece from the ordinary sectional binary is simply the fact that part one is repeated. Rather than A-B, the design is A-A-B. It is referred to as the barform.[2]

The two parts of the form exemplify a pattern of repetition followed by contrast. In some barforms the repetition is varied rather than exact. In Ex. 6-8 it will be noted that phrase 5 is a restatement of phrase 2. Thus the same phrase is used to close each of the two parts. While this aspect of the design is not an inevitable characteristic of barform it is to be found quite commonly. A parallel case is the Lutheran hymn, *A Mighty Fortress Is Our God.*

Historical Note   Ordinarily the repetition of a part is of no significance in formal analysis. If we make an exception here it is only because barform has for centuries been recognized as a distinct entity. Indeed, it has a longer history than any other single form. It appeared during the early Middle Ages in the music of the Eastern Church, having been foreshadowed in the ancient Greek odes. Later it became the basis of the *canzo* of the troubadours in Provence and from there it moved to northern France to become the trouvères' *ballade.* The German minnesingers, and after them the meistersingers, cultivated this form above all others and it is from these that the name "barform" derives. In medieval German nomenclature the first part and its repetition were called the *stollen* ("stanzas"), the second part *abgesang* ("aftersong"). These terms are often used today, in English as well as German, but some writers prefer to adopt the names of the parts of the ancient Greek odes: Part one is called the strophe, its repetition the anti-strophe, and part two the epode.

After the decline of the meistersinger the form continued to appear in Protestant chorales and folk songs. Barforms familiar to all are *Dixie* and *The Star-Spangled Banner.* Barform is not of particularly frequent occurrence in the art

---

[2] We retain the name because it is in common use although it is actually a misnomer (see Manfred Bukofzer, *Music of the Baroque Era.* New York: Norton, 1947, p. 356.)

music of the eighteenth and nineteenth centuries,[3] but Wagner made much of it in his opera *Die Meistersinger von Nürnberg*, the *Trial Song* in Act I and the *Prize Song* in Act III both being highly developed, if somewhat irregular, examples.[4]

EXERCISES

4. Contrast:

a. Continuous binary form with sectional binary form
b. Simple sectional binary with rounded sectional binary
c. Simple sectional binary with barform

5. Examine the compositions in sectional binary form listed below, answering the following questions:

(1) Which measure marks the end of part one?
(2) How is division into two brought about in each case?
(3) What is the design of the composition?
(4) Which type of sectional binary (simple, rounded, barform) is represented by each piece?

A	B
a. Chopin: *Prelude No. 7*	a. Bach: *Jesu Meine Freude*, First Movement
b. Beethoven: *Op. 22*, Second Movement, mm. 1–12	b. Schumann: *Album No. 6*
c. Beethoven: *Op. 26*, Scherzo (omit Trio)	c. Hindemith: *Un Cygne*
d. *WJ*, No. 5, mm. 8–24	
e. *WJ*, No. 6, mm. 5–28	
f. *Chorale No. 1*	
g. *Chorale No. 6*	

6-5. THREE-PART FORMS

The sectional ternary form: division by double harmonic movement and by design

[3] On the other hand, A. Lorenz, in his *Das Geheimnis der Form bei Richard Wagner* (1924–1933) claimed that the barform was the basic formal principal of Wagner's operas and Dr. S. Levarie has interpreted parts of Mozart's *Marriage of Figaro* as barforms (in *Mozart's Le Nozze di Figaro.* Chicago: University of Chicago Press, 1952).

[4] When Walther concludes the antistrophe on V rather than on I, Hans Sachs comments that to do so is painful to the meistersingers (*"das macht der Meistern Pein."* Act III, Scene 2).

Ex. 6-9.   MENOTTI: *The Medium*, Act I

Measures 1–12 comprise a three-phrase period completing a harmonic movement in the area of the tonic, forming part one. Phrases 4, 5, and 6 (mm. 13–25) have a special quality of their own contrasting with that of the previous phrases: The melody is made up almost entirely of new motives; the rhythmic character and instrumentation, though not clearly indicated here, are in the original completely changed. With phrase 7 (m. 26 and ff) a return to the beginning is effected. The chief characteristic of the design, then, is statement, digression, restatement.

Because of their contrasting quality, phrases 4–6 strike the listener as a part in themselves. The result is a three-part form, the first division being accomplished by the completion of a harmonic movement, and the second by contrast in the melody, texture, rhythm, and so forth—that is, contrast in design. The three parts constitute a ternary form. The first part is harmonically "closed": It is therefore sectional. The form is referred to as a sectional ternary, the design indicated by the letters A-BA.

The sectional ternary is probably the most common of all three-part forms, occurring again and again in folk songs, hymns, familiar community songs, and popular tunes (for example, *Drink to Me Only with Thine Eyes* and *The Bluebells of Scotland*).

This form is a near relation of the rounded sectional binary which is similar in both tonal structure and design (see Ex. 6-7). The distinction between the two lies in the relationship of the digression to the rest of the piece. In Ex. 6-9 the digression (B) is clearly and strikingly contrasting in character to A. This contrast is strong enough to set B apart in the mind of the listener as distinct in itself. Even if B can be related motivically to A (as it can in mm. 21, 24, and 25 of Ex. 6-9), it will form a part in itself if it is strongly contrasting in character. Examination of Brahms' *Intermezzo in E Minor, Op. 118, No. 2,* will provide ample evidence for this point. Still, even if B is not strikingly contrasting in character to A, it will be heard as a part in itself if its material is not based on that of A.

> Only if B is derived melodically or motivically from A and only if it continues in the same general character (as in Ex. 6-7) does it merge with the return of A into a single part and result in a binary form.

The full sectional ternary form: division by three complete harmonic movements

Ex. 6-10.   SCHUMANN: *Kinderscenen No. 6*

Two very short phrases combine to form a symmetrical period (mm. 1–4), completing a harmonic movement with the feminine perfect authentic cadence. The subsequent eight bars (mm. 5–12) are a symmetrical period in the subdominant key, completing a harmonic movement and ending with a masculine perfect authentic cadence. Measures 13–16, not included in the illustration, are exactly like part one. On the basis of the three complete harmonic movements, Ex. 6-10 divides itself into three parts. The design coincides with this division.

Part One (A)	*Part Two (B)*	*Part Three (A)*
I → II₆–V–I	V–I → II₅⁶–V–I	I → II₆–V–I
	of IV	

When a composition consists of three complete harmonic movements the third part is as a rule either exactly like or a varied repetition of the first part. The middle may or may not be of a contrasting character. The symbolic designation is A-B-A. Since all parts are harmonically "closed," the form is called a full sectional ternary.

The continuous ternary form: division into three parts by design alone

Ex. 6-11.   MOZART: *Im Frühlingsanfang, K. 597*

Phrases 1 and 2 (mm. 1–8) are a symmetrical period with a progressive harmonic movement ending with a strong cadence on V (m. 8). Phrase 3 (mm. 8–12) exhibits a chord succession prolonging V and supporting a melody of a contrasting nature. Interruption now occurs. The harmonic and melodic movement returns to the beginning, this time cadencing on the tonic. The tonal structure, then, consists of a single harmonic movement interrupted at m. 12. The design, on the other hand, divides the piece into three parts. Measures 1–8 become part one due to the divisive strength of the masculine perfect authentic cadence in m. 8. Measures 9–12 become part two due to the contrasting nature of the phrase melody. The remainder is part three.

To acknowledge the continuity of the harmonic movement, the form is called a continuous ternary. The design is graphically represented as AB || A′.

Formal Ambiguity The basic tonal structure of the continuous ternary is identical to that of the continuous rounded binary (see Ex. 6-3):

$$I \rightarrow \underbrace{V_7\text{–}I \ldots V_7}_{\text{of } V} \parallel I \rightarrow V\text{–}I$$

The designs of the two forms are also very similar, both being expressed as AB || A′. As with the sectional ternary and sectional rounded binary, the difference between the two forms lies in the nature of the material that makes up section B. In the continuous binary form, the melodic and motivic material of B is clearly taken from A so that unless there is a striking contrast in character between them, B will not be heard as a distinct part in itself. In the continuous ternary, on the other hand, B is made up of new material or contrasts strikingly in some other way and hence becomes the middle part of a three-part form.

Since the only clear distinction between the continuous rounded binary and the continuous ternary lies in the nature of the material used for the digression (section B), from time to time one comes across a composition for which it is difficult to make a definite decision. Fauré's charming song *Nell, Op. 18, No. 1,* is a case in point. The vocal melody of the digression, beginning with m. 19, is contrasting to that previously heard but not strikingly so, and certain motives are vaguely suggestive of motives in part one. The accompaniment, though at first slightly more complicated than previously, continues with the identical pianistic figure. It is easy to work out a plausible argument in favor of either form. Such ambiguous cases should not annoy the student. On the contrary, they serve to reinforce the contention presented earlier that, however numerous the formal similarities among a number of works, the good composer does not create a piece of music by forcing his ideas to fit a stereotyped pattern. Often his labor results in a work which falls neatly into one of our categories; often it will fit none. And sometimes it seems to hover indecisively between two of them.

For other examples of continuous ternary form using the basic tonal structure of Ex. 6-11, the student is directed to Brahms' piano *Intermezzi, Op. 118, No. 4* and *No. 6; Op. 119, No. 1,* and Mendelssohn's *Song without Words, Op. 19, No. 2.* Some continuous ternary forms, however, use a different tonal structure. Rather than establishing V as a secondary tonic, part one may progress to the dominant of whichever chord begins part two. For instance, part one of Schubert's *Moments Musicaux, Op. 94, No. 2,* progresses from I to IV. This IV is taken to be V/♭VII, ♭VII (enharmonically expressed) being the key of part two.

Other continuous ternary forms mark the end of part one with a strong cadence on III. Rather than a chord succession prolonging V, part two then becomes a progressive movement, leading from this III to the interrupting V which immediately precedes part three. Such a movement is to be found in Mendelssohn's *Song without Words, Op. 85, No. 1,* in F major (see Ex. 5-9) though it is more characteristic of compositions in the minor mode.

Still other tonal structures are to be found among the continuous ternary forms of the great composers. We will consider some of these in more detail in Chapter 8. For now it is enough to emphasize that the usual tonal structure is that of Ex. 6-11 and the fact that

> the division into three is brought about entirely by design: the first division due to a strong conclusive cadence marking the end of part one, and the second due to the contrasting nature of part two.

EXERCISES

6. Contrast:

a. Sectional ternary and full sectional ternary
b. Sectional ternary and continuous ternary
c. Continuous ternary and rounded continuous binary
d. Sectional ternary and rounded sectional binary

7. Examine the compositions in ternary form listed below, answering the following questions:

(1) Which measure marks the end of part one and which the end of part two?
(2) How is division into three brought about in each case?
(3) What is the design of the composition?
(4) Which type of ternary (sectional, full sectional, continuous) is represented by each piece?

A	B
a. Beethoven: *Op. 26,* First Movement, mm. 1–34	a. Schumann: *Album No. 3*
b. Beethoven: *Op. 22, Menuetto* (omit *Minore*)	b. Schumann: *Papillons No. 5*
c. MF, No. 9	c. Chopin: *Mazurka No. 24*
d. Chopin: *Prelude No. 13*	d. Haydn: "Clock Symphony," Finale, mm. 1–28
e. WJ, No. 18	
f. WJ, No. 19	

6-6. COMPOSITIONS IN MORE THAN THREE PARTS

Ex. 6-12. SCHUMANN: *Nachtstücke, Op. 23, No. 4*

After a brief introductory figure, part one, a symmetrical period, presents a complete harmonic movement based on interruption. Part two is a complete harmonic movement in the key of the mediant. Part three is a slightly varied repetition of part one. So far, then, the form is like the full sectional ternary, A-B-A. The subsequent passage is a progressive harmonic movement leading through ♭III and ♭VI to V₇, cleverly semicadencing with the introductory figure. Contrasting in melody and texture it becomes part four. Part five is another restatement of part one, with further changes. The design of the piece is A-B-A-CA and the form can be called a sectional five part. The derivation of this five-part form is clearly from the (full) sectional ternary. The basic idea of repetition after contrast has simply been applied twice rather than once, as in the ternary.

The design of A-BA-BA, as in Chopin's *Nocturne in E flat Major, Op. 9, No. 2,* does not result in a true five-part form. It is, rather, a ternary with repetition, exact or varied, of the last two parts (A-BA-BA equals A-‖ : BA : ‖).

The four-part form, such as Schubert's *Impromptu in E flat Major, Op. 90, No. 2,* is also derived from the ternary, in this case the sectional ternary, form. The contrasting middle part of the ternary A-BA returns as the fourth and final part, resulting in the design A-BA-B′.

Pieces in more than five parts occur from time to time, particularly in the piano works of Schumann. As a rule these multipartite pieces are assembled by several applications of the principle of repetition and contrast as found in the ternary forms. There is no need to discuss them here, for anyone who has followed this study so far will have no trouble in discovering their forms for himself.

6-7. THE ONE-PART FORM

The one-part form with complete harmonic movement

Bach's *Prelude No. 2 in C minor* from the *Well-Tempered Clavier,* Vol. 1 (Ex. 6-13) shows none of the devices that we have enumerated as

Ex. 6-13. BACH: *WTC,* Vol. 1, *Prelude No. 2* (harmonic skeleton)

divisive. Its four phrases are clear enough, but none of these except the last ends with a strong conclusive cadence. The cadenzalike six measures marked "presto" and the single bar marked "adagio" notwithstanding, the design exhibits no contrasts which could separate the single harmonic movement into more than one part. The piece, then, a four-phrase asymmetrical period, is divided by neither design nor tonal structure. It is a one-part form.

The one-part form with progressive harmonic movement

Ex. 6-14. CHOPIN: *Prelude, Op. 28, No. 2*

Some of Chopin's preludes have only a single part. Example 6-14 gives a skeletal outline of one of these. This piece is remarkable in many ways, not least of which is the tonal structure. The vast majority of tonal music begins by establishing a tonic and, after a move away from that tonic, returning to it again. Here no tonality is established until the final two bars. Once these two bars have sounded, the listener realizes that the goal of the preceding harmonic movement is an authentic cadence on an A minor triad. It is then simple enough, by applying hindsight, to label all the preceding harmony as if it were in the key of A minor. This is what has been done in Ex. 6-14. But until the whole piece has been played through, it is impossible to know for certain what tonality the opening phrases express. For the first phrase, either E minor or G major is as plausible, or even more so, than A minor. The piece, then, actually shows a progressive harmonic movement and is a period consisting of three similar phrases. None of these phrases reaches a strong conclusive cadence except the last and no contrasts in design occur. It is therefore a one-part form in three sections with the design AA'A''.

The one-part form with interrupted harmonic movement

A more common type of one-part form is that based on an interrupted harmonic movement. Chopin's *Preludes No. 1* and *No. 4* are so constructed. These are both symmetrical periods, the interruption occurring at the end of the antecedent phrase, with extended consequents, especially in the case of the first prelude. Their design is A ‖ A'. They cannot be considered two-part forms because an interrupted harmonic movement does not have the requisite divisive strength to separate a composition into two real parts. Instead, they are to be considered one-part forms in two sections.

The one-part form with twice interrupted harmonic movement

Ex. 6-15. CHOPIN: *Prelude, Op. 28, No. 9*

Table of Standard Forms

Form	Description
1. One part	Single harmonic movement (complete, progressive, or interrupted); no divisive aspect in design either through strongly conclusive cadences or striking contrasts.
2. Continuous binary	Single harmonic movement divided by design (conclusive cadence).
a. simple	Design: AB or AA'.
b. rounded	Design: AB ‖ A'.
c. balanced	Design: AA'. Part two closes with a transposed restatement of the passage that ends part one.
3. Sectional binary	Double harmonic movement, that is, two complete or interrupted harmonic movements.
a. simple	Design: A-B or A-A'.
b. rounded	Design: A-BA.
c. barform	Design: A-A-B. Part one repeated, part two not repeated.
4. Sectional ternary	Double harmonic movement the second of which is further divided by design (contrast). Design: A-BA.
5. Full sectional ternary	Triple harmonic movement, that is, three complete or interrupted harmonic movements. Design: A-B-A.
6. Continuous ternary	Single interrupted harmonic movement divided by design (conclusive cadence and contrast). Design: AB ‖ A'.
7. Sectional four part	Same as sectional ternary plus transposed restatement of part two as part four. Design: A-BA-B'.
8. Sectional five part	Same as sectional ternary plus new part four and restatement of part one as part five. Design: A-BA-CA.

The *Prelude in E Major* shows a harmonic movement twice interrupted, the harmonic sequence each time taking a different course toward the interrupting V. Like Ex. 6-14 it is a one-part form in three similar sections but is to be distinguished from that work by its two interruptions of the harmonic movement. The design is therefore represented as A ‖ A' ‖ A". The *Prelude in F Major, No. 23*, is similarly constructed as is, on a much larger scale, the *Nocturne in D flat Major, Op. 27, No. 2*.

6-8. THE SIX-STEP METHOD OF ANALYSIS

As with the six steps leading to identification of the larger unit outlined in section 5-7, the student is urged to follow the systematic method presented below until he has gained experience in analytical techniques.

Step 1. Consider the successive phrases, note their cadences, and come to a conclusion regarding the tonal structure of the piece, deciding whether it exhibits a single, double, triple, or other harmonic movement. If single, is the harmonic movement complete, interrupted, or progressive? In a double harmonic movement, of which type is each?

Step 2. Consider the design from the cadential point of view, noting the presence or absence of any divisive conclusive cadence.

Step 3. Consider the design from the motivic and melodic point of view, noting the presence or absence of contrasting phrases and phrases that are restatements of other phrases. (A restatement differs from a repetition in that the former is a recurrence after contrast while the latter is an immediate recurrence. Restatements are important elements of form; repetitions are not.) Represent the design graphically by means of letters: A-BA, A-B-A, A ‖ A′, and so on.

Step 4. In the light of steps 1, 2, and 3, come to a conclusion regarding the number of parts into which the piece will separate.

Step 5. Considering steps 1 and 4, decide whether the form is continuous, sectional, or (if there are three or more parts) full sectional.

Step 6. Decide whether or not the piece coincides in a general way with any of the commonly used standard forms listed in the table.

6-9. APPLICATION OF THE SIX-STEP METHOD OF ANALYSIS

Ex. 6-16.   FAURÉ: *Lydia, Op. 4, No. 2*

Used by permission of Hamelle et Cie, Paris, copyright owner.

For the purpose of demonstration, Gabriel Fauré's *Lydia*, a song for voice and piano, will be analyzed. Example 6-16 presents the song reduced for piano alone. The original has two stanzas that are not, as in our example, indicated by repetition signs but are written out completely. Comparison of the original second stanza with the first will show certain slight changes in the voice part not reproduced here. These changes occur only to accommodate the words of the second stanza to the music of the first. Such slight changes, often necessary in strophic songs, have nothing to do with form and can therefore be disregarded. (See Ex. 6-16.)

Step 1. After two introductory bars played by the piano alone, the voice enters with four successive phrases (mm. 3–19); each consists of four bars except the last, which has five. The piano introduction recurs, this time as an interlude, and stanza two is sung, after which a fifth phrase, for piano, concludes the song. The cadences are: Phrase 1, imperfect authentic on III; phrase 2, semicadence on V; phrase 3, semicadence on V_5^6/VI; phrase 4, perfect authentic on I; phrase 5, imperfect authentic on I.

Before going further we must pause to consider phrase 5. It indubitably presents a complete harmonic movement, $I \rightarrow IV_2^4 \; V_4^6 \; I$. Are we then faced with the necessity of considering this a piece with double harmonic movement, the first covering the first four phrases with their repetition, and the second only this final phrase? Before answering this question, let us consider the relative strength of the cadences. The strongest cadence of the piece is the masculine perfect authentic on I which concludes phrase 4, and it is this cadence which completes the harmonic movement that began with the first phrase. The final phrase, beginning and ending with the tonic chord, is a chord succession whose purpose seems to be not to add to the "argument" of the piece, but only to reinforce the conclusion. The harmonic movement has been from I through III, V, and VI, back to I. The final chord succession, prolonging and emphasizing this I, is therefore not a new harmonic movement but merely an appendage to the other. As such it is, appropriately enough, called a *coda* (Italian: "tail"). The fact that the voice is silent during the coda confirms our interpretation but does not influence it. Even if the voice had taken part, phrase 5 could only have been interpreted as a coda.

Discounting the coda, then, the tonal structure is that of a single harmonic movement, complete.

Step 2. No divisive conclusive cadence is present, the only cadence possessing the requisite strength being that which closes phrase 4.

Step 3. Although the motive a reappears either direct or inverted in each phrase except the coda (marked by overhanging brackets), the phrase melodies are not enough alike to warrant calling them similar phrases. The rising thirds in the lower staff of the coda are related to the similar rising thirds of phrase 3 (m. 11), but the right hand plays an entirely new melody. In graphically representing the design of a composition, a convenient indication of the coda is to place its letter or letters in parentheses. Thus, the design of Fauré's *Lydia* is

$$\text{ABCD- } \left(\begin{smallmatrix} E \\ C \end{smallmatrix}\right)$$

the two letters arranged vertically denoting simultaneity.

Step 4. Steps 1 and 2 provide no basis for separation into parts. The result of step 3 is the realization that, though the melody is partially unified motivically, it provides continuous contrast. In the absence of any restatement, this contrast is not divisive, particularly since it is not far reaching. Tempo, meter, and the general style and mood remain unified. The song is therefore in one part.

Step 5. Since we are dealing with a one-part form this step is unnecessary. All one-part forms are by nature continuous.

Step 6. The form coincides generally with the standard uninterrupted one-part form. The existence of a coda makes no difference in analysis. Any musical form is likely to be provided with a coda.

A full consideration of a given piece of music undertakes both a formal analysis and identification of its larger units. Example 6-13, which is in genre a strophic song of two stanzas, is a four-phrase asymmetrical period (the song proper) plus a single phrase (the coda); it is a one-part form with coda, the design of which is:

$$\text{ABCD- } \left(\begin{smallmatrix} E \\ C \end{smallmatrix}\right)$$

EXERCISE

8. Following the six-step method, analyze the following music.

A	B
a. Chopin: *Prelude No. 20*	a. Couperin: *La Bandoline*, mm. 1–8
b. Beethoven: *Op. 14, No. 2,* Second Movement, mm. 1–20	b. Schubert: *Who Is Sylvia?*
c. *WJ, No. 13*	c. Schumann: *Album No. 5*
d. *WJ, No. 12*	d. Chopin: *Mazurka No. 5*
e. *MF, No. 15*	e. Chopin: *Prelude No. 4*
f. Beethoven: *Op. 2, No. 3,* Second Movement	f. Wolf: *Das verlassene Mägdelein*
g. Chopin: *Prelude No. 17*	g. Ives: *The Cage*
h. *Chorale No. 59*	
i. *Chorale No. 131*	

7

Theme and Variations

*Bach
Goldberg
+
Beethoven
Diabelli;
to 115*

7-1. SECTIONAL AND CONTINUOUS VARIATIONS

The chief characteristic of the theme and variations lies in the principle of repetition. A theme is stated, then repeated a number of times, each time in a new guise. The theme and variations does not lack contrast, but the contrast is not juxtaposed to the restatement, as in the rounded binary and the ternary forms. Rather, the contrast is merged with the restatement.

There are two chief categories of the theme and variations. *Sectional variations* are those based on a theme that consists of one or more periods with, usually, a pause or clear caesura at the end of the theme and of each variation. *Continuous variations* are those based on a theme comprising only a phrase or two (usually covering a total of from four to eight bars), the variations following each other uninterruptedly. The former are represented by the theme and variations (or variations on a theme) and the eighteenth-century doubles; the latter by the ground bass (*basso ostinato*), *chaconne*, and *passacaglia*.

Historical Note on Sectional Variations   Sectional variations are one of the oldest instrumental practices, having been in continuous use since their appearance in the early sixteenth century in the lute and keyboard music of Spain and England [see Nos. 122, 124, and 134 in *Historical Anthology of Music (HAM)*]. Some isolated examples are of even earlier origin, such as the fourteenth-century *Le Moulin de Paris* (in RCA Victor album, *The History of Music in Sound*, vol. 3).

Often the theme and variations form part of a larger work, a movement in a sonata or suite, but they appear frequently as independent compositions. In all

96

periods it has been common practice for a composer to borrow the theme which he sets out to vary, either from folk song or from the work of another composer, as in Brahms' *Variations and Fugue on a Theme by Handel, Op. 24,* or Dohnanyi's *Variations on a Nursery Song.* But when the set of variations occurs as part of a larger work, the theme is usually an original creation of the composer.

In the eighteenth-century keyboard suite (see Chapter 10, Historical Note), particularly those of French origin, certain dance movements were provided with a very simple type of variation. The movement was played through, then repeated with new ornaments in the melody. The second version was called the double. Sometimes more than one double was written, as in the second Courante of Bach's *English Suite No. 1,* which has two. Sometimes the composer went further than merely to provide new ornaments for the double of a dance. In the doubles of Bach's courante just referred to, the bass lines as well as the melodies are varied.

In addition to the use of the term described above, the name "double" sometimes occurs in the eighteenth century as a synonym for "variation." Thus, the airs in Handel's *Suites No. 4* and *No. 5* for harpsichord are provided with doubles which in no way differ from his works expressly entitled "variations."

7-2. FIXED AND VARIABLE ELEMENTS OF A THEME

It is obvious that a varied repetition of a theme will change some aspects of the original and retain others. To change everything would destroy the element of repetition; to retain everything would leave the original unvaried. We shall examine the air known as "The Harmonious Blacksmith" chosen by Handel for the variations that close his *Suite No. 5* for harpsichord. Reference to this air (Ex. 6-1) reveals certain features which might be changed or which might be maintained.

1. Key: E
2. Mode: major
3. Form: simple continuous binary
4. Length: part one, two bars, repeated; part two, four bars, repeated
5. Basic tonal structure:

$$||: I \rightarrow \underbrace{\text{V--I}}_{\text{of V}} :|| \; ||: I \rightarrow \text{V--I} :||$$

6. Precise harmonic sequence:

$$||: I \; V \; I \mid V_6 \; VI_6 \; VII \; III \; \underbrace{II_6 \; V \; I}_{\text{of V}} :||$$

$$||: I_6 \; IV \; I_6 \; I \mid IV \; I_6 \; IV \; I_6 \; V_4^6 I \mid V \; I_6 \; II_6 \; I_6 \mid II_6 \; I_6 \; VII_6 \; I \; V_7 \mid I :||$$

7. Tempo: not indicated; presumably *moderato*
8. Melody

9. Bass

✗ 10. Texture: homophonic, mostly four-part chordal style

Example 7-1 is part one of each of the doubles.

Ex. 7-1.   HANDEL: *Suite No. 5 in E Major*

Examination of the five doubles which follow the air reveals that of the features listed above seven remain fixed throughout. These are key, mode, form, length, basic tonal structure, and tempo. Changes in the precise harmonic sequence take place, though these are few and unimportant. The only features subjected to real variation are the melody, the bass, and the texture.

The fixed and variable elements of Handel's "Harmonious Blacksmith" variations are not those of every set of variations. In his *Aria with Thirty Variations*, commonly called the "Goldberg Variations," Bach sometimes varies the mode and the (presumable) tempo in addition to melody, bass, precise harmonic sequence, and texture. Other sets of variations sometimes go further and vary the basic tonal structure and the key. In his *Piano Variations in F Major, Op. 34*, Beethoven changes key with each variation, though such a procedure is admittedly very exceptional. Normally both the form and length of the theme remain fixed throughout the variations. Exceptions to this observation will be discussed later.

To sum up, it is usual for the composer to retain as fixed the length and form of the theme throughout his variations. The other elements—key, mode, basic tonal structure, precise harmonic sequence, tempo, melody, bass line, and texture—may or may not be subjected to variation during the course of the work. Of these the most commonly varied features are the melody, the bass, the texture, and the precise harmonic sequence.

7-3. PROCEDURES IN SECTIONAL VARIATIONS

Reference to Ex. 7-1 will reveal the various procedures used by Handel in constructing his variations on "The Harmonious Blacksmith."

Ornamental variation

The melody of the theme is made up for the most part in eighth notes. Double 1 turns these into sixteenth notes, ornamenting the melody in a simple manner (Ex. 7-1a).

Simplifying variation

Double 2 continues the sixteenth-note motion but transfers it to the left hand as an accompaniment to a simplified version of the melody in eighth notes (Ex. 7-1b).

Figural variations

Doubles 3 and 4 are constructed from a three-note triplet motive (marked by overhanging brackets in Ex. 7-1c and d). When a variation is thus built from a particular figure or motive—which may or may not be derived from a part of the theme—it is spoken of as a figural variation. Sometimes more than one motive is employed. Double 5 is another figural variation in which the motive employed is a scale through an octave, sometimes ascending and sometimes descending.

The theme of Bach's "Goldberg Variations" has a bass consisting of slow-moving notes mainly constructed from segments of the downward scale. This bass is simple and easily grasped by the listener. The melody, on the other hand, is so elaborate and laden with ornamentation that only after repeated hearings is one able to keep it in mind. This matters not the least to Bach, for he builds these variations on the bass of the theme rather than on the melody. He makes use of the principle of the ornamental variation, but applies it to the bass.

Ex. 7-2.   BACH: "Goldberg Variations" (some bass lines)

Melodic variation   — same bass + general harmonic scheme

Once the aria has been played, its melody is abandoned until the variations are completed, after which it returns *da capo* to bring the work to a close. In this piece many variations, then, provide new melodies while retaining the same bass and general harmonic scheme, a procedure known as the melodic variation. (See also Beethoven's *Sonata, Op. 109*, Third Movement, Variation I.)

Contrapuntal variation

In the "Goldberg Variations" counterpoint is prominently exhibited in several ways. These can be grouped under four headings.

Ex. 7-3. BACH: "Goldberg Variations"

IMITATIVE Example 7-3a illustrates a type of contrapuntal variation in which motivic imitation plays an important role.

CANONIC When two voices are written in canon, the second is a strict imitation of the first. Every third variation of the "Goldberg Variations" is so written, nine canonic variations in all. Variation 3 is a canon at the unison, that is, the second voice imitates at the pitch of the first voice. Variation 6 is a canon at the second, the imitating voice being placed a second higher than the leading voice. Variation 9 is at the third (see Ex. 7-3b), Variation 12 at the fourth, and so on.

FUGAL Example 7-3c illustrates a variation which proceeds along the lines of a fugue. The fugue will be explained in Chapter 14. Here we can only point out its presence.

ADDITIVE Example 7-3d shows the beginning of variation 30, the final variation of the work. This variation has been constructed by Bach as a contrapuntal *quodlibet* (Latin for "what you please"), a piece which combines various tunes or fragments of tunes. Bach uses two songs popular in his day, *Ich bin so lang nich bei dir gewest* ("It's been so long since I've been with you") and *Kraut und Rüben haben mich vertrieben* ("Cabbage and turnips have driven me away") which he combines with each other and superimposes over the bass of the theme. Since the fragments have been added to the pre-existing bass, this type of contrapuntal variation is called "additive." In other music the additive variation does not ordinarily make use of borrowed melodies, but combines newly invented counterpoints with the melody of the theme (see Ex. 7-4).

Characteristic variation

Bach has introduced into the "Goldberg Variations" several characteristic variations, so called because each one takes on a special character, such as a march or dance of some kind. Variation 7, for instance, has the quality of a *siciliano* with its distinctive rhythm

Variation 11 is like a *gigue* in fast 12/16 time, and Variation 19 a minuet. Variation 16 is particularly interesting in that its two halves are utilized to imitate first the slow, dignified opening and then the fast fugal section of a French overture (see Section 14-10).

The sets of variations by Bach and Handel discussed so far have yielded up the commonly used procedures to be found in the variations of the great composers. But no pretense is made of having exhausted all possibilities. The variations of certain composers—Beethoven and Brahms in particular—contain many isolated procedures invented for particular pieces which do not readily form themselves into groups or categories. The student is urged to study the variations of these composers, especially Beethoven's *Diabelli Variations, Op. 120,* and to make his own discoveries.

The list of variation procedures given before can be misleading if one supposes that every variation must fall into one and only one category. It is not uncommon for variations to partake of features of two or even three types. For instance, double 3 of the "Harmonious Blacksmith" variations is listed as a figural variation. Nevertheless, the perpetual fast-moving triplets give it the nature of a *gigue*. It is at once a figural and a characteristic variation. In the Finale of Mozart's *Quartet in D Minor, K. 421,* the second variation alternates every four bars between the figural and the melodic types.

7-4. FORM IN SECTIONAL VARIATIONS

Form of the theme   A glance through a great number of the sectional variations of the composers of the last two centuries reveals that most themes contain a double bar with repetition signs somewhere near their middle. One must, however, avoid the hasty conclusion that two repeated halves inevitably indicate one of the binary forms. It is true, of course, that the first part of the binary form is often repeated before the statement and repetition of the second part. But a one-part or ternary form can also be subjected to a similar repetition scheme. For instance, the theme of the *Allegretto con Variazioni* from Mozart's *Clarinet Quintet, K. 581,* is a sectional ternary form with a repetition scheme as follows: || : A- : || || : BA : ||. The theme of Beethoven's *Twenty-Four Variations on Vieni Amore* (without opus number) is a one-part form, a contrasting symmetrical period with repeated antecedent and repeated consequent, as is the theme of Brahms' *Handel Variations, Op. 24.* It is necessary, then, to disregard the repetition scheme and to focus one's attention on the tonal structure of the theme and its design before coming to a conclusion regarding the form of the theme. Still, most themes chosen by the great composers for treatment by variation do in fact exhibit one of the binary forms.

Form of each variation

It has been pointed out that one of the aspects of the theme that is usually maintained throughout the variations is its form. Most variations, then, like most themes, are binary forms. Not infrequently, variations occur which seemingly change the form of the theme in that they do not retain the double bar and repetition marks which appear at the presentation of the theme. Often this change is only an apparent one, the repetition of each half of the theme having been written out rather than indicated by the repetition sign. The composer does this in order to incorporate certain changes the second time. Sometimes only small changes appear in the repetition (as in double 2 of the "Harmonious Blacksmith" variations), sometimes important ones (as in the Finales of Beethoven's *Sonatas, Op. 109* and *Op. 111*). In variations for two instruments, such as violin and piano, the material first given to the violin might be given to the piano in the repetition or vice versa (for example, Mozart, *Violin Sonata, K. 305,* Second Movement, Variation 6). When the repetition itself is thus varied, one speaks of a double variation.

Nevertheless, variations which really do change the form of the theme occur occasionally. In the latter half of the nineteenth century this device became common and was used along with changes of key and length. Indeed, almost none of the original features of the theme were regularly maintained, each variation being more in the nature of an independent development on some motive or other distinctive feature of the theme. Richard Strauss' *Don Quixote* (1897) is a theme with variations of this kind. Some maintain that this species should not be called "Variations on a Theme" at all, but "Developments on a Theme." When the form of the theme is abandoned, the resulting variation is termed "free" in contrast to the regular strict type.

Elgar's *Variations on an Original Theme, Op. 35,* known as the "Enigma Variations" (1899), represents a mid-point between strict and free variations. All elements of the theme are subjected to variation throughout the piece. Its sectional ternary form, however, though not rigidly adhered to, exerts a definite influence on the form of each variation. All manner of varied repetitions of different passages, introductions, extensions, and codettas are brought in, creating differences in length and outward appearance of the form. Yet through it all the ternary form can be traced in each variation.

The finale

The problem of finding a satisfactory means of concluding a set of variations is one which has admitted a great number of solutions. Handel, in his "Harmonious Blacksmith" variations, provides no special finale, simply ending with the last and most brilliant variation. In the "Goldberg Variations," Bach concludes by repeating the theme *da capo.* Not infrequently the last variation gives place to a fugue which concludes the work, as in Brahms' *Variations and Fugue on a Theme by Handel, Op. 24,* or Benjamin Britten's *Young Person's Guide to the Orchestra (Variations and Fugue on a Theme by Henry Purcell).* In his *Variations on a Theme by Haydn, Op. 56,* Brahms concludes with a ground bass (see Section 7-8). Occurring more often than any other one type, however, is the addition of a coda. Sometimes the coda is quite short, as in the variations on the "Austrian Hymn" from Haydn's *Quartet, Op. 76, No. 3,* but not infrequently it is lengthy and devotes itself to a free development of all or part of the theme. Beethoven's *Twenty-Four Variations on Vieni Amore* conclude with a developing coda which is exactly four times the length of the theme.

EXERCISE

1. Examine the following sectional variations and answer the questions listed below regarding each.

A	B
a. Beethoven: *Op. 14, No. 2,* Second Movement	a. Mozart: *Theme with Variations from Sonata, K. 284*
b. Beethoven: *Op. 26,* First Movement	

(1) Compare the theme with each variation. Indicate which of the following elements are fixed and which are varied in each variation: key, mode, form, length, basic tonal structure, precise harmonic sequence, tempo, melody, bass, texture.

(2) In what way are the varied elements of the two sets of variations changed?

(3) Which procedure is used for each variation? Does any variation fail to fall

neatly into one of the categories listed in Section 7-3? If so, describe the procedure used.

(4) How is the problem of the finale dealt with?

7-5. SHAPE IN SECTIONAL VARIATIONS

A good composer will not be satisfied to string together a number of variations at random with no attention to the order in which they appear, for to do so would result in a lack of coherence despite the unity of material. Common ways of achieving a coherent arrangement of the variations can be summarized under four headings.

Rhythmic crescendo

A glance back at Ex. 6-1 and Ex. 7-1 will show that the rhythmic movement of Handel's "Harmonious Blacksmith" variations gradually increases from eighth notes in the air itself to thirty-second notes in the final variation. The consistent use of notes of smaller and smaller value is known as a "rhythmic crescendo" and imparts to the work as a whole a unity over and above that of the separate variations. A particular double is thus more than just an interesting variant of the theme, for it has an integral part in the whole work, helping along the gradual increase of intensity that builds steadily from the beginning to the end.

The rhythmic crescendo often occurs in works in variation form, not usually throughout the whole work as is the case here, but extending over several of the variations.

Grouping

The five variations in Handel's work actually make up only three groups: doubles 1 and 2 belong together due to their sixteenth-note motion, and doubles 3 and 4 belong together because of the similarity of their triplet figure; at one end double 5 stands alone, balancing the theme which stands alone at the other. Grouping of the variations into larger parts is a second road toward unity.

Logical scheme

In Bach's "Goldberg Variations," every third variation is constructed as a two-voice canon at a different interval. Here we encounter a logical scheme used as one means of organizing the entire set of variations.

In his *Quartet, Op. 76, No. 3,* Haydn has written a set of additive variations on the "Austrian Hymn." The melody is left intact throughout the four variations (see Ex. 7-4), but passes from the first violin (theme) to the second violin (Variation 1), to the cello (Variation 2), to the viola (Variation 3), and back to the first violin (Variation 4).

Benjamin Britten's scheme in his *Young Person's Guide to the Orchestra* is to construct the successive variations in such a way as to emphasize and demonstrate the various orchestral instruments, beginning with those at the top of the orchestral score (flutes and piccolo) and continuing systematically through the string basses.

In none of these cases is the logical scheme the only means of over-all organization, but it serves as one factor making a definite contribution to a unified whole.

Increasing complexity

In the case of the variations on the "Austrian Hymn," the effect of the logical scheme is aided by Haydn's having placed his variations in an order of increasing complexity.

Ex. 7-4.   HAYDN: *Quartet, Op. 76, No. 3, Second Movement*

The theme first appears with straightforward four-part harmony. Variation 1 is a contrapuntal duet between the two violins, violin II playing the melody and violin I adding a counterpoint above it (Ex. 7-4a). Variation 2 stresses the violins and cello while the viola plays only occasional bass notes. The melody is given to the cello (Ex. 7-4b). Variation 3 is still mostly in three voices, but the voices are divided up among the four instruments, each voice having greater independence than previously, and the element of chromaticism heightens the sense of urgency (Ex. 7-4c). Finally, in the last variation, the four instruments play continually and in their upper registers, providing an elaborate contrapuntal texture to support the melody. To this last variation is appended a five-bar coda in which the texture is gradually simplified and the music descends to a normal playing register.

The following diagram, admittedly oversimplified, is meant to show the total shape of the piece regarding the degree of textural complexity. It has nothing to do with dynamics, for the theme and all the variations are to be played softly.

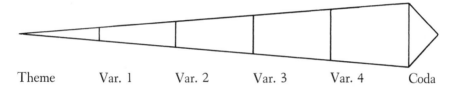

Theme   Var. 1   Var. 2   Var. 3   Var. 4   Coda

Diagram of Shape of Haydn's Quartet, Op. 76,
No. 3, Second Movement

The device of gradually increasing the complexity of the successive variations is somewhat akin to that of the rhythmic crescendo, for in both cases the variations tend to become steadily more engaging, more intense, though not necessarily louder. It is also possible to reverse either procedure by a rhythmic diminuendo or a gradual decrease in complexity.

Arnold Schoenberg's, *Variations on a Recitative for Organ, Op. 40,* has a rather complex shape. The work consists of a theme, ten variations, a cadenza, and a finale which bears some resemblance to a fugue.[1] The theme and the first three variations group themselves together by a steady increase in tension achieved through a rhythmic and dynamic crescendo. Variation 4 brings in a quieter, slower movement; Variation 5 is fast and light; Variation 6 returns to the serene character of Variation 4. These three, then, form a second group: Two calm variations surrounding a scherzo. With Variations 7, 8, and 9 a rhythmic and dynamic crescendo combine with increasing com-

---

[1] Although the score does not expressly call it so, in conversation Schoenberg referred to this finale as a fugue.

plexity to build toward a second climax. This tapers off for Variation 10, a very slow, extremely quiet movement. A brilliant cadenza introduces the finale, the over-all effect of which is of increasing complexity and rhythmic crescendo to a point of climax (m. 14 from the end). The music then seems to crouch down within itself and gather up its energy for the grandiose outburst of the last few bars (see Ex. 2-6).

A simplified diagram illustrates the shape of Schoenberg's organ variations:

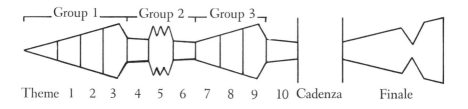

Theme 1   2   3   4   5   6   7   8   9   10 Cadenza   Finale

Diagram of Schoenberg's Organ Variations

In summary, the chief methods by which a coherent shape in sectional variations is attained are as follows. Any of these methods may, of course, be used in combination.

1. *Grouping.* If each variation is a self-contained unit unrelated to the other variations, the work is apt to be sprawling and disconnected. But if two or more variations are constructed with enough similarity to be perceived as a group, the total number of parts in the work can be considerably reduced. Fewer parts will greatly increase comprehensibility.

2. *Logical scheme.* A plan, logical and systematic in itself, imposed on the variations, can do much in the way of tying them together. Bach's series of canons and Haydn's passage of the theme from instrument to instrument are examples of such logical schemes.

3. *Rhythmic crescendo or diminuendo.* A gradual build-up of intensity or excitement can sometimes be achieved by introducing into successive variations notes of smaller and smaller value. Or, conversely, a gradual relaxation by the systematic use of notes of larger value can be effected. In this way, each variation becomes an integral part of a larger unit.

4. *Increase or decrease in complexity.* Similar in effect to 3 above is the gradual increase in complexity of texture—two-voice counterpoint moving to three voice, then to four voice, is a simple means of achieving greater complexity. A more subtle means would be a greater degree of independence in the voice parts within the texture of a fixed number of voices. A gradual decrease in complexity is to be had by reverse methods.

Contrast

Sometimes variations are juxtaposed not to obtain maximum unity, but to achieve the greatest possible variety. For instance, in Beethoven's *Diabelli Variations, Op. 120*, Variations 29, 30, and 31 are clearly a part in themselves, grouped together to achieve coherence, with the preceding Variation 28 acting almost like a transition to this section. Earlier, however, many adjacent variations exhibit a high degree of contrast, for example, Variations 13, 14, and 15, or Variations 18, 19, and 20.

EXERCISE

2. Re-examine the variations of Exercise 1 of this chapter. Do these variations exhibit a coherent shape? By what method or methods is coherence attained? Make a diagram.

7-6. MODIFICATIONS OF SECTIONAL VARIATIONS

Variations on two themes   Some works present not one, but two themes as subjects for variation. The themes are sometimes contrasting, but not infrequently they are motivically related and share the same key, though often they differ in mode. Since it takes so much longer to get through two themes than one, composers generally write only a very few variations for each theme. Haydn's exquisite *Piano Variations in F Minor* are a notable example. Here, theme B, called Trio by Haydn, is in the same key, but opposite mode, as theme A. Each theme is presented, then alternately twice varied, a lengthy coda concluding the piece. A twentieth-century example of variations on two themes occurs as the second movement of Schoenberg's *Quartet No. 3, Op. 30*.

Variations on two themes are sometimes referred to as "double variations." It is preferable to reserve this term for variations in which the repetition of each part is itself varied (see Section 7-4).

Variation rondo

From time to time composers have contrived to write movements that combine essential features of different forms. The basic principle of the rondo (see Chapter 9) is the regular recurrence of a *refrain* which contrasts with interspersed *episodes*. One occasionally comes across sets of variations that include insertions in the form of episodes, either between each variation or between a group of variations. There is no term universally applied to this type of hybrid form. For convenience we shall refer to it as the variation rondo.

A well-known example of the variation rondo is the *Andante* of Haydn's *Piano Trio in G Major* which is a theme and two variations separated by episodes.

Refrain 1	Episode 1	Refrain 2	Episode 2	Refrain 3
Theme I A	New (related to theme) I♭ B	Var. 1 I A	New VI C	Var. 2 I A

Mozart, too, used this form, though somewhat differently from Haydn, in the last movement of his *Piano Concerto in C Minor, K. 491*. This movement contains three episodes. The first, in the relative major key, is inserted between Variation 3 and Variation 4. The second, in the tonic key major mode, occurs between Variations 4 and 5, and the third between Variations 5 and 6. Each episode contains new material, the third including a solo cadenza for the piano. After Variation 6 a coda is added.

Isolated modifications by Beethoven

On several different occasions Beethoven invented special modifications of the variation form to suit his purpose for a particular work. These forms are interesting and instructive, but as they do not appear again in other works, it is not necessary to go into more than one in detail here. The student is nevertheless urged to study the scores and discover for himself what Beethoven has done in the slow movements of *Symphonies No. 5, No. 7,* and *No. 9,* and in the slow movement of the *Quartet in A Minor, Op. 132*.

The particular work to be discussed here is the Finale to the *Symphony No. 3* ("Eroica"). This movement is unique in a number of ways. First, it makes use of both "strict" and "free" variations; second, the theme is preceded by an introduction; and third, perhaps most striking of all, the melody of the theme is not introduced until the third variation.

The movement opens with a stormy unison passage in the strings, emphasizing III, which soon settles down to a V_7. This constitutes the introduction and occupies eleven bars. We then hear the theme—or what we presume to be the theme—played in unison (mm. 12–43). It is a symmetrical period with both antecedent and consequent repeated, but although this is its first presentation, the repetition of each phrase is varied. Variations 1, 2, and 3 are strict in that they keep to the form and key of the theme. They are of the additive type and at the same time gradually increase in complexity and create a rhythmic crescendo that goes from eighth notes to triplets to sixteenth notes. Variation 3, along with the added sixteenth-note counterpoint in the first violins, introduces in the woodwinds the actual melody of the theme (mm. 75–107), for what we have heard previously turns out to be only its bass.

Ex. 7-5. BEETHOVEN: *Symphony No. 3*

The gradual increase in complexity that occurs from the original presentation of the bass of the theme through Variation 3, in addition to the rhythmic crescendo, ties together this portion of the movement, so that it plainly forms a part in itself. Moreover, all the variations have been strict ones and have expressed the main tonality of E♭ major. As the third variation closes (m. 107), a new and different part begins. The new part is devoted to free variations. Except for Variation 5, the form of the theme is disregarded, new keys appear, and the variations are sometimes separated from each other by passages called *transitions* which lead from one to another. One of these transitions does, in fact, open the new part and lead into the submediant key, C minor. Variation 4 (mm. 117–174), expressing VI, is like a fugue, using as its subject the first four notes of the bass theme to which a new ending is appended. Its counterpoint is taken from Variation 1. The variation ends with a semicadence (V_7/VI). The fifth variation (mm. 175–210) expresses VII (D major). It is an ornamental variation on the melody of the theme. D major acts as the dominant of G minor (VII = V/III) and Variation 6 (mm. 211–256) expresses the latter key. It is a melodic variation: A new melody, with a dancelike Hungarian quality, is superimposed over a recurring bass figure made up of the first four notes of the bass of the theme. The seventh variation (mm. 257–277) is short and might almost be considered a transition. It begins with a statement of the theme—bass and melody—in the major mode of VI, then treats the first phrase in sequence through the minor mode of VI and so through II to V_5^6 and thence to I_6. From this point until the end of the movement, the main key of E♭ major is maintained.

Variation 8 (mm. 277–348) corresponds to Variation 4 in that it is like the beginning of a fugue. This time, however, the bass subject is inverted and appears with a new counterpoint in the manner of a double fugue (see Section 14-7). The melody also makes its appearance in this section in a rhythmically altered version. Gradually the bass of the theme becomes less and less prominent, being reduced to a three-note motive and treated in diminution, and before the variation is completed it disappears entirely.

With Variation 9 (mm. 348–380), an abrupt change occurs and the third part begins. The tempo slows from *allegro molto* to *poco andante* and the melody of the theme, with new harmonies and a new bass, is played expressively by the woodwinds, then taken up by the strings. An accompaniment of triplets is added, and the variation rises to a climax ushering in Variation 10 (mm. 380–396), which continues Variation 9 more broadly and fully, with the melody in the bass instruments. With 9 and 10, the "strict" type of variation returns except that the repetitions are omitted for Variation 10. The final coda (mm. 396–473), based on the melody of the theme, is in several sections, the fourth of which brings back the introduction and the quick tempo so that the movement ends brilliantly and triumphantly.

Particularly remarkable is Beethoven's treatment of the bass of the theme. At the beginning of the movement it is the most prominent feature, first played alone; later in the movement it dominates many of the variations, even acting as the subject of the two fugal portions. Gradually disappearing during the second fugue (Variation 8) it remains absent during the rest of the movement, which is completely given over to the melody. In the final variation the melody itself becomes the bass.

Variations 1 through 3 are characterized by dependence on the formal structure of the theme and remain in the home key. Variations 9 and 10 do likewise. Variations 4 through 8, on the other hand, display the "free" type of variation and express VI, ♭VI, VII, and III, only the final fugue emphasizing the tonic. Thus the variations group themselves into three parts as a kind of sectional ternary form.

Outline Summary of Beethoven's Symphony No. 3, Finale

Bars	Section	Material	Description	Tonal Structure
1–11	Intro.	Independent	Unison flourish, slowing to halt on V_7.	$\underbrace{V_7\text{–}I}_{\text{of III}} \to V_7$
Part One				
12–43	Theme	Bass only	Varied repetitions	$I \to V\ I$
44–59	Var. 1	Bass & counterpoint	Additive var., eighths	$I \to V\ I$
60–75	Var. 2	Bass & new counterpoints	Additive var., triplets	$I \to V\ I$
75–107	Var. 3	Bass & new counterpoints, plus melody	Additive double var., sixteenths	$I \to V\ I$
Part Two				
107–116	Trans.	Motive from melody	Sequential	$I \to V/VI$
117–174	Var. 4	Motive from bass & counterpoint from Var. 1	Fugue	$\underbrace{I \to V_7}_{\text{of VI}}$
175–210	Var. 5	Melody	Ornamental double var. with 4-bar extension	$\underbrace{VI\ V_7\ I \to V_7\ I}_{\text{of VII}}$
211–256	Var. 6	Motive from bass	Melodic var. over recurring bass figure	$\underbrace{I \to IV \to I}_{\text{of III}}$
257–277	Var. 7	Melody, antecedent only	Sequential, quasi-transition	$VI\natural\text{–}\flat \to II\ V_2^4\ I_6$
277–348	Var. 8	Bass motive inverted; new counterpoint; melody, antecedent	Double fugue; bass motive in diminution	$I \to V_7$
Part Three				
348–380	Var. 9	Melody	Ornamental double var., new bass; slow tempo.	$I \to V_7\ I$
380–396	Var. 10	Melody	Additive var., repetitions omitted, melody becomes bass	$I \to V_7\ I$
Coda				
396–404	Sec. 1	Melody, antecedent	Melody hidden in uppermost voice	$I \to V_7/IV$

Outline Summary of Beethoven's Symphony No. 3, Finale—(Continued)

Bars	Section	Material	Description	Tonal Structure
404–420	Sec. 2	Melody, antecedent	Melody hidden in uppermost voice	$IV \rightarrow V\ I$ of III
420–430	Sec. 3	Melody, antecedent	Melody hidden in uppermost voice	III
431–435	Sec. 4	Introduction	Intro. flourish transposed; fast tempo	$III \rightarrow V_7$
435–473	Sec. 5	Motive from melody; new	Brilliant conclusion	$I \rightarrow V_7\ I$

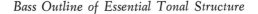

Bass Outline of Essential Tonal Structure

EXERCISES

3. Contrast:

a. Double variations and variations on two themes
b. Variations on two themes and variation rondo

4. Examine at least one of the following works:

a. Haydn: *Piano Variations in F Minor*
b. Haydn: *Piano Trio in G Major,* First Movement
c. Mozart: *Concert Rondo, K. 382*
d. Mozart: *Piano Concerto in C Minor, K. 491,* Third Movement
e. Beethoven: *Symphony No. 5,* Second Movement
f. Beethoven: *Symphony No. 7,* Second Movement
g. Beethoven: *Symphony No. 9,* Third Movement
h. Beethoven: *Quartet in A Minor, Op. 132,* Third Movement

7-7. SUMMARY OF SECTIONAL VARIATIONS

We speak of sectional variations when the theme and each variation is a complete little piece in itself. The theme is often binary form, but whether it is one part, binary, or ternary it will in many cases be laid out in two repeated halves. Usually there will be a distinct stop between variations.

"Strict" variations keep the form of the theme and, normally, the key and length as fixed elements. Other elements may or may not be modified in the course of the variations. In "free" variations the form and length of the theme are as variable as the other elements.

An attempt to list all the possible procedures used by the great composers in constructing different types of variations would result in a cumbersome list of mammoth proportions and be of little use to the student. Some common procedures are the (1) ornamental, (2) simplifying, (3) melodic, (4) figural, (5) contrapuntal (imitative, canonic, fugal, additive), and (6) characteristic, but no variation is necessarily limited to only one category.

Composers have often attempted to achieve an over-all coherence to their sets of variations by means of (1) grouping certain ones together, (2) setting in motion a rhythmic crescendo or diminuendo which operates over some or all of the successive variations, (3) devising a series of variations which evince steadily increasing or decreasing complexity, and (4) imposing some kind of logical scheme which permeates the whole set.

Historical Note on Continuous Variations   Since the early seventeenth century, continuous variations have tended to group themselves into two types. In one, the fixed element is a persistently recurring series of harmonies, in the other it is a bass melody.

The idea of the constantly repeating bass melody, called a ground bass or *basso ostinato* (Italian: "obstinate bass"), can be traced back to the thirteenth century. The well-known canon *Sumer is icumen in* is one of the earliest extant compositions to make use of this technique. In the sixteenth century the ground bass is to be found in connection with the dance (see *HAM, No. 103*) and during the seventeenth century it came into prominent use not only in dance music but in vocal music as well. Early baroque composers such as Caccini, Monteverdi, Landi, and Frescobaldi are among those who composed vocal continuous variations. Often the ground-bass melody was not regularly repeated in its original form but was constantly varied. Nevertheless, in spite of the different versions in which it appeared, its skeletal outline would engender the same series of harmonies at each repetition. Thus the continuous variations in which the fixed element is a persistently recurring series of harmonies came about. Such a procedure will be referred to as *variations on ostinato harmonies.*

Appearing about the beginning of the seventeenth century is a type of continuous variation that used a standard bass pattern of moderately slow tempo in triple meter, moving stepwise through the interval of a descending fourth, either diatonically or chromatically, sometimes concluding with a drop down to the lower octave. Compositions of this type were called *chaconne* or *passacaglia* indiscriminately by baroque composers. Sometimes the terms were also applied to variations on *ostinato* harmonies in which the standard bass pattern is absent or only hinted at:

The major diatonic form was used by Monteverdi in the duet *Pur ti miro* that concludes his *L'Incoronazione di Poppea* (1642) and the minor chromatic by Purcell as the bass of the song *When I Am Laid in Earth* from *Dido and Aeneas* (1689). Both diatonic and chromatic versions of the descending scale fragment, or slight variations of them, occur commonly in the works of composers of the seventeenth and early eighteenth centuries. Many *bassi ostinati*, on the other hand, are highly elaborate melodies. The descending scale fragment can be detected, however, as the basis of many of these as well.

Compositions making conspicuous use of this standard bass pattern, meter, and tempo were sometimes called *chaconnes* even when not written as continuous variations. Usually this type of *chaconne*, specialized in by French baroque composers, was in the form of a rondeau (see Chapter 9), as in Louis Couperin's *Chaconne in G Minor* for organ (in Bonnet, *Anthology of Early French Music* or *HAM, No. 212*), but Handel's *Chaconne in F Major*, an independent keyboard piece, has a unique form.

During the late eighteenth century, interest in continuous variations of either type was negligible, but it revived again in the nineteenth century with Beethoven's *Thirty-Two Variations in C Minor* for piano. Beethoven's successor in this field was Brahms, whose two most celebrated continuous variations occur as the Finales to his *Variations on a Theme by Haydn* and his *Symphony No. 4*, the first a ground bass, the second variations on *ostinato* harmonies. In this century the continuous variation is of very common occurrence, two notable examples being the *passacaglia* from Hindemith's *Nobilissima Visione*, and the fourth scene of Act I of Berg's opera, *Wozzeck*.

7-8. PROCEDURES OF CONTINUOUS VARIATIONS

The ground bass

Ex. 7-6. RAISON: *Organ Mass on the Second Tone, Trio en Passacaille*

Beginning on the last beat of m. 2, the bass presents a melody[2] four bars in length that is repeated five times. In two of these statements (mm. 11 ff and mm. 23 ff), the theme undergoes striking variation. Otherwise it remains virtually in its original form. This bass melody supports two contrapuntal voices which, at each statement, continue their melodic motion beyond the

[2] Taken from the Gregorian chant *Acceptabis sacrificium,* the communion antiphon for the tenth Sunday after Pentecost. This melody, extended to double its length, was also used by J. S. Bach as the ground bass for his great organ *Passacaglia.*

final note of the theme in order to cadence with the first or second note of the subsequent statement. Thus the movement flows uninterruptedly.

The ground bass normally remains in the lowest voice throughout and is not transposed to a different pitch, as in Ex. 7-6. But in his *Passacaglia in D Minor*, Buxtehude transposes the middle statements first to III, the relative major key, then to V. In his continuous variations, Bach never transposes ground-bass melodies to different keys. In the organ *Passacaglia*, however, he does transfer the theme in two variations from the bass to the uppermost voice and immediately after places it in a middle voice (mm. 89–113).

With the foregoing observations in mind, we can attempt to list the characteristics of a set of continuous variations of the ground-bass (*basso ostinato*) type.

1. A melody, normally in the lowest voice, is repeated a number of times.

2. Ornamentation of this bass melody may or may not be introduced during the course of its repetitions.

3. The melody is fairly short, usually a single phrase, and normally no more than eight bars in length.

4. The bass melody is not ordinarily transposed to a different pitch, though on occasion transpositions take place.

5. The recurring melody supports other voices that supply a changing fabric above it by added melodic counterpoints, motivic figuration, chordal harmonies, or any other means the imagination of the composer has devised.

6. The supporting voices often cadence at a different point from the ground-bass melody in order to keep up a continuous flow.

Variations on ostinato harmonies

Ex. 7-7.   HANDEL: *Suite No. 7 in G Minor, Passacaille*

Example 7-7 presents the theme and three of the fifteen variations of the *Passacaglia* which closes Handel's *Suite No. 7 in G Minor* for keyboard. Comparison of the basses will show that it is possible to trace the original bass line in the lowest voice of each variation. However, since the bass is changed in virtually every variation it does not have the effect of a recurring melody as the ground bass does. Rather it is the repetition of the precise harmonic sequence that shapes each variation.

The characteristics of a set of continuous variations on *ostinato* harmonies include the following:

1. A theme, usually comprising a single phrase, is sounded.

2. While the theme has a distinct melody and bass line, these are not necessarily fixed elements of the successive variations. Rather the precise harmonic sequence constitutes the fixed element. On occasion slight changes in the precise harmonic sequence occur.

3. Successive variations normally follow each other without a perceptible break, thus insuring a continuous flow.

4. Any of the types of sectional variations (see Section 7-3) are likely to occur here, but emphasis is on those of homophonic texture rather than the contrapuntal types.

The most celebrated set of continuous variations on *ostinato* harmonies is undoubtedly the great *Chaconne* which closes Bach's *Partita in D Minor* for unaccompanied violin. The two great nineteenth-century examples are Beethoven's *Thirty-Two Variations in C Minor* and the Finale of Brahms' *Symphony No. 4*. The latter, however, is only partially constructed by means of *ostinato* harmonies, some of the variations being based on the melody of the theme with modified harmony.

7-9. SHAPE IN CONTINUOUS VARIATIONS

Since the themes of continuous variations are short (eight bars or less), they are generally provided with many variations. In a piece with a short theme varied a great number of times it is extremely important—perhaps more so than in the case of sectional variations—to utilize shape to gather the variations into groups which can give a unified impression to the movement as a whole. In continuous variations a particular group is generally even more coherent than in sectional variations, for here there is no pause between the end of one variation and the beginning of the next.

The twenty variations of Bach's *Passacaglia* are grouped together into three parts. The variations of part one cohere by virtue of their gradually increasing intensity and excitement. There is a rhythmic crescendo operating until the establishment of continuous movement in sixteenth notes at Variation 6. The principle of increasing complexity is then applied through the next three variations. Variation 9 introduces a new and vigorous motive which leads into the brilliant runs of Variation 10, continued in Variation 11 with the bass melody leaping to the uppermost voice. Variation 12 is the most brilliant of all, with rapid pedal figures imitated in the manual parts.

The variations of part two (Variations 13–15) are all without pedal and should therefore presumably be played on a different manual with a decrease in volume. The musical texture bears out this assumption for it becomes less and less complex, Variation 15 consisting only of delicate arpeggio figuration.

Part three (Variations 16–20) enters abruptly with the return of the ground bass in the pedals and introduces majestic organ figuration in the manuals. Variation 17 is a whirlwind of rapid sixteenth-note triplets which are slowed down to regular sixteenths for the passionate final variations. For a finale, Bach treats the first four bars of the *Passacaglia* theme as the subject and, with the addition of a new theme, presents a double fugue which brings the work to a mighty and solemn close.

A diagram of the shape of the *Passacaglia* might look something like this:

Part One   Part Two   Part Three
(Theme, Var. 1-12)   (Var. 13-15)   (Var. 16-20)

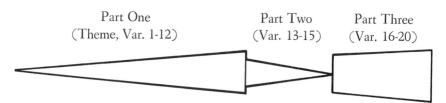

The grouping of these variations manifests on a large scale the symmetry of the "golden mean," a type of symmetry we saw working on a small scale in Ex. 3-3. The theme appears a total of twenty-one times. The largest group consists of thirteen appearances. The remaining eight are divided into two groups, one of three, the other of five. In length, part two is to part three as part three is to their sum (3:5 ∼ 5:8); and the sum of parts two and three is to part one as part one is to the whole (8:13 ∼ 13:21).

7-10. SPECIAL APPLICATIONS OF THE GROUND-BASS PRINCIPLE

The ostinato figure

Ex. 7-8.   STRAVINSKY: *Symphony of Psalms,* Third Movement (trumpet and cello parts omitted)

In Ex. 7-8 the ground bass is not a complete melody but only a motive. It is referred to either as a ground motive or an *ostinato* figure.

The *ostinato* figure is too short to serve as a bass for a series of variations superimposed over it, as the regular ground bass does. Therefore it cannot act as the structural basis for a composition. Rather, it occurs as a technical procedure for certain sections within a composition of another form. For instance, the third movement of Stravinsky's *Symphony of Psalms* uses the *ostinato* figure of Ex. 7-8 only for the final section. Beethoven's *Symphony No. 9* uses an *ostinato* figure in one section of the coda to the first movement (see Section 12-2). Brahms uses the *ostinato* figure a number of times, one of the most prominent being as the bass to the second theme in the Finale of his *Symphony No. 1.* Chopin uses the idea for the rocking left-hand accompaniment of his *Berceuse, Op. 57,* and in the middle section of the grandiose *Polonaise in A flat Major, Op. 53*. Indeed, the faded glories of boogie-woogie are none other than an application of the same principle.

The free ground bass

Ex. 7-9.   BACH: *Partita on "O Gott, du frommer Gott"*

Bach's *Partita on "O Gott, du frommer Gott"* for organ comprises nine different settings of the hymn tune. The excerpt in Ex. 7-9 presents the first twelve measures of the second setting.

In mm. 1–2 a bass melody is heard alone, then repeated in mm. 3–5 as support for a modified version of the chorale. A third statement of this bass melody begins in m. 5 but is lengthened and modified in mm. 6–7. Measures 7–8 are derived motivically from the bass theme, yet they constitute an essentially different melody, as does m. 9. The melody returns in mm. 10 and 11, but again its ending is altered in order to cadence on III rather than on I. Throughout the rest of the piece various other changes take place in the melody.

It cannot be denied that this piece is constructed over a recurring bass melody, but the melody is treated freely. It is lengthened, separated by interludes, transposed in part or in its entirety. We speak of such irregular bass melodies as free ground basses. The procedure is not at all uncommon during the baroque period. Many of the slow movements of Vivaldi's concertos consist of a *cantabile* melody over a free ground bass and Bach, in the slow movements of his *Italian Concerto* for harpsichord and his *Violin Concerto in E Major*—to name only two cases among many—has imitated Vivaldi's practice.

The soprano ostinato

Occasionally the concept of the persistently recurring melody is applied to the uppermost voice rather than to the bass of a composition. A striking case is the exquisite *Agnus Dei* from Verdi's *Requiem Mass*. A two-phrase melody, constructed as a thirteen-bar period, recurs five times, alternating between presentations by soprano and mezzo-soprano soloists, who sing it in octaves, and the full chorus.

The melody is first sung without accompaniment by the soloists, then repeated, as Variation 1, by the chorus and orchestra. Variation 2, in the minor mode, brings in a harmonized orchestral accompaniment. Variation 3, sung by the full chorus in three parts (sopranos and altos moving in octaves), is abridged to consist of only the consequent of the period. Variation 4, for soloists, is given a flowing accompaniment in the orchestra which continues in Variation 5, the latter abbreviated in the manner of Variation 3. A short coda concludes the piece.

A contemporary use of the soprano *ostinato* is the *Dirge* from Benjamin Britten's *Serenade for Tenor, Horn, and Strings*.

EXERCISES

5. Contrast:

a. Continuous variations and sectional variations
b. Variations on a ground bass and variations on *ostinato* harmonies
c. Ground bass and *ostinato* figure
d. Ground bass and free ground bass
e. *Basso ostinato* and *soprano ostinato*

6. Examine in detail the following compositions.

A (one or more)	B
a. Purcell: *When I Am Laid in Earth* from *Dido and Aeneas* (in HAM, No. 255 and elsewhere)	a. Purcell: *Thy hand, Belinda* beginning at m. 9
b. Bach: *Passacaglia* for organ	

c. Bach: *Crucifixus* from *Mass in B Minor*

7. Examine in detail the following compositions.

A (one or more)	B
a. Bach: *Chaconne* from *Partita II* for solo violin	a. Bach: *Chaconne* from *Partita II in D Minor*
b. Beethoven: *Thirty-Two Variations* for piano	
c. Handel: *Passacaille* from *Suite VII in G Minor*	

8. Examine in detail the following compositions.

A (one or more)	B
a. Bach: *VC,* Second Movement	a. Schubert: *Der Doppelgänger* (from *Schwanengesang*)
b. Bach: *Magnificat, No. 5*	b. Beethoven: *Quartet, Op. 135,* Second Movement, mm. 143–190
c. Vivaldi: *Concerto in A Minor for Two Violins, Op. 3, No. 8* (in original form or arranged for organ by J. S. Bach)	c. Hindemith: *Piano Sonata No. 2,* First Movement, mm. 63–89
d. Schubert: *Der Doppelgänger*	
e. Debussy: *String Quartet,* Second Movement	

7-11. SUMMARY OF CONTINUOUS VARIATIONS

We speak of continuous variations when the theme is not a complete little piece in itself, but only a phrase, possibly two, and the successive variations appear with little or no perceptible break between them.

Continuous variations fall into two main types:

1. *Variations on a ground bass.* A melody in the lowest voice persistently recurs while the upper voices supply an ever-changing texture above it.

2. *Variations on ostinato harmonies.* The precise harmonic sequence persistently recurs throughout the variations, but neither the melody nor the bass of the original theme necessarily reappears during their course.

The principle of the ground bass is sometimes utilized to different ends.

1. *Ostinato figure.* The ground bass is a recurring bass motive rather than a complete melody. It does not control the formal structure of the composition, but acts as a bass line for certain sections within a composition in another form.

2. *Free ground bass.* The ground bass is a melody that recurs but not so exactly or persistently as the regular ground bass. Appearances of the ground bass might be separated by interludes, and the melody itself is subjected to various changes.

3. *Soprano ostinato.* The recurring melody is in the uppermost voice rather than the lowest.

8

The Ternary Forms

The discussion of ternary forms in Chapter 6 was chiefly concerned with methods of analysis. Our interest was centered upon dividing a composition into parts and discovering the general category, if any, into which it might fall. The time has now come for a second look at the ternary forms—some of the details, some unusual procedures, and, especially, the *composite ternary form.*

Historical Note on Ternary Forms Compositions in ternary form existed as far back as the early Middle Ages. The textual arrangement of certain parts of the Mass, such as the Kyrie and Agnus Dei, conveniently accommodates a musical form based on the principle of statement, digression, restatement. The Kyrie of Gregorian Masses XII and XVI are among those ternary forms that can be traced back to the twelfth century and may well be of even earlier origin. The Agnus Dei of Mass XV is another. Nevertheless the ternary form did not occupy a conspicuous place in musical composition during the Medieval and Renaissance periods of music history. Only occasionally does one come across its use before the seventeenth century (for example, the chansons of Clément Janequin).

In the early part of the seventeenth century, the ternary form began to make more frequent appearances, as in arias from the cantatas and operas of Luigi Rossi (1598–1653) and Monteverdi. The famous duet *Pur ti miro* from the latter's *Poppea* is a fully developed ternary form with repetition of the middle part (ABBA). During the course of the seventeenth century, composers of opera, cantata, and oratorio began to rely more and more on the three-part plan for their arias. The third part often would not be written out but merely indicated by the words *da capo* which directed the performers to repeat the first part, the soloist, to be sure, ornamenting it differently the second time.

The first half of the eighteenth century saw the rise of an instrumental genre analogous to the *da capo* aria and occurring in some of the dances of the late baroque suite. A first dance could be followed by a second of the same type, after

126

which the first would be performed again. An example is to be found in the two minuets of Bach's *French Suite No. 3.*

It was the instrumental dance, specifically the minuet (or scherzo) and trio (that is, the second minuet), that offered the most conspicuous use of the ternary idea during the late eighteenth and early nineteenth centuries. Nevertheless, ternary forms are encountered in other genres: *Dalla sua pace* from Mozart's *Don Giovanni* and the first movement of Haydn's *Quartet, Op. 76, No. 5.* In addition to the conventional minuet and trio, a spot particularly favored by the classical composers for the ternary form was the slow movement of a sonata, trio, quartet, or symphony, as occurs in Haydn's *Symphony No. 92* ("Oxford"), Mozart's *Piano Sonata in D Major, K. 576,* and Beethoven's *Quartet, Op. 135.*

Throughout the nineteenth century, composers continued to favor the ternary form for the slow movements of their large multimovement instrumental works. In addition, it is to be encountered again and again in songs and especially in short piano pieces. Many of the piano compositions of the romantic composers, whether they were called nocturnes, preludes, romances, intermezzi, or some fanciful or descriptive title, exhibit one of the ternary forms. Nor is its use uncommon in this century. Prokofiev's *Piano Sonata No. 7,* Second Movement, Berg's *Lyric Suite* for string quartet, Third Movement, and Bartók's *Piano Concerto No. 3,* Second Movement, are but a few instances that come readily to mind.

8-1. CONNECTION OF PARTS ONE AND TWO

With the sole exception of the full sectional ternary, parts two and three of the ternary form are normally connected, for part two ends with a V_7 or some other chord which leads into the beginning of part three (see Ex. 6-9). In addition, many ternary forms include connective passages between parts one and two. There are four chief methods by which the composer can span the gap between these parts.

The link

Ex. 8-1. SCHUBERT: *Impromptu, Op. 90, No. 2*

The first three bars of Ex. 8-1 show the final cadence of part one. Measure 82 consists of a single major triad on G♭, III of the main tonality.

Enharmonically, this chord acts as V of B minor, the key of part two. In this case a single chord, V in the new key, III in the original key, has joined part one with part two. This chord serves as a link between the end of the first part and the beginning of the next. In Ex. 8-2 the link consists of three tones that lead smoothly into the first note of the melody of part two.

Ex. 8-2.   MOZART: *Sonata, K. 576*

The elision

Ex. 8-3.   HAYDN: *Symphony No. 92* ("Oxford")

In Ex. 8-3 parts one and two are connected by the device of the elided cadence (see Section 2-4). The device is used to bring about a continuity of movement between the two parts. Often, however, it does more as in Ex. 8-3. The sudden beginning of part two in the opposite mode and in a contrasting character introduces an element of surprise.

The broken cadence

Ex. 8-4. SCHUBERT: *Moments Musicaux, Op. 94, No. 4*

Rather than ending the first part with a complete conclusive cadence, Schubert, in Ex. 8-4, proceeds as if he is going to do so, then suddenly breaks off before sounding the final tonic chord. A grand pause follows and then the middle part begins. The opening chord of part two resolves the chord that was sounding when the break occurred. A similar procedure is used by Chopin in his *Nocturne in F Major, Op. 15, No. 1.* In other situations the grand pause is sometimes filled in by a harping on a single tone, a brief flourish, or some other linking device. Such a link does not eliminate the broken cadence. The link as described above comes *after* the completion of the perfect cadence, whereas here it comes *instead* of its completion.

The transition

Ex. 8-5. BRAHMS: *Ballade, Op. 118, No. 3*

In Ex. 8-5, the final cadence of part one (mm. 31–32) is followed by a passage nine bars in length which connects it with part two (mm. 41 ff). Part one is in G minor, part two in B major, that is III by change of mode. Brahms concludes part one not on a G minor triad but on G major (the "Picardy third"). To this G major triad he adds the note f', turning it into V_7/IV, following it by IV and VII_7 (mm. 32–33). These two bars are repeated, after which mm. 36–40 prolong the seventh chord on G which has been treated as V_7/IV. With the entrance of the first B major triad of part two (m. 41) the listener realizes that the seventh chord on the note G has served as a musical pun, being the enharmonic equivalent of a chord of the augmented sixth (E♯-G-B-D) on VII/V in B.

The passage does more than merely effect an interesting and striking modulation from I to III. Instead of presenting us with an abrupt contrast as we go from part one to part two as Haydn had done (Ex. 8-3), Brahms gradually diminishes the energetic movement through mm. 32–37. In m. 38 he brings in a new flowing figure which anticipates the accompaniment of part two. Beyond this he introduces in mm. 38, 39, and 40 the motive (marked in brackets) from which the chief melody of part two is to be constructed. This type of passage is termed a transition or bridge.

The transition, like the link, serves to connect two parts of a composition. The connection by means of the link is achieved as expeditiously as possible, while the transition, taking longer, has time to prepare the listener for the new part.

EXERCISES

1. Contrast:

a. Elision and broken cadence

b. Link and transition (bridge)

2. In the following pieces, how are parts one and two connected?

A	B
a. *WJ, No. 19*, mm. 20–22	a. Chopin: *Mazurka No. 49*, mm. 20–23

A	B
b. Chopin: *Prelude No. 15*, mm. 26–28	b. Chopin: *Prelude No. 22*, mm. 15–17
c. Beethoven: *Op. 2, No. 3*, Second Movement, mm. 10–11	c. Brahms: *Intermezzo, Op. 118, No. 2*, mm. 15–16
d. Beethoven: *Op. 7*, Second Movement, mm. 23–25	d. Brahms: *Intermezzo, Op. 119, No. 2*, mm. 33–36
e. *WJ, No. 4*, mm. 43–47	

8-2. CONNECTION OF PARTS TWO AND THREE

The retransition   When a transition is employed to connect parts two and three its function is to modulate from the key in which part two closes to that in which part three begins. Since part three is a restatement of part one, such a transition is referred to as a retransition.

Dovetailing of parts two and three

In most ternary forms, part two or the retransition closes on V_7, sometimes VII, which resolves directly into the opening I of part three (that is, the return of part one). But it is also possible for part three to begin before the harmonic movement has reached the V_7 (or VII) which ordinarily precedes it.

Ex. 8-6.   SCHUMANN: *Romance, Op. 28, No. 2*

Part two of Schumann's *Romance* in F♯ major, for instance, reaches
the VII/V. But rather than moving on to V or V₇ before part three begins,
the VII/V moves to

6-5
4-3
⌣
V

(that is, I⁶₄–V) *as* part three begins. The tonic chord that completes the
harmonic movement is not sounded until the middle of the second bar after
part three has begun. There is a conflict here between tonal structure and
design, a conflict that results in a tight dovetailing of parts two and three.

Some dovetailing occurs by other means. Example 8-7 shows the opening
phrase of part one (Ex. 8-7a), then skips to the last bar and a half of part two,
continuing with the opening phrase of part three, the return of one
(Ex. 8-7b).

Ex. 8-7.   SCHUMANN: *Frauenliebe und -Leben, No. 2*

Comparison of the two opening phrases shows the second (mm. 29 ff) to have an identical vocal melody but a different bass line. The original bass line moves upward in half steps from the note G to B♭, where it supports the V_7. In m. 28 the bass is on the note *d*, supporting the V_5^6 chord. Contrary to the listener's expectations, this note *d* moves downwards to *d♭* where it supports the first chord of part three not as a I, but as a seventh chord on I in third inversion. It then proceeds downward by half steps to reach the V_7 (m. 31). The descending bass line, governing the harmonies which underlie the return of the melody of part one, serves to hide the seams between parts two and three.

Alternate harmonies for close of part two

As was mentioned above, the normal way of closing part two is by reaching the V_7 (or VII). Sometimes, however, other chords are substituted. Such substitutions are almost obligatory when the opening theme of part three does not begin on I but on V. In such cases part two is likely to reach V/V or VII/V. In Schumann's *Carnaval, Op. 9*, this situation occurs several times, the student being directed in particular to *No. 2* and *No. 3*. In the fourth piece, *Valse Noble*, the first part (in B♭ major) begins with a diminished seventh chord on VII in third inversion, moves to a V_7, thence to I_6, and so forth (Ex. 8-8a). Part two, expressing the submediant key (G minor) concludes with a V_7 in that key: the notes D-F♯-A-C. By reinterpreting the note F♯ as G♭ and a simple move of the soprano note *d″* to *e♭″*, Schumann arrives at the diminished seventh chord on VII which initiates the return of part one. Though an unusual procedure, the connection between the second and third parts could hardly be smoother (Ex. 8-8b).

Ex. 8-8.   SCHUMANN: *Carnaval, No. 4*

The preceding have all been illustrations of methods designed to bridge the gap between parts two and three so smoothly and subtly that the listener is hardly aware part three has begun until it is well under way. But the composer may desire to surprise the hearer by jumping abruptly into the beginning of part three. In that case, part two may cadence on a chord calculated to lead the listener's expectations in a direction other than that which the music is about to take.

Ex. 8-9.   ROSSINI: *Stabat Mater, No. 2*

Part two of the *Cujus animam* from Rossini's *Stabat Mater* expresses VI, the relative minor key. It comes to a semicadence on the dominant of that key (V/VI), while the voice descends stepwise unaccompanied. Melodically, the voice part returns smoothly to the initial phrase (m. 4 of Ex. 8-9), but the entrance of the orchestra on I comes as a pleasant surprise.

EXERCISES

3. Terms to define:
   Retransition
   Dovetailing of parts
4. In the pieces for Exercise 2 of this chapter, how are parts two and three connected?

<table>
<tr><td align="center">A</td><td align="center">B</td></tr>
<tr><td>a. Measures 29–31</td><td>a. Measures 38–40</td></tr>
<tr><td>b. Measures 72–76</td><td>b. Measures 31–34</td></tr>
</table>

A	B
c. Measures 41–43	c. Measures 25–30
d. Measures 37–51	d. Measures 67–72
e. Measures 59–65	

8-3. THE PRELUDE AND POSTLUDE

Ex. 8-10.   **a.** CHOPIN: *Mazurka, Op. 17, No. 4*

b. MENDELSSOHN: *Song without Words, Op. 30, No. 3*

Example 8-10 illustrates passages with which certain ternary forms by Chopin and Mendelssohn begin. In the first case (Ex. 8-10a) the pianist strums on a single chord, VI_6, decorated with nonharmonic tones. In the second (Ex. 8-10b) he plays a simple but complete harmonic movement, I–V_7–I. At the end of each piece the identical passage returns. In neither case does the passage bear any specific relationship to the composition it encloses. It seems to act as a frame for a piece rather than as an integral part of it. We refer to such a passage as a prelude when it precedes a composition and a postlude when it follows, the two usually occurring together in a single work. The use of the prelude and postlude is virtually confined to short songs and lyric piano pieces of the romantic composers.

8-4. THE INTRODUCTION

Introduction to the first phrase   Many ternary forms begin the first phrase with an introduction accomplished by one of the methods described in Section

4-1. Such an introduction is always very short, sometimes only a bar or less in length, and rarely more than four bars.

The single phrase introduction

Some ternary forms are provided with short introductions which are not part of the first phrase but which exist as independent phrases. These are rarely more than a single phrase in length.

Ex. 8-11.   GERSHWIN: *Prelude No. 3 in E flat Minor*

As the ternary forms are not customarily provided with lengthy introductions, those of large proportions will be discussed in Chapter 12.

8-5. THE CODA

In the course of the last two chapters we have had an introduction to the coda, a term referring to a section that is added to the end of a composition as a kind of appendage. At this point we shall take another look at the coda, considering it first from the point of view of tonal structure, then of design.

Tonal structure of the coda

CODA PROLONGING THE FINAL I BY CHORD SUCCESSION   The last five bars of Ex. 6-16 illustrated the coda in which the I, upon resolving the final V_7 in the perfect authentic cadence, is prolonged by a chord succession. (See also Ex. 5-5, last four measures.)

CODA PROLONGING THE FINAL I BY MEANS OF A TONIC PEDAL   Rather than a straightforward chord succession, many codas prolong the final I by means of a tonic pedal point. Normally, of course, the pedal point is in the lowest voice. Example 8-12 illustrates another possibility.

This ternary form ends with a coda that prolongs the final I by means of a double pedal point (root and third of I) in the upper voices.

Ex. 8-12. PROKOFIEV: *Sonata No. 7, Op. 83,* Second Movement

CODA DELAYING THE FINAL I BY MEANS OF DECEPTIVE CADENCE

Ex. 8-13. CHOPIN: *Nocturne, Op. 48, No. 1*

The ternary form of Ex. 8-13 behaves as if it will close with a conventional perfect authentic cadence (m. 71). But when the moment for the final I arrives, it is transformed into $V_2^4/\flat II$ (m. 72). Thereupon it progresses through $\flat II_6$ to V_7 and only then is the final I heard (m. 74). The deceptive cadence with which the coda begins delays by two bars the final resolution of V_7 to I.

In its first bar (m. 72) this coda emphasizes the chord of the "Neapolitan sixth." More often, the tonal structure of the coda is devised to stress subdominant or submediant harmonies. The last four bars of Ex. 5-5, for instance, dwell on IV. The slow movement of Brahms' *Symphony No. 2* is a ternary form with a coda which begins with the deceptive cadence V_7–$\flat VI$ and which continues to emphasize this $\flat VI$ throughout the coda. The prevalence of both IV and $(\flat)VI$ in many codas seems to be calculated by the composer as a means of establishing tonal equilibrium. Most compositions involve harmonic motion that begins on I, moves to III or V, or to III and then to V, then returns to I. The coda can reflect this move to III (up a third) by a move to VI (down a third) as in Brahms' *Nicht mehr zu dir zu gehen*. A move to V (up a fifth) is balanced by a move to IV (down a fifth), occurring in the aria *It is enough* from Mendelssohn's *Elijah*. On the other hand, the coda might reiterate a harmonic movement made earlier in the piece. In Berlioz' *Symphonie Fantastique,* the middle part of the waltz appears suddenly in $\flat VI$. This striking harmonic turn is recalled for a few bars in the coda (mm. 36 ff from the end).

Design of the coda

CODA EXTENDING THE FINAL PHRASE   The coda illustrated by the last four bars of Ex. 5-5 does no more than extend the final phrase by a continuation of the accompanimental figuration. There is no need to indicate such extensions of the final phrase by a separate letter in the symbolic representation of the design.

THE SINGLE PHRASE CODA   The coda of Ex. 6-16 consisted of a single phrase, made up almost entirely of new material. While the coda of new material is not rare, more commonly the composer makes use of material heard before. Often this is chosen from part one, but as frequently it is part two that provides the basis for the coda, as in Chopin's *Prelude No. 13*. The point of this procedure has to do with unity, for the effect is that of a kind of reconciliation of the mood of the second part with that of the first and third. From time to time the coda, even when only a single phrase in length, makes reference to both parts one and two. Example 8-14 presents the coda to the composition from which Ex. 8-4 was taken. It begins with a reference to part two, then concludes by a return to part one. The design of the piece is represented by the letters ABA-(BA).

Ex. 8-14. SCHUBERT: *Moments Musicaux, Op. 94, No. 4*

THE LARGE CODA The coda to the Finale of Beethoven's "Eroica Symphony" is quite long and consists, as we have seen, of a number of sections. Codas to ternary forms, too, are sometimes long and divide themselves into sections. As with the shorter codas, the basis for the longer codas may be new or may come from one or more of the parts of the ternary form itself. Brahms concludes the second movement of his *Symphony No. 3* with a long coda in three sections. Section 1 (mm. 108–115) introduces an entirely new melody. Section 2 (mm. 115–121) recalls part two. Section 3 (mm. 122–134) is based on part one. The design of the entire movement would be symbolized by the letters ABA-(CBA).

THE CODETTA The term "coda" refers to an appended section at the end of a composition or movement. When a part within, say, a ternary form has such a "tailpiece" it is referred to as a codetta (see Chopin, *Prelude No. 12*, mm. 17–20).

8-6. SUBDIVISION OF A PART: THE SECTION

Let us examine the *Andante cantabile* from Tchaikovsky's *Symphony No. 5*. The movement opens with an eight-measure phrase consisting of a series of long, slow chords. These serve as an introduction to the familiar French horn melody. This melody leads directly into a passage marked *con moto* (mm. 24–32) in which the horn is joined by the oboe in a motivic interplay based on a new motive. The original horn melody is resumed, this time by the cellos, and leads into another tune (mm.45–61) based on the motive of the *con moto* section previously heard. This comes to a perfect authentic cadence on I, the first strong conclusive cadence heard so far, marking the end of part one.

It is clear then, that part one is itself divisible into several sections. After the introduction, the horn melody with its accompaniment—that is, the *first theme*—makes up section 1 (mm. 8–24). The *con moto* passage with the motivic interplay is section 2 (mm. 24–32). The return of the first theme played by the cellos comprises section 3 (mm. 32–44). Section 4 (mm. 45–61)

Outline Summary of Tchaikovsky's Symphony No. 5, Second Movement

Bars	Division	Description	Basic Tonal Structure	Design Symbol
1–8	Introduction	Chords in low strings (quasi-transition from first movement)	$VI–IV–I–V_7–I$	– –
8–61	Part one	Two themes, alternating	$I–III–I$	A
8–24	Sec. 1	First theme (horn)	$I \rightarrow VII^4_3–III\sharp$	a
24–32	Sec. 2	Anticipation of second theme (horn and oboe)	$III\sharp$	b
32–44	Sec. 3	First theme modified (cellos)	$I \rightarrow V^4_3$	a'
45–61	Sec. 4	Second theme (violins)	$I \rightarrow V_7 I$	b'
61–66	Transition	Repetitions and sequence of final cadence of part one.	$I \rightarrow V_7/III$	– – –
67–110	Part two	Third theme	$V_7/III \rightarrow V_7/VII–V^4_2$	B
67–99	Sec. 1	Gradual increase of tension as third theme repeats in sequence and imitation.	$V_7/III \rightarrow V_7/VII$	c
99–109	Sec. 2	Climax toward which sec. 1 was heading. Restatement of "motto" theme of the whole symphony, previously heard in first movement. Subsides to become the retransition.	V^4_2	d
110–170	Part three	Modified restatement of part one.	$I_6 \rightarrow V^6_5/V–IV\flat^{(+6)}–I$	A'
110–127	Sec. 1	First theme (violins)	$I_6 \rightarrow V^4_3$	a
127–141	Sec. 2	First theme (winds)	$I_6 \rightarrow V^4_3$	a
142–157	Sec. 3	Second theme (full)	$I \rightarrow V_7$	b'
158–170	Sec. 4	"Motto" theme as in part two, sec. 2, subsiding to become transition to coda	$V^6_5/V–IV\flat^{(+6)}–I$	d
170–184	Coda	Based on second theme	I (pedal)	b'

consists of the *second theme* which is based on the motive previously heard in section 2.

In representing in detail the design of a composition with subdivisions, it is necessary to differentiate the letters standing for a part from the letters standing for a section (a subdivision of a part). To do this we use capital letters for the parts and lower-case letters for the sections. Thus Tchaikovsky's *Andante cantabile*, part one, is indicated by the letter A and the sections into which it is subdivided by aba'b'.

EXERCISES

5. Contrast coda with codetta.
6. Describe the tonal structure and design of the codas of the following:

A	B
a. *WJ, No. 19,* last 3 measures	a. Brahms: *Intermezzo, Op. 118, No. 2,* mm. 38–48
b. Chopin: *Prelude No. 15,* last 5 measures	b. Brahms: *Intermezzo, Op. 119, No. 2,* last 6 measures
c. Beethoven: *Op. 7,* Second Movement, last 6 measures	
d. *WJ, No. 4,* last 7 measures	

7. Analyze in detail, making outline summaries, the following:

A	B
a. Chopin: *Prelude No. 12*	a. Beethoven: *Quartet, Op. 135,* Third Movement
b. Chopin: *Prelude No. 13*	b. Brahms: *Intermezzo, Op. 119, No. 2*
c. Beethoven: *Op. 7,* Second Movement	

8-7. INSTRUMENTAL COMPOSITE TERNARY FORM: MINUET (SCHERZO) AND TRIO

The minuet and trio, or scherzo and trio, familiar as one of the middle movements of most sonatas, trios, quartets, and symphonies of Haydn, Mozart, and Beethoven, is a structural complex. The minuet or scherzo is a complete composition in itself (see Ex. 10-3). It usually exhibits a rounded binary form, but sometimes it is one of the ternaries. The Minuet from Mozart's *Serenade, K. 525 ("Eine kleine Nachtmusik"),* for instance, is a sectional ternary on a miniature scale. In any case, in the music of the classical composers it is almost always in two repeated halves—‖ : A : ‖ ‖ : BA : ‖. The same observations hold true for the trio (see Ex. 6-3 and Ex. 6-7).

In performance, the minuet or scherzo is played, the trio follows, and then the minuet or scherzo is restated *da capo* without the repetitions. This practice lends to the two pieces an over-all aspect of a large full sectional ternary form:

A	B	A
‖:a:‖ ‖:ba':‖	‖:a:‖ ‖:ba:‖	aba'

Since this large form comprises two smaller forms, it is called a composite ternary.

EXERCISE

8. Examine the *menuetto* (scherzo) and trio from any or all of Beethoven's first twelve piano sonatas (except *Op. 14, No. 2*).

8-8. INSTRUMENTAL DERIVATIONS FROM COMPOSITE TERNARIES

The repeated trio   Beethoven lengthened the scherzos of his *Symphonies No. 4* and *No. 7* by the simple device of restating the trio after the scherzo proper had been played *da capo* and following this restatement with still another scherzo *da capo*, finishing with a short coda. The resulting design can be diagramed A ‖ : BA : ‖. Such a representation is not misleading as is the diagram A-B-A-B-A, for in these symphonies although the listener hears the scherzo three times and the trio twice, these are no more than repetitions within an over-all ternary form. We are not dealing with a genuine five-part form.

Two trios

In his *Clarinet Quintet, K. 581,* Mozart employs two different trios which result in a composite five-part form: A-B-A-C-A. A number of Beethoven's successors used this procedure to arrive at lengthy movements. The most famous example of the resulting composite five-part form, however, is not a minuet or scherzo at all, but the "Wedding March" from Mendelssohn's incidental music to *A Midsummer Night's Dream*. In this instance the first *da capo* of A is much abbreviated.

Many of the scherzos in the symphonies and chamber music of Schumann have two trios. Brahms also made use of the idea from time to time, as in his powerful *Scherzo, Op. 4*, for piano. In his *Symphony No. 2*, the two trios of the *Allegretto grazioso*, though contrasting in character, are derived from the melody of the first part. The tune of the first trio is arrived at by applying a different meter and rhythm to the original melody, with only a few changes of the actual notes. The melody of the second trio, in a still different meter, grows out of motives occurring at the end of the original melody, or rather, from the motives as they appeared in the version of the first trio. Thus, while the first trio can be said to be a result of the original theme, the second trio is a result of the first trio.

Ex. 8-15. BRAHMS: *Symphony No. 2,* Third Movement

The chain of waltzes

The eminent Viennese waltz composers Johann Strauss, both father and son, Joseph Lanner, Emil Waldteufel, and others, generally followed a single procedure in their popular dances. They assembled a series of five contrasting waltzes preceded by an introduction in slow tempo that might anticipate motifs from the ensuing waltzes. Between the introduction and the first waltz came a few bars, called the "entry" (*Eingang*) which marked the waltz time. After the series of waltzes a lengthy coda was added based on the melodies of the various waltzes and ending brilliantly. The whole complex of the typical Viennese waltz, then, was introduction, entry, waltz A, waltz B, waltz C, waltz D, waltz E, finale (based on A and/or B, C, D, E). The introduction and coda are important in tying together an otherwise unrelated series of dances.

One of Chopin's waltzes for piano (*Op. 18*) is almost a chain of waltzes. It too consists of a series of five waltzes, but the fifth is like the first. The result is a composite five-part form, designed A-B-C-D-A, with introduction and coda.

Other possible groupings of the various parts of sectional forms can be easily discovered by a cursory perusal of march and ballet music or by an analysis of the potpourri overture to many a once-popular "grand opera" and to the operettas of Gilbert and Sullivan. From the formal point of view these pieces are always extremely simple to understand, for the parts are precise and clear cut. The listener has no trouble in identifying them and can, therefore, easily grasp the design whether or not the formal scheme is a usual one. Special mention, however, will be made of certain designs of an unusual kind which are occasionally found in the greatest music.

Isolated derivations from the composite ternary

In considering the nature of his musical material, the composer might decide that none of the standard forms, if used in its usual way, will suit him. Since there can be no compulsion on the composer to use one of the established designs, it should not be surprising when variations from the fixed norm appear.

Thus, in his *Sonata, Op. 106* ("*Hammerklavier*"), Beethoven has a scherzo with two trios. But the second trio follows immediately after the first, omitting the first *da capo*. The result is represented as A-B-CA. Mozart had arrived at much the same design in the Finale of his *Sonata, K. 570*.

In his *Rhapsody in E flat Major, Op. 119, No. 4,* Brahms arranges the parts in the order A B C B A, a pattern sometimes referred to as an *arch* (or *chiastic*) form. Chopin's *Waltz, Op. 34, No. 1,* is also an arch form: A B C D C B A-(BA).

The celebrated *alla turca* which closes Mozart's *Piano Sonata in A Major, K. 331,* is a composite ternary with a distinctive feature: Between each large division and before the coda is heard a two-phrase period, of contrasting mode and character, which acts as a kind of refrain. Thus:

A	Refrain	B	Refrain	A	Refrain Coda
‖ : a : ‖ ‖ : ba : ‖		‖ : a : ‖ ‖ : ba : ‖		‖ : a : ‖ ‖ : ba : ‖	

EXERCISE

9. Analyze:

A	B
a. Beethoven: *Op. 26, Third Movement; also one or more of the following:*	a. Schumann: *Album No. 14*
b. Schumann: *Nachtstücke, Op. 23, No. 3*	b. Chopin: *Mazurka No. 3*
c. Schumann: *Carnival Jest from Vienna, Op. 26,* First Movement	c. Chopin: *Mazurka No. 5*

A	B
d. Chopin: *Waltz in A Minor, Op. 34, No. 2*	d. Beethoven: *Sonata, Op. 28,* Third Movement
e. Mendelssohn: *Song without Words, Op. 53, No. 5*	e. Brahms: *Intermezzo, Op. 118,* No. 2
f. Beethoven: "Eroica Symphony," Second Movement	

8-9. VOCAL COMPOSITE TERNARY FORM: DA CAPO ARIA

The aria *Cara Sposa* from Handel's opera *Rinaldo*[1] illustrates a baroque *da capo* aria. It begins with a largo movement in E minor in simple binary form. Part one of this movement extends to m. 46 where it closes with a perfect authentic cadence on III. Particularly striking is the use of the orchestra. It does not supply a subordinate accompaniment to the voice part so much as provide a musical texture of equal importance to the part allotted the soloist. There are two passages in the first part where the orchestra plays alone. First, the long opening phrase (mm. 1–12) is given to the orchestra, the soloist not entering until m. 12. Again, with the semicadence on V in m. 24, the orchestra plays alone (mm. 24–28). This second orchestral passage reproduces mm. 4–6 of the first orchestral passage. Because in the baroque aria passages given to the orchestra alone are generally based on the opening passage, that is, on the return of material previously heard, we speak of them today as *ritornellos*. This aria, then, begins with an orchestral ritornello (mm. 1–12), continues with voice and orchestra (mm. 12–24), introduces a second ritornello for orchestra (mm. 24–28), and continues with voice and orchestra to the conclusive cadence on III which closes part one (m. 46). Part two begins with voice and orchestra and continues to a conclusive cadence on I in m. 72. Another orchestral ritornello occurs at this point, reproducing all but the first three bars of the opening ritornello and bringing the largo movement to a close on I. So far, then, the aria is constructed as a complete composition in itself—a simple binary form with the design AA′ and the basic tonal structure:

$$V\text{–}I$$

$$I \rightarrow \text{of III} \rightarrow V\text{–}I$$

Rather than concluding here, however, the aria continues with an allegro movement of a completely contrasting character. It, too, is in two parts (mm. 82–86 and mm. 86–91) but unlike the largo it does not exhibit a complete harmonic movement. It is, instead, a progressive movement from

[1] Reproduced in *Masterpieces of Music before 1750,* ed. by Parrish and Ohl. New York: Norton, 1951, No. 44.

III to VII (VII is also V/III) in part one and thence to a perfect authentic cadence on V at the conclusion of part two. At the end of the allegro, the words *da capo* direct the performers to return to the beginning of the largo.

Tonal structure of the baroque da capo aria

It is apparent that the *da capo* aria is analogous to the minuet (scherzo) and trio in that it is a composite ternary form assembled from two binary forms placed together according to the principle of statement, digression, and restatement. Regarding tonal structure, the chief difference between them lies in the middle portion. In the instrumental composite ternary, the trio is a complete composition in itself showing harmonic independence—that is, it is a single complete harmonic movement. In the *da capo* aria, on the other hand, the middle portion is usually not a single complete harmonic movement, but rather progresses from one key to another. Handel's *Cara Sposa*, like many baroque *da capo* arias in the minor mode, begins the middle portion in III and moves through another key (in this case VII) to a perfect authentic cadence on V. Bach does the same in the aria *Buss' und Reu'* from the *St. Matthew Passion*. A procedure frequently occurring in major-mode arias is to begin the middle portion on VI and progress to an authentic cadence on III, the dominant of VI (*St. Matthew Passion, Ich will dir mein Herze schenken*). Often, then, the middle portion begins in the relative key, for III is the relative major of a minor key, VI the relative minor of a major key.

The following diagram sums up the previous observations. While it cannot be said that the *da capo* aria usually shows one of the following tonal structures, these are, at least, of fairly common occurrence.

A	B	A
	V–I	
Major: I → V–I	VI → ⌣ of III	I → V–I
	V–I	
Minor: I → V–I	III → ⌣ of V	I → V–I

Design

CONTRAST   In *Cara Sposa* the middle portion contrasts greatly with the outer portions, appropriately so since the text carries an entirely different emotion. The largo is an expression of grief, the allegro of defiance. However, should the words continue with approximately the same sentiment, as is often the case, the middle portion usually presents no striking contrast. In many cases, in fact, the second part shows strong motivic resemblances to the first (see *St. Matthew Passion, Ich will dir mein Herze schenken* and *Können Tränen*).

THE RITORNELLO   A distinctive feature of the late baroque aria, common to both *da capo* and other arias, is the orchestra ritornello. The first portion of an aria invariably begins and ends with a ritornello. In addition, more or less brief snatches of the ritornello appear as interludes from time to time during the singing of this opening portion. Generally speaking, the middle portion makes little use of the ritornello idea.

From the thematic point of view, these ritornellos are of two types. The more common type is that which is based on the vocalist's melody (see *HAM*, *No.* 258), either identical to it or a variation of it. The other type is that which is entirely different from the singer's part, but which is designed so that it can be heard simultaneously with it.

In illustration of the first type, Ex. 8-16 shows the opening ritornello and the beginning of the soloist's part of a baroque *da capo* aria. The first bar of the ritornello is an ornamentation of the first of the vocal melody.

Ex. 8-16.   BACH: *St. Matthew Passion*, Part One

The second type is illustrated in Ex. 8-17, which shows the opening of the ritornello and of the voice part. While there is no thematic connection between the two, the ritornello is designed in such a way that it can, at least in its opening measures, be sounded simultaneously with the vocal melody.

Ex. 8-17. HANDEL: *Radamisto,* original version, Act III

THE ABRIDGED RESTATEMENT Composers sometimes substitute an abridged restatement of the first portion rather than allowing it to return *in toto*. Abridgements are made by omitting or compressing portions (see, for instance, *Arm, Arm Ye Brave* from Handel's *Judas Maccabaeus*).

Composite ternary in other vocal types

While the *da capo* device is found mainly in connection with the baroque solo aria, it is sometimes applied to other vocal media. For example, the charming duet for soprano and alto in Bach's *Cantata No. 78* (*Jesu der du meine Seele*) is in structure a typical *da capo* aria, as is the exquisite double chorus which concludes his *St. Matthew Passion*.

EXERCISE

10. Analyze in detail:

A (one or more)	B
a. Handel: *The Trumpet Shall Sound* from *Messiah*	a. Pergolesi: *Il nocchier nella tempesta* from *Salustia*
b. *HAM, No. 244*	
c. *HAM, No. 258*	

8-10. SUMMARY

The ternary forms of the great composers have often received certain treatment calling for special discussion. This treatment involves the connection of parts. To increase the effect of continuity through the three parts of a ternary form, composers have often connected parts one and two by the following devices:

1. *Link*: A short melodic fragment or a chord or two ties the end of part one, after the completion of its final cadence, to the beginning of part two.

2. *Elision*: The cadence of part one is elided so that part two begins as part one ends.

3. *Broken cadence*: The final cadence of part one is broken off before the resolution of its V_7, leaving a gap which arouses the listener's expectations of something to follow; the first chord of part two resolves the last chord of part one.

4. *Transition*: A modulating passage, at least a phrase in length, leads gradually from part one to part two.

Parts two and three do not always call for a special connecting device since part two frequently ends on V_7, or a substituted chord, which in itself prepares the ear for the return of the first part. Sometimes, however, a retransition connects parts two and three. Occasionally parts two and three are harmonically "dovetailed," that is, part three begins with the final V of part two instead of waiting for its resolution to I.

Ternary forms are seldom provided with introductions longer than a single phrase, but both short and long codas are frequently found. In contrast to the nineteenth-century prelude and postlude, which act as a relatively independent frame for a composition, the introduction and coda are integral parts of it. (The distinction between the coda and the postlude can be most easily perceived by listening to a composition having both, such as Chopin's *Mazurka, Op. 17, No. 4.*) Whether long or short, the coda either prolongs the final I which closes part three or, opening with a deceptive cadence, delays this final I. In doing so the coda often emphasizes IV or (♭)VI, occasionally ♭II or some other chord. Usually it takes its material from the ternary form itself though not uncommonly the coda introduces new material.

In large ternary forms, each part frequently comprises a number of sections. A part may have its own short coda, termed in this case a codetta.

Statement, digression, restatement—the basic ternary principle—can be applied to other forms to create the composite ternary form. This is represented in vocal music mainly by the *da capo* aria, and in instrumental music by the minuet and trio with its derivations. In both cases two binary forms are normally involved: The first is stated, then the second, followed by a restatement of the first.

9

The Rondo

The word "rondo" is a generic name referring to those compositions that are distinguished by frequent recurrence of a *refrain*. The refrain is normally a self-contained, harmonically "closed" passage. It begins the rondo and reappears at least twice. The passages between appearances of the refrain are called *episodes* or *couplets*.

Historical Note on the Baroque and Classical Rondo   The rondo can be traced as far back as the medieval rondel, a poetic form used by the troubadours of Provence during the twelfth and thirteenth centuries. Consequently it has a long history prior to the era of tonal music. Its first appearance during the period under discussion here was in the music of the French composers of the seventeenth and early eighteenth centuries. (This early rondo will be distinguished from later ones by the retention for the former of the French spelling *rondeau.*)

The rondeau was sometimes used by Bach in his instrumental suites where he adapted the form to a specific dance style. For instance, in the *Partita No. 3* for solo violin he includes a *Gavotte en Rondeau* with four couplets, and in the *English Suite No. 5* for harpsichord the first *Passepied* is a typical French rondeau with two couplets. The light attractive nature of these dance melodies is particularly appropriate to the rondeau, which is, in essence, a piece for entertainment rather than one with deep emotional content. This cheerful, witty quality remained characteristic of many of the classical rondos of Haydn, Mozart, and Beethoven, and hence came to be thought of as "rondo style." Actually, however, the classical composers by no means limited their pieces in rondo form to this one style, and the "rondo style" appears in compositions in other forms.

The refrain of the classical rondo may have any character. Many, as we have just observed, are gay or humorous. Others are of the gently flowing *amabile* type (see Beethoven's *Piano Sonata, Op. 90*, Finale), wistful or melancholy (Mozart's *Rondo, K. 511*), shadowy and mysterious (Mozart's *Sonata, K. 457*, Finale, and

150

Beethoven's *Sonata Pathétique, Op. 13,* Finale). If, as sometimes happens, a rondo is not the finale but the slow movement to a sonata or symphony, the theme is likely to be a long-breathed melody expressive of peace and quietude (Beethoven's *Symphony No. 4, Adagio*). But whatever the mood, the rondo refrain will always have a definite, clearly melodious character. It is not fragmentary or made up of figuration, but instead is more in the nature of what is called a tune.

The catalogues of works by Haydn, Mozart, Beethoven, and Schubert contain relatively few independent rondos. Their main use of the form was in connection with sonatas, chamber music, symphonies, and concertos. The rondo form, with its regular recurrence of the refrain set off by easily grasped episodes, is particularly appropriate to those lighthearted finales designed to leave the audience in a happy frame of mind. When, then, a rondo forms part of a large work, it is usually the last movement of that work.

9-1. THE RONDEAU

Ex. 9-1.   D'AQUIN: *Suite No. 3, La Joyeuse*

From *Suite No. 3* in E minor, edited by Y. Pessl (in a volume of dance suites for the harpsichord). Copyright Edward B. Marks Music Corporation. Used by permission.

The essentials of a complete French rondeau of the eighteenth century are given in Ex. 9-1. The refrain is a double period based on interruption of the harmonic movement $(I \rightarrow V \parallel I \rightarrow V_7 - I)$ and completes a harmonic movement in E minor. Couplet I is a four-phrase period completing a harmonic movement on III (G major). A link leads back to the refrain. Couplet II is a five-phrase period based on a progressive harmonic movement from VII (D major) to V (B minor). The refrain is again restated. The refrain (A) and the two couplets (B and C) sounded in this order result in the design A-B-A-C-A: a small five-part form.

D'Aquin's rondeau illustrates the form used by many of the late seventeenth- and early eighteenth-century French composers. In the hands of François Couperin and Rameau, too, it was as simple. The refrain, a complete little piece in itself, was written out only once, the performers understanding that it was to be repeated between each couplet. There were no standard number of couplets, but there were always at least two, insuring a minimum of three appearances of the refrain.

Except for contrast of key, the couplets rarely differ greatly in quality from each other or from the refrain. The general sameness of character is often increased by actual thematic resemblances between refrain and couplet, as in Ex. 9-1.

EXERCISES

1. Analyze:

A	B
a. *VC,* Third Movement	a. Couperin: *La Bandoline*

2. Examine *HAM, No. 265b* and *No. 277.*

9-2. THE TYPICAL CLASSICAL RONDO

Design Among the various designs to be found in the rondos of the classical composers, the one which appears more often than any other was

derived from the French rondeau of three couplets by the simple expedient
of transposing couplet I to the tonic key and allowing it to serve as couplet III:

Refrain	Episode 1	Refrain	Episode 2	Refrain	Episode 3	Refrain
A	B	A	C	A	B′	A

Such is the basic design of many classical rondos, and its close relationship
to the rondeau of the seventeenth and early eighteenth centuries is obvious.
But the similarity stops there. Leaving aside the difference in musical styles
between the classical and the baroque periods, the usual classical rondo gives
the listener an entirely different impression from the old rondeau. The
difference lies in the effect of continuity found in the classical rondo. The
rondeau, being extremely simple, made no use of transitions to connect the
couplet with the refrain. The most that can be expected is a short link. The
result is a chain of self-contained units following each other in sequence.
In the classical rondo, on the other hand, although the refrain is harmonically complete in itself, often the episodes are not. Being "open" at
one end, they lead smoothly back to the return of the theme. Usually it is
by means of retransitions that the return is made and these retransitions
often become important sources of the rondo's charm. Through skillful use
of the retransition the constantly returning theme is not met by the listener
with boredom, but with a pleasant sense of recognition.[1]

The refrain

Other than the fact that the normal rondo theme is harmonically closed,
there is no general description of its structure that will hold true enough of
the time to be significant. Schubert's *Sonata in A Major, Op. posth.*, has a
rondo refrain in binary form: a double period, the consequent repeated.
The refrain of the last movement of Beethoven's *Sonata, Op. 14, No. 2*, is a
short sectional ternary (A-BA).[2] Whatever the form the refrain is a period
of some kind, not a single phrase.
This period, returning as it does a number of times, is often treated to

---

[1] Still, it is not wise to insist overmuch on generalizations about the rondo, for
the name is given to various compositions of widely differing character and design.
There is a misconception shared by many music lovers that the classical composers,
especially Haydn and Mozart, were bound by rigid rules from which they could deviate
only at their peril. Nothing could be further from the truth, as even a cursory study of
their rondos would at once prove. The fact of the matter is that the "rules" of classical
rondo writing are like those of any other form; they are simply deductions made later
by scholars who observed what Haydn or Mozart did in a number of cases.

[2] Beethoven called this movement *Scherzo* because of its humorous style. Its form,
however, is that of a rondo.

variation (see the variation rondo, Section 7-6). Some of the returns may be shortened either by actual omission or by the elimination of repetitions.

The first (and third) episode

The chief task of the first episode is to express a contrasting key, usually V or III. This may be accomplished without definite melody by the use of scales, arpeggios, or figuration. Or the first episode may present a melody that contrasts with the tune of the refrain. On the other hand, it may be the refrain melody transposed into the new key.

Ex. 9-2.   HAYDN: *Piano Sonata in C Major, No. 48,* Second Movement

The first episode is almost always in the same meter and tempo as the refrain.

If the rondo is in a major mode, the usual procedure is to let the first episode express V (as in Ex. 9-2). If the rondo is in a minor mode, the first episode is also apt to be in the dominant key, but it might very well express III (the relative major) instead. When the first episode returns near the end as the third episode it is customarily transposed from the key in which it formerly appeared to I. Thus, near the end of the piece the tonic is emphasized with unmistakable clarity.

The second episode

The second episode is generally larger than any other single section and is a self-contained unit, often a complete binary or ternary form. Frequently its change of key is marked by a new signature, and if a change of tempo or meter should occur within the rondo it is likely to take place here. In all, it presents much more of a contrast to the chief quality of the rondo than do the other sections.

In a major-mode rondo, the key expressed by the second episode is IV, VI, or the minor mode of I. In a minor-mode rondo, the second episode is likely to be the major mode of I, or possibly IV. But again, there is no rule other than the fact that some change of key or mode will almost certainly appear.

The transition and retransitions *Refrain (Trans.) Epis. Retrans.*

In a few rondos the conclusive cadence of the refrain is followed immediately by the first episode with no transition at all, as in the old rondeau, though there may be a link to connect the two. Usually, however, there is provided between each refrain and its ensuing episode a modulatory transition such as was described in connection with the ternary form (see section 8-1). The transition may consist of no more than figuration of some kind or may continue with motives taken from the refrain melody. Sometimes, however, the transition has a definite melody of its own.

The retransition connects an episode with a return of the refrain. As usually handled by the classical composers, the retransition glides smoothly and almost imperceptibly into the melody of the refrain.

Ex. 9-3.   MOZART: *Sonata, K. 333, Third Movement*

Example 9-3 illustrates the first part of a typical classical rondo. The theme itself is a symmetrical period that is repeated with a few ornamentations (the repetition is not included in the illustration). The transition that follows presents at m. 16 a new melodious idea, and at m. 21 a modulating figure in triplets that introduces the dominant key. The first episode can hardly be said to have a melody. It consists of a single motive, marked by overhanging brackets, repeated three times, the second and third times in a varied form. In m. 28 it becomes a running figure in sixteenth notes which continues throughout the next two bars. These come to an authentic perfect cadence on V at m. 36 connecting by elision with the retransition. Over chromatically rising thirds the note f'' is tapped out in a distinctive rhythm which appears in augmentation in the bass as a pedal point. A brief flourish in mm. 39–40 deflects this f'' into upper regions but it soon returns and gracefully becomes the first note of the refrain melody.

There is a special transitional device, the false return, which Beethoven seems to have particularly enjoyed using. After an episode, usually the second, the retransition is designed to lead not back to I but to another key, often IV, in which the refrain melody seems to return. But after a few bars the real refrain begins in I and the listener finds that what he had thought was the refrain was only an anticipation of its initial phrase. At times the device has the effect of a joke on the listener. As used in Ex. 9-4, however, it is not in the least amusing but results in a peculiar poignancy. It is as if the second violin longs to play the "sweetly melancholy" theme. It manages two bars of the melody but the first violin takes over. Trying again, the second violin succeeds this time in playing four bars only to be forced to give in to the first violin who, after all, knows which is the right key.

Ex. 9-4. BEETHOVEN: *Quartet, Op. 132*

In the classical rondo scheme episode 3, like the refrains which precede and follow it, is in the tonic key. Since the normal purpose of the transition is to modulate from the key of one section or part to the key of the next, one might well question the necessity of a transition between the last episode and its surrounding refrains. In some cases the composer does simply omit the transition. Usually, however, the transition is utilized as a means of providing temporary relief from tonic harmonies. The transition in this case is constructed to set up chords other than I as secondary tonics. Usually it strays quickly into rather remote regions, such as ♭VI or ♭III, or moves restlessly from secondary tonic to secondary tonic.

In the E major rondo which concludes Beethoven's *Sonata, Op. 90,* the retransition between the final appearances of the episode and refrain begins on I, passes to ♭VI and thence through ♭VII to II. The supertonic in turn progresses to V which is elaborately prolonged to cover nine bars, at length slipping almost imperceptibly into the refrain.

Ex. 9-5. BEETHOVEN: *Sonata, Op. 90,* Second Movement (harmonic outline of retransition, mm. 201–231).

The whole retransition covers a space of thirty bars. This provides the relief of harmonies distant from I and a degree of emotional contrast as well. Both episode and refrain have here a quiet, gently flowing character. The retransition builds to a climax, quickly subsides to a pianissimo passage of a mysterious quality, then, with a great up and down swell on II and V_5^6 glides into the refrain. After the retransition's tortuous path the reappearance of the refrain comes as a soothing return to a familiar landscape.

Basic tonal structure

In all but a very few classical rondos, each appearance of the refrain is in the tonic key. The first episode expresses III or V, the former usually but not always being reserved for minor-mode rondos, the latter for pieces in either major or minor modes. The second episode not infrequently remains in the tonic key with a change to the opposite mode. Otherwise, it might express IV or VI. The third episode transposes the first episode to I. The tonal structure of the usual classical rondo, then, can be expressed succinctly as:

A	B	A	C	A	B'	A
I	V	I	I	I	I	I
	(III)		(IV, VI)			

Form

A glance at the schematic representation of the most-used rondo form, A-BA-C-A-BA shows that the seven sections group themselves quite naturally into three parts:

Part One	Part Two	Part Three (Equals Part One)	(Plus Coda)
A–B A I V I (III)	C I, IV, or VI	A–B' A I	

In this light one perceives an over-all composite sectional-ternary structure, part three being a partly transposed version of part one, both surrounding a central part. The individualized treatment of the second episode (that is, part two) often bears out this ternary conception of the rondo.

EXERCISE

3. Analyze:

	A		B
a.	Beethoven: *Op. 13*, Finale	a.	Beethoven: *Sonata, Op. 13*, Third Movement
b.	Beethoven: *Op. 2, No. 2*, Finale		
c.	Beethoven: *Op. 2, No. 3*, Finale		

9-3.   OTHER DESIGNS IN THE CLASSICAL RONDO

Isolated designs   Though the rondo just discussed is found more often than any other one type in the music of Haydn, Mozart, Beethoven, and Schubert, it is not at all unusual to find different designs, some involving a greater number of episodes, others involving fewer episodes. Sometimes two episodes are placed adjacently, omitting the normal return of the refrain between them. Below are listed some of the various designs to be found isolated among the works of the classical composers.

A B A C A D A B′ A	Mozart: *Sonata, K. 281*, Finale
A B A C A B′—(Transition)	Mozart: *Sonata, K. 310*, Finale
A B C A D A—(A)	Haydn: *Trio in G Major*, Finale ("*Rondo all' Ongarese*")
A B A C A D A—(BCDA)	Beethoven: *Violin Sonata No. 4, Op. 23*, Finale
A B A C D A E A B′—(A)	Mozart: *Rondo, K. 494*
A B A B′ A—(Transition and New)	Mozart: *Sonata, K. 457*, Finale

The small rondo form

There is a particular rondo structure which appears often enough to warrant special mention. It consists in abbreviating the normal rondo structure by omitting the return of the first episode. The result is the design A B A C A, referred to as a small rondo.[3]

Immediately the perplexing question arises: How can a small rondo be distinguished from the five-part form, which is also an A B A C A design, or from the minuet or scherzo with two trios? The distinction lies in the continuity of the rondo. The five-part form, including the rondeau with two couplets, and the scherzo with two trios are built up mostly by placing self-contained sections or parts alongside each other with frequent complete cadences and a minimum of transitionary passages. While there may be a retransition from B back to A, B being harmonically closed, this retransition will begin after a definite and conclusive cadence. In the rondo, on the other hand, the episodes are usually "open," or at least lead into the retransition with no perceptible break. Thus, while the fundamental designs are identical, the total effect of the two forms is different.

The appellation "small rondo form" seems to imply that its use will result in a short rondo. This is not necessarily the case, however. The term is used merely to indicate an abbreviation of the usual design. Actually one of Mozart's longest rondos exhibits this form, the *Rondo in A Minor* for piano,

---

[3] Some theorists call this the "second rondo," the "first rondo" being our ternary form (ABA), and the "third rondo" being the typical classical one (ABACAB'A).

K. 511. Its great size is due to the fact that each section is in itself quite long, the refrain alone consisting of thirty bars of 6/8 time in an andante tempo. And the first episode with its retransition consists of fifty bars. Each of these sections is itself a ternary form, with statement, digression, and restatement.

The small rondo form only occasionally appears as a fast final movement of a sonata, an unusual example being Beethoven's *Op. 14, No. 2.* But if a slow movement is to be cast in a rondo form, it is usually a small rondo that is chosen, examples being the slow movements of Mozart's *Eine Kleine Nachtmusik* and *Sonata, K. 457,* and of Beethoven's *Sonata Pathétique, Op. 13,* and *Quartet, Op. 74.*

Particularly interesting is Mozart's application of the small rondo form to vocal music. On a small scale, his song, *An Chloe,* is a little "rondino" with a delightful variation of the refrain upon its third appearance. On a larger scale, Donna Elvira's aria *Mi tradì quell' alma ingrate* from *Don Giovanni* is a small rondo form in which a single motive appears in both voice part and accompaniment during the refrain and both episodes. When the refrain and all episodes are based on the same theme we speak of a "monothematic rondo." The *Agnus Dei* from the *Mass in C Major, K. 317* ("Coronation"), is also a small rondo.

The sonata rondo

Frequently the second episode of a classical rondo does not present new material but is devoted instead to a development of the ideas heard in the refrain or episode 1, or, in some cases, a transition. In this case, episode 2 takes on the aspect of the development section of sonata form, to be discussed in Chapter 11. For that reason our discussion of the sonata rondo must be postponed until then, although the basic design of this hybrid form is simple enough:

Refrain	Episode 1	Refrain	Episode 2	Refrain	Episode 3	Refrain
A	B	A	Development (of A, B, or transition)	A	B′	A
						plus Coda

The final refrain and coda

Sometimes the final refrain is not stated in its entirety. Rather, its beginning is heard, and then it merges with the coda. Looked at from another point of view, one can hold that in these situations there is no final refrain but that the coda begins with the opening passage of the refrain. Which point of view best expresses a particular situation resolves itself around the question of the length of the partial restatement of the refrain. For example, in the rondo that closes Mozart's *Piano Concerto in D Minor, K. 466,* the final statement of the refrain (mm. 346–352) is abruptly cut off after only six bars, at which point the coda begins. A plausible argument for considering those six bars not as a return of the refrain but as the actual beginning of the coda could easily be made. In the *Concerto in C Major, K. 415,* Mozart has shortened the refrain by omitting its repetition by the orchestra, but has not cut out any essential part of it. Although the coda connects with the refrain's ending without a perceptible break, it would not seem that this case justifies considering the final appearance of the refrain as no more than the beginning of the coda. On the contrary, it is a genuine reappearance which then merges with the coda.

EXERCISES

4. Analyze:

Last Movement — Pathétique

A	B
a. Beethoven: *Op. 13,* Second Movement	a. Haydn: "Clock Symphony," Finale

form of theme
key scheme
most imp. diversion

9-4. CLASSICAL RONDOS LACKING CONTINUITY

We have emphasized that the difference between the classical rondo and a similarly designed derivation from the ternary form is that the former exhibits a general continuity of movement while the latter does not. Having absorbed this distinction, we discover that some classical rondos—so labeled by their composers—do not display the continuity described as distinctive of the classical rondo, but are loaded with full stops. They seem to be in this respect more like the old French rondeau than a composition of the classical era.

To explain this seeming discrepancy one must remember that our description of the typical classical rondo is based not on eighteenth-century books of musical theory, but on deductions drawn from observation of what Haydn and Mozart actually did. These are the men who, along with certain lesser figures, created the classical rondo. Therefore it stands to reason that when they first began to compose rondos their starting point was not *our* idea of the classical rondo but something more like the French rondeau. (See, for instance, the rondo Finales to *Sonatas, K. 26* and *K. 30,* by the nine-year-old Mozart.) When Beethoven and Schubert began to compose, their idea of the rondo was based on those of Haydn, Mozart, and their contemporaries. It is for this reason that their rondos generally conform to

our idea of the typical classical rondo, whereas Haydn's and Mozart's sometimes do not.[4]

Historical Note on the Rondo after the Classical Period   The chief ap-
pearance of the rondo form during the romantic era was as a concerto finale (see
Section 13-3). Otherwise, the majority of romantic composers had little use for the
form. Among the works of Chopin and Weber are a few piano rondos in a virtuoso
style. Mendelssohn wrote a brilliant *Rondo Capriccio* for piano and orchestra. But
Wagner and the Italians were writing only opera, and the arch-romanticists Berlioz
and Liszt, turning their attention to program music and new forms and genres,
had little use for the worn-out rondo.

In the piano music of Schumann there are a number of rondolike structures.
The *Novellett in E Major, Op. 21, No. 7*, for instance, is an eight-part form with
the design A-B-CA-D-A-CA. The fourth piece, *Grillen*, that is *Caprices*, of the
Phantasiestücke, Op. 12, is, in design and tonal structure, a typical classical rondo.
Yet these pieces cannot be considered real rondos, nor does Schumann call them
so. The classical composers had taken what was originally a form made up of a
number of separate sections—with the seams still showing—and worked it into a
continuous and coherent whole. Schumann's structures consist, like the old
rondeau, of a series of little pieces in a row, but unlike the rondeau his pieces stand
in strong contrast to each other with little relationship between them. They are
delightful music, but are not real rondos despite the rondo principle underlying
their structure.

The only romantic composer who showed a decided interest in the rondo was
the classically oriented Brahms. Most of his works in rondo form are of the sonata
rondo type (see Section 9-3). A notable example of a simple rondo by Brahms is
the great *Rondo alla Zingarese* which forms the Finale to the *Quartet for Piano
and Strings, Op. 25*. Using four distinct episodes, in addition to a cadenzalike section before the final appearance of the refrain, the result is a work of twelve sections. The many sections, however, seem to group themselves according to mode
into three parts.

Outline of Brahms' Piano Quartet, Op. 25, Fourth Movement

	Part One	Part Two	Part Three
	(Minor)	(Major)	(Minor)
Tonal Structure	I → V I III I	I VI → III I → V I	I → V (V) I
Design	A B A C A	D E C D	B Cadenza A (E C D)

At the very end of the nineteenth century, Richard Strauss wrote a symphonic poem, *Till Eulenspiegel's Merry Pranks*, which claims in its title to be a
rondeau "after the old-fashioned rougish manner." "Thus," writes Leichentritt,

[4] But see Beethoven, *Quartet, Op. 18, No. 4*, Finale, for an exception.

"the listener is warned to accept the rondo as one of Till's 'merry pranks.' "[5] Indeed, if this is a rondo at all, it is one only in the sense that two motives, representing the hero, make frequent reappearances throughout the work. Another interesting rondo of the late nineteenth century is the great Finale to Mahler's *Symphony No. 5.*

Certain twentieth-century composers have continued to compose rondos which, for all their change in musical style, do not show any outstanding alteration of design from those of the classical era. In tonal structure, to be sure, novelties are to be found. Hindemith closes his *Sonata No. 1 for Organ* with a small rondo form in E♭. While the second episode expresses a key conventional enough in the late eighteenth and early nineteenth centuries (♭VI), the first episode is in the key of A, a tritone distant.

Other rondos of the twentieth century are in Stravinsky's *Firebird Suite* (*Rondeau des Princesses*), Berg's *Wozzeck* (Act I, Scene 5; Act II, Scene 5), and even in some early twelve-tone music, such as Schoenberg's *Quartet No. 3,* Finale.

9-5. SUMMARY

The principle of the rondo lies in the statement of a passage of music, the refrain, and its return at intervals after contrasting episodes or couplets. It is, then, allied to the ternary forms whose chief characteristic is also statement, digression, and restatement. In the rondo, however, more than one restatement is always present.

The rondeau of the seventeenth and early eighteenth centuries was an aggregation of a number of miniature pieces with little contrast between them other than that of key. They were assembled as refrain, couplet 1, refrain, couplet 2, refrain, and so on, either without connective passages between them or with no more than a simple link. Some of the rondos of Haydn and Mozart are similar to these, but the typical classical rondo was given a much more continuous aspect by the judicious use of transitions, especially retransitions leading into the return of the refrain. While many different designs are to be found in the rondos of the classical composers, the typical design is arranged as a composite ternary form.

[5] Hugo Leichentritt, *Musical Form.* Cambridge, Mass.: Harvard University Press, 1951, p. 120.

10

The Binary Forms

Historical Note on the Binary Forms and the Suite During the late seventeenth and early eighteenth centuries, instrumental music depended on the binary form to a greater extent than on any other. Virtually all stylized dance pieces, of which baroque sonatas and suites are full, as well as many slow movements of concertos and other large works exhibit binary forms.

The binary form is characteristic of the individual pieces of the French and German lute and keyboard suites (for example, Chambonnières and Froberger; see No. 35 in *Masterpieces of Music Before 1750*, New York: Norton, 1951) during the second half of the seventeenth century. A baroque suite consists of a number of dances, all in the same key. While there is no standard number or type of dances used consistently, many suites include an *allemande, courante* (or *corrente*), *sarabande,* and *gigue*.

Dance Type	Meter	Tempo and Character
Allemande	Duple	Moderate; sombre, stately
Courante	Triple	Moderately fast; *corrente* faster
Sarabande	Triple	Slow; stately
Gigue (*Giga*)	Compound duple (6/8 or 12/8)	Fast and vivacious

Most suites comprise at least four pieces, some as many as twenty or more. Additional dances often appearing, especially in the eighteenth century, are as follows:

164

Dance Type	Meter	Tempo and Character
Bourrée	Duple	Lively
Gavotte	Duple (usually 4/4, each phrase starting on third quarter)	Moderately fast
Minuet	Triple	Moderate; stately
Passepied	Triple	Lively

Bach's *French* and *English Suites* all include the *allemande, courante, sarabande,* and *gigue* in that order as well as a few other dances. These are inserted between the *sarabande* and *gigue* or occasionally between the *courante* and *sarabande.* Some of the dances are provided with doubles. In addition, each of the *English Suites* opens with a prelude.

In Germany the suite was also called a *partita,* in France an *ordre,* and in England a *lesson.*

The two-part form was by no means limited to music in dance style. Some of the preludes of Bach's *Well-Tempered Clavier* are constructed along these lines as are many sonata movements (for example, each of the three movements of the *Organ Sonata No. 1*) and cantata sinfonias (for example *Ich steh' mit einem Fuss im Grabe, No. 156*). Much of the vocal music of the baroque era is also in binary form.

Bach and Handel made occasional use of the balanced and rounded binary forms, but relied mainly on the simple binary. Domenico Scarlatti, on the other hand, consistently wrote balanced binaries. In the late eighteenth century it was the rounded binary that came into normal use, particularly in the instrumental minuet and scherzo, though the other types were not totally absent. Throughout the nineteenth century, the binary form—especially the rounded type—is frequently found. Usually, however, it was used either on a small scale, as we have already seen in certain of Schubert's songs and Chopin's preludes, or as one division of a composite ternary form. A sole exception is the operatic aria which, during the latter half of the eighteenth century, had dropped the undramatic *da capo* idea. Instead many arias and some ensemble numbers were constructed as large composite binary forms: A slow part followed by a fast one (for example, *Batti, batti* from Mozart's *Don Giovanni*). This scheme, ideally suited to the depiction of a dramatic change in emotion or situation, continued through the first half of the nineteenth century as a standard form for the operatic aria. The slow part was often called *cavatina,* the fast part *cabaletta,* each frequently being introduced by a recitative. (See Bellini, *Come per me sereno* from *La Sonnambula.*) One of the last examples and most often sung of the *cavatina-cabaletta* construction is the *Ah, fors' è lui* and *Sempre libera* from Act I of Verdi's *La Traviata.* In this century, however, it has been revived by Stravinsky for the closing scene of the first act in his opera, *The Rake's Progress.*

10-1. SUBDIVISION OF BINARY FORMS

Let us examine two binary forms, a simple binary by Bach and a rounded
binary by Haydn.

Ex. 10-1.   BACH: *French Suite No. 3*, Minuet

Example 10-1 illustrates a late baroque keyboard minuet in simple binary
form. Dominating is a melody of the *perpetuum mobile* type constructed from
the motives, a, a′, and b. Part one is a two-phrase period comprising a progres-

sive movement from I to III. Beginning where part one leaves off, part two progresses from III to a perfect authentic cadence on V (m. 24). Measures 25–26 emphasize IV and, by means of a sequential repetition, emphasize V again (mm. 27–28). In m. 29 this V becomes a seventh chord (V_5^6) leading back to I.

Aside from the cadence in mm. 15–16 which divides part one from part two and that which closes the minuet, the design shows one perfect authentic cadence. This occurs at mm. 23–24. Although the strength of this cadence would seem to be as great as that on III which brings part one to a close, the cadence is weakened to the point of being nondivisive by two factors. First, motive a which acts as a bridge in the left hand provides continued motion in eighth notes. Compared with the definite conclusive quality of the three-quarter notes played by the left hand in m. 16, the steady eighth-note motion tends to weaken the divisive effect of this cadence. The second factor is that on the third beat of the bar, e is introduced as a passing tone leading into the beginning of the next phrase, and this passing tone propels the listener on. Other factors in design are not divisive. Unity of tempo, texture, and rhythm prevails, and the melodic motives of part one are, with the exception of motive c and its derivatives, the same as those of part two.

The attentive listener will sense that the quality of the music from m. 17 to m. 31, while not contrasting, is subtly different from that which precedes and follows it. The effect results from the greater degree of tension manifested in this section. Undoubtedly the difference is partially due to the introduction of the new, rhythmically interesting motives c and c″. More than that, however, is the effect of the secondary tonics which occur here on both IV (mm. 25–26) and V (mm. 22–23; 27–28). By emphasizing first one chord, then another, as tonic, the harmony brings about a sensation of energetic movement. Combined with the steady rise of the melody (mm. 25–30) just before the relaxing return of the tonic (m. 31), these secondary tonics imbue the section with great vitality. Due to the distance from the tonic that the harmony travels in bringing in secondary tonics, the sections opening part two are called the departure or digression and the section in which the main key reappears is called the return. Example 10-2 is a harmonic outline of the piece.

Ex. 10-2. BACH: *French Suite No. 3,* Minuet (harmonic outline)

Ex. 10-3.   HAYDN: *Quartet, Op. 76, No. 5,* Third Movement

Example 10-3 is one of Haydn's minuets in rounded binary form. Part one is a phrase with a progressive harmonic movement from I to V. It will be remembered that in the rounded binary when part one closes on V, part two begins by prolonging this V until the restatement begins (see Section 6-4). Example 10-3 accomplishes this prolongation by an interesting use of a succession within a succession. The digression leaves the cadential V by treating II as a secondary tonic (mm. 9–10), these bars repeating sequentially on I. This I is immediately treated as the dominant of IV (mm. 11–12). Measures 13–15 outline the notes of the supertonic triad, preceding each with a lower appoggiatura, leading into the return of V (see Ex. 10-4).

Ex. 10-4. HAYDN: *Quartet, Op. 76, No. 5,* Minuet (harmonic outline of departure)

Two features of part one should be particularly noted: (1) the three-note motive in m. 4, marked with an overhanging bracket, and (2) the *sforzando* on the third beat of m. 6. Haydn has provided himself with a three-note motive and a misplaced accent—two bits of material which Haydn exploits fully. He begins his digression by combining the two, with the result that mm. 9–11 are rhythmically askew: Four bars of 2/4 meter are injected into three bars of 3/4. A unison cascade on the first two notes of the motive follows, during which one loses track of the 3/4 meter altogether. This passage leads into the restatement. Thus the entire digression is constructed by *motivic development* from the two fragments of material chosen from part one.

The digression, with its rhythmic surprises, is both exciting and humorous. The modified bars of the restatement (mm. 23–24) provide a further surprise for they are played a delicate *piano* rather than *forte* with a *sforzando* as they had first appeared. And now, as if angry at having been excluded from the graceful ending of the restatement, the cello bursts in with the three-note motive and the misplaced accents, the other instruments immediately joining the fray. Thus while part one is balanced by the first phrase of the expanded restatement, the digression is balanced by the second. The complete design of Ex. 10-3 is, therefore, an unusual AB||A'B'.

Certain features occurring in one or both of the Bach and Haydn examples just examined should be noted.

1. Part one is shorter than part two.

2. Part one can be a single phrase or it can be a period, divisible into sections. Part two is divisible into sections.

3. Part two is based wholly or partially on material first heard in part one.

4. (a) When part one ends on III, part two begins with a progressive movement connecting this III with the V that ushers in the return to the tonic key. (b) When part one ends on V, part two begins with a prolongation of this V until it ushers in the return to the tonic key. In Ex. 6-2 and Ex. 6-3 this prolongation was accomplished for the most part by a simple extension of the V with a dominant pedal point in the lowest voice. But we have now observed that

> the prolongation may take the form of a chord succession beginning and ending with V.

5. The initial section of part two, in its task of progressing to or prolonging V, is given to bringing about a feeling of energy with an increase of tension. This is done partly by harmonic restlessness due to the establishment of a series of secondary tonics, and partly through increased rhythmic and textural complexity. The increase in tension may continue through more than just the initial section of part two, as happens in the example from Bach. The sections opening part two, given over to such increase in tension, can be referred to collectively as the departure or the digression.

Examination of many binary forms of the great composers of the tonal era reveals that the observations deduced from the two previous examples may be considered typical for the binary forms as a whole. Nevertheless, it will be advantageous to consider the binary form as used by Domenico Scarlatti for one of his harpsichord sonatas. We shall examine the *Sonata in A Minor*, No. 175 in Kirkpatrick's catalogue, by means of a summary outline.[1]

This outline reveals a much longer and more complex structure than either of our previous binary-form examples. While Scarlatti's sonatas are normally balanced binaries, they do not follow a stereotyped pattern in details. The particular sonata outlined here, then, cannot be considered typical. It illustrates, rather, one way of subdividing the parts of a balanced binary form. In other sonatas the transposed restatement of part two might

---

[1] This sonata is reproduced in *HAM, No. 274,* and in Scarlatti, *Sixty Sonatas,* ed. by Ralph Kirkpatrick. New York: Schirmer, Vol. 1, No. XXI.

Outline Summary of Scarlatti's Sonata in A Minor, K. 175

Bars	Division	Basic Tonal Structure	Design Symbol
1–51(52)	Part One	$I \rightarrow$ V–I of V♯	A
1–16	Section 1: opening section	$I \rightarrow$ V	a
16–32	Section 2: modulating section	$I \rightarrow$ V$^6_5$–I V–I–V of IV of V	b
32–41	Section 3: closing section	$I \rightarrow$ IV–V–I of V♯	c
41–51(52)	Section 4: codetta	I–IV–V–I of V♯	a'
52–103	Part Two	V → V–I♯	A'
52–66	Section 1: departure	V–I V– –V/V of II	d
66–84	Section 2: departure	V → IV–V	b'
84–96	Section 3: closing section	I♯ → IV–V–I♯	c
96–103	Section 4: codetta	I♯–IV–V–I♯	a'

involve more or fewer sections. The departure might be reduced drastically, or more than one codetta might appear. Scarlatti's balanced binary form served him as a broad framework within which he constructed a great variety of designs.[2]

10-2. CONNECTION OF PARTS ONE AND TWO

Ex. 10-5. SCHUBERT: *Twelve Ländler, No. 1*

[2] For a detailed examination of form in Scarlatti's sonatas see Ralph Kirkpatrick, *Domenico Scarlatti*. Princeton, N. J.: Princeton University Press, 1953, Chap. XI.

Just as parts one and two of the ternary forms are often connected for greater continuity, so are parts one and two of the binary forms.

In Ex. 10-5, part one ends with the perfect authentic cadence (mm. 28–29) and is followed by a three-bar transition (mm. 30–32) leading into part two. (See also Bach, *WTC, Prelude No. 10,* mm. 21–22.)

More commonly the link is used as a connective device (Bach, *WTC, Prelude No. 4,* m. 14). The use of elision or broken cadence is extremely rare, an exceptional case being the elision in m. 6 of *WTC, Prelude No. 23.*

10-3. CODETTA AND CODA

The outline summary of Scarlatti's *Sonata, K. 175* (section 10-1), shows that section 4 of each part is a codetta. The longer simple and rounded binaries also include occasional codettas, as in the Minuet of Haydn's *Symphony No. 101* ("Clock"), mm. 20–28; mm. 72–80.

Frequently the binary form concludes with a more or less lengthy coda. When the two parts are repeated, the coda usually begins after the repetition of the second part. Occasionally, however, it is included in the repetition (*WTC, Prelude No. 24,* last five-and-one-half bars).

EXERCISE

1. Analyze the following music. Subdivide those parts that are susceptible to subdivision and label each section appropriately. Construct a harmonic outline.

A	B
a. MF, No. 11	a. Scarlatti: *Sonata, K. 158*
b. MF, No. 10	b. Scarlatti: *Sonata, K. 159*
c. Beethoven: *Op. 2, No. 3, Scherzo* (omit Trio)	c. Handel: *Flute Sonata No. 4,* Second Movement
d. WTC, Prelude No. 23	d. Wolf: *In der Frühe*
e. WTC, Prelude No. 24	
f. MF, No. 17	

10-4. THE COMPOSITE BINARY FORM: OPERATIC ARIA

Let us examine the soprano aria *Tacea la notte placida* from Verdi's *Il Trovatore.* After a five-bar introduction Leonora begins an andante, 6/8 meter, in Ab minor, quiet and restrained. With the words *"dolci s'udiro e flebili"* the mode changes to major, the mood becomes expansive. These two passages, then, contrasting in nature, comprise a small simple continuous binary form. The following stanza constitutes a repetition, slightly varied, of the first, and leads by deceptive cadence into a climactic coda, ending with a perfect authentic cadence in A♭ major. The meter now changes to 4/4, the tempo to *allegro giusto* and, after a lengthy orchestral introduction, we hear a brilliant coloratura aria, a sectional ternary form, its repetition, and coda.

Verdi's *Tacea la notte placida* contains two independent and contrasting forms, placed adjacently to comprise a composite binary form. The first half in slower tempo is called the *cavatina*, the half in quick tempo is the *cabaletta*.

It will be remembered that the composite ternary form of the *da capo* aria and the minuet (scherzo) and trio is the result of a combination of two independent forms according to the principle of statement, digression, restatement. Like *Tacea la notte placida*, many operatic arias of the late eighteenth and early nineteenth centuries show an analogous composite binary form. The two halves are always of a contrasting character. Usually they are placed as in Verdi's aria, the cavatina before the cabaletta, and it is only when they are so arranged that these terms are used. Sometimes, however, depending on the text, the slower half follows, as happens in Leporello's celebrated *Madamina* in Mozart's *Don Giovanni*.

EXERCISE

2. Analyze one or more, omitting recitatives:
a. Mozart: *Magic Flute, No. 4* ("O zittre nicht")
b. Mozart: *Don Giovanni, No. 4* ("Madamina")
c. Beethoven: *Fidelio, No. 9* ("Abscheulicher!")

10-5. SUMMARY

As in the ternary forms, the parts of a binary form are often susceptible to subdivision—part one frequently, part two almost always. Ordinarily the initial section of part two, referred to as the departure or digression, is particularly interesting. This is the section which, in prolonging the V which concluded part one or progressing from the final III of part to the V, moves restlessly from secondary tonic to secondary tonic, resulting in an effect of tension or vitality. Upon the return of the tonic key, or shortly thereafter, this tension is released.

As in ternary forms, the parts of a binary form may be connected by a link or transition. Each part may close with a codetta, and a coda often concludes the whole.

Many operatic arias consist of a combination of two independent forms of a contrasting character. The result is termed the composite binary form.

11

The Sonata Form

Historical Note on Sonata and Sonata Form ⌐Today the term "sonata" is usually reserved for works performed by one or two players only. Sonatas for three performers are called trios, those for four quartets, those for orchestra symphonies. Although the number of instruments may vary, such works are similar in form, and our discussion will refer to them all as sonatas.

The sonata as a distinct genre can be traced back to the middle of the sixteenth century. About this time, the style and technique of the French chanson, a polyphonic composition based on imitative counterpoint and comprising a number of distinct sections, was transferred to the organ and thence to the instrumental ensemble to become the *canzon da sonar,* a "chanson to be sounded [on instruments]." This term was later abbreviated to sonata and frequently contrasted with toccata, a piece to be played on a keyboard, and cantata, a piece to be sung. In 1580 and 1586, Giovanni Croce and Andrea Gabrieli, respectively, published pieces entitled *sonate,* each of which comprised five to ten contrasting sections played continuously as one movement. In the early part of the seventeenth century, other Italian composers (for example, S. Rossi, C. Fontana, M. Neri) were writing sonatas with fewer sections, each of these enlarged—that is, sonatas in several movements. The history of the sonata now becomes extremely complex due to the enormous number and types of compositions being written in various countries by many composers. Here it will suffice to point out that from the conflicting trends in sonata construction there emerged at the beginning of the eighteenth century two generally observed standard movement schemes: the four-movement sonata and that in three movements.

The three-movement scheme—two fast movements surrounding a slow one—has been common since the beginning of the eighteenth century when it was used not only in chamber music but as the standard scheme of the Italian opera overture, the sinfonia. Outside the sinfonia this three movement scheme has sometimes been restricted to works for one or two performers, for example, sonatas

174

for piano or organ, and sonatas for violin or some other instrument and piano. The four-movement scheme, on the other hand, has been associated since the time of Beethoven with sonatas requiring any number of performers from one (Beethoven's *Op. 2*) to several hundred (Beethoven's *Symphony No. 9*).

When a sonata has four movements, either of two schemes is likely to be found. The slow-fast-slow-fast pattern was used a great deal in the seventeenth and early eighteenth centuries by Torelli, Corelli, Handel, Bach and others, but has only rarely occurred since then (Brahms, *Horn Trio, Op. 40*; Franck, *Violin Sonata*). The four-movement scheme of the classical and romantic composers, first established in some of the symphonies of Johann Stamitz and other Mannheim composers around 1750, comprises two fast movements surrounding two middle movements. One of these middle movements is generally slow, the other is a minuet or scherzo.

From time to time sonatas with schemes of more or fewer than the standard three or four movements are to be found. One-movement sonatas are represented by the eighteenth century Italian keyboard composers, especially Domenico Scarlatti. It is now known, however, that Scarlatti ordinarily grouped his sonatas in pairs so that the majority of them should more properly be thought of as forming sonatas in two movements. The sonata consisting of a single movement was revived in the nineteenth century by Liszt (*Piano Sonata in B Minor*) and is not infrequent in the twentieth century (Sibelius, *Symphony No. 7*, Berg, *Piano Sonata*, Schoenberg, *String Trio*). It should be noted that often the sonata which is ostensibly in one movement actually contains several movements played continuously without pauses (Barber, *Symphony in One Movement*, Schoenberg, *Chamber Symphony No. 1*). Two-movement sonatas were written by the classical composers, but after Beethoven they are not found among the great music of the nineteenth century unless Schubert's *Symphony No. 8* ("Unfinished") is included in this group. The two-movement sonata is not uncommon in this century (Schoenberg, *Chamber Symphony No. 2*, Webern, *Symphony, Op. 21*).

Sonatas in more than four movements were written rather frequently in the seventeenth century, such as those of Vitali (fast-slow-fast-slow-fast), but later works comprising so many movements are more properly classed with the suite. The *serenades, cassations, notturni,* and *divertimenti* of Mozart, Haydn and many other late eighteenth-century Austrian composers are of this type, generally including at least six movements (two minuets and two slow movements in addition to the outer fast movements). Beethoven's *Septet, Op. 20*, is properly included in the serenade category, along with his two *Serenades, Op. 8* and *Op. 25.* Schubert's *Octet*, based on Beethoven's *Septet*, is another example. Still, the sonata proper sometimes includes five and, occasionally, more movements. The greater number comes about by the addition of a movement to the standard four-movement scheme. Beethoven's *Symphony No. 6* ("Pastoral") adds the storm scene, his *Quartet, Op. 132*, a short march, Berlioz's *Symphonie Fantastique* the "March to the Scaffold," Schubert's *Piano Quintet in A Major* a set of variations on his song *The Trout.* Beethoven's *Quartet in C sharp Minor, Op. 131*, precedes the standard four movements with a slow fugue and places a short transitional movement before the slow movement and another before the finale. The result is a seven-movement work played without pause.

Sometimes a single theme appears in more than one movement of a work. For example, in Brahms' *Violin Sonata No. 1*, the second episode of the rondo which concludes the sonata makes use of the same theme which opened the slow movement. Such treatment is termed "cyclic." The cyclic principle was common very early in the evolution of the sonata (for example, in the sonatas of Legrenzi in the latter half of the seventeenth century), but the principle waned and was not revived and further developed until the romantic movement. Berlioz' first two symphonies (*Fantastique* and *Harold in Italy*) make use of a single theme (the *"idée fixe"*) that appears in each movement. Brahms sometimes restates the opening theme of the first movement during the finale (*Symphony No. 3; Clarinet Quintet*). The Finale of Bruckner's *Symphony No. 8* includes a simultaneous statement of the principal themes of the three preceding movements. During the last half of the nineteenth century French composers (Franck, Saint-Saëns, d'Indy, and others) particularly emphasized cyclic treatment in their sonatas.

Any discussion of the formal aspect of the sonata must make clear the distinction between the movement scheme and the sonata form. The movement scheme, as used above, refers to the number and tempo or type (for instance, minuet) of the individual movements comprising the whole sonata. The sonata form is a standard form exhibited by certain single movements. Not every movement in a sonata is a sonata form. Some are binary forms, others are ternaries, rondos, and so on. Sonata form is a form which, throughout history, has played such a large rôle in the various sonata movements that the name has been attached to it.

The particular form known today as sonata form (also often called sonata-allegro form and sometimes first-movement form) has, from the second quarter of the eighteenth century, been associated with the Italian opera sinfonia, as well as with the sonata. The vast majority of movements in both the sonatas and overtures of the late seventeenth and early eighteenth centuries were continuous binaries—simple, balanced, and sometimes rounded. Around 1720, a few sonata movements of certain composers, though still in continuous binary form, began to take on all the essential characteristics of what was later to become standardized as sonata form. Examples of such movements are the Finales of Veracini's *Violin Sonatas No. 1* and *No. 6* (1721), the first movement of Francesco Conti's Overture to *Pallade Trionfante* (1721), and the second movement of the *Violin Sonata, Op. 1, No. 9*, by G. B. Somis (1722). During the 1730s this rudimentary sonata form became more and more frequent and was the preferred form for the first movements of the opera *sinfonie* of the Neapolitan composers G. B. Pergolesi and Leonardo Leo. By 1742, it had found its way to Berlin in the "Prussian" sonatas of C. P. E. Bach. In the latter half of the eighteenth century and the first quarter of the nineteenth century, sonata form was so prevalent throughout Europe that it constituted the most important single form, extending its influence beyond the sonata as far as the realm of opera (for example, Mozart's *Don Giovanni*, Nos. 3 and 15). But this is not to say that sonata form was a fixed, unchangeable blueprint according to which composers constructed their works. On the contrary, the form remained stable only in its broadest outlines. Each of the great classical composers treated it according to his own creative impulses and in constantly fresh ways. Only after Beethoven did the sonata form tend at times to petrify into a stereotype, as it seems to have in the first movement of Grieg's *Piano Concerto in A Minor*.

Throughout the classical and romantic periods it is the first movements of sonatas, chamber music, and symphonies that are usually, but by no means always, sonata forms. Any of the other movements may or may not be in this form. Slow movements and finales are very often in this form; exceptionally a minuet or scherzo may be (Mozart, *Quartet, K. 387,* Beethoven, *Symphony No. 9,* Brahms, *Symphony No. 4*). The classical overture is ordinarily either a sonata form or its relative the sonatina, which we will discuss in Chapter 12.

The sonata form has found a place in certain music of the twentieth century (Hindemith, Prokofiev, Bartók). Although Schoenberg managed to follow its design even in twelve-tone works (*Quartets No. 3* and *No. 4*), it seems hardly likely that the form will be found useful by present-day atonal composers.

11-1. THE GENERAL ASPECT OF SONATA FORM

The sonata form originated as a type of continuous binary form, the two parts of which, like those of the rounded and balanced binary, are subdivided in a particular way. Example 11-1, the first movement of a Neapolitan opera overture dating from the year 1739, illustrates the sectional pattern of the first part of a typical sonata form.

Part one extends to m. 36 and is subdivided into four sections. The first, because of its opening position, is called the first theme or the principal theme. It is a two-phrase group, the first phrase repeated, and ends with a semi-cadence. The next section (mm. 13–20) is a single phrase that, by a series of sequences, modulates to the dominant key and semicadences there. The chief purpose of this section is to introduce the key of the next section. It is, then, a transition or bridge.

The next section, called the second theme or the subordinate theme (mm. 20–28), begins and ends in the dominant key. In this example it states a melody differing in its initial three-and-one-half bars from the first theme. Though melodic contrast between first and second themes occurs with great frequency, it is not a *sine qua non* of the sonata form. Often, in what are called monothematic sonata forms, the two themes are similar and elements of a melody may be used in both principal and subordinate themes alike, as indeed happens here in mm. 24–25. What is essential to this form is that the second theme be in some key other than the tonic.

The final section (mm. 28–36), a single phrase repeated, concludes part one, hence its name "closing theme." It continues the key of the second theme, beginning immediately after its conclusive cadence. In this example the closing theme has a melody that contrasts still further. Again, one must not look for melodic contrast in the closing themes of all sonata forms. Some closing themes—and this is true for some first and second themes as well—exhibit no clearly melodic aspect whatsoever, consisting instead of arpeggios, scales, or some other figuration appropriate to the performing medium [see the Finale of Beethoven's *Sonata, Op. 27, No. 2* ("Moonlight")].

The chief musical material of the piece is set forth or "exposed" in the four sections of part one. The first part of a sonata form is therefore called the exposition. The four sections of the exposition (first theme, transition, second theme, and closing theme) appear in the majority of cases as they do in Ex. 11-1. It is not rare, however, for there to be more or fewer sections, as will be demonstrated in future examples.

Ex. 11-1. LEO: *Achille in Sciro, Sinfonia*

The second part of the sonata form opens like that of any other binary form with a departure or digression prolonging the concluding V of the exposition or, in cases where part one ends on III, progressing to V. As in the rounded binary, this V brings about interruption of the harmonic movement, followed by a return to the beginning and a complete harmonic movement on I.

The terms universally employed today for the departure and return are, when used in connection with the sonata form, development and recapitulation, respectively. The term "development" indicates that the section is often devoted to motivic development based on themes heard in the exposition. The term "recapitulation" implies a return of a number of themes rather than a single one.

In its over-all aspect the sonata form can be outlined in this manner:

Part One			Part Two	
Exposition			Development	Recapitulation
PT tr	ST	CT		PT tr ST CT
	V–I	V–I		I → V–I V–I
I →	of V(III)	of V(III)	$x\ x\ x\ x\ V_7$	

Since the sonata form grew almost imperceptibly out of the various types of continuous binaries, the practice of repeating each part was at first regularly followed. But in many of their later works, Haydn and Mozart dropped the repetition of part two, and Beethoven and Schubert did the same. Only in a few works of the latter composers (Beethoven's *Sonatas Op.* 78 and *Op.* 79, and Schubert's *Sonata in A Major, Op.* 120, for instance) are the development and recapitulation sections also repeated. In the Finale of the *Sonata, Op.* 57 ("Appassionata"), Beethoven repeats the development and recapitulation sections, but not the exposition. As a rule, however, the exposition was repeated by all classical composers and often by the romantics as well. On the other hand, when sonata form is used for an overture, neither part is customarily repeated.

Having outlined the main features of sonata form, we shall consider it in greater detail in the next sections.

11-2. THE FIRST THEME

Example 11-2 is the first theme from the exposition of the opening movement in Brahms' *Symphony No. 1 in C Minor*.

Ex. 11-2. BRAHMS: *Symphony No. 1 in C Minor*, First Movement

The first phrase acts as an introduction. Phrase 2 presents the theme's first real melody, A, which ends with a semicadence on V (m. 46). Thematically similar, phrase 3 makes this V a secondary tonic by means of the imperfect cadence $VII_6/V–V$ (mm. 50–51). Phrase 4 presents a different melody, B, and closes with another semicadence on V (mm. 56–57). Phrase 5, similar to 4 though extended, closes the harmonic movement with a perfect authentic cadence on I (mm. 69–70). The four phrases of mm. 42–70 have formed a contrasting double period. Phrase 6 takes up the melody A again, semicadencing in mm. 77–78. Phrase 7 is similar and closes the second complete harmonic movement with a perfect authentic cadence on I. Phrases 6 and 7, then, are recognizable as a symmetrical parallel period. The seven phrases which comprise the first theme thus form themselves into two groups preceded by an introduction, and are characterized by a design involving statement, digression, and modified restatement. It will be observed that the double period (mm. 42–70) encompasses both the statement and digression, while the second period presents the modified restatement.

The "symmetry" of the double period lies in the balancing of the two-phrase antecedent by the two-phrase consequent. Each phrase, however, is longer than the preceding one (four bars, five-and-one-half bars, six bars, thirteen bars). Similarly, in the period that follows, the eight-bar antecedent is followed by an eleven-bar consequent. The enormous drive of this powerful theme is partly due to the constant growth in the length of its phrases.

The exposition of a sonata form comprises the first part; the principal theme comprises the first section of that part. A subdivision of the principal theme is referred to as a subsection. The introduction and two groups of Brahms' first theme, then, become three subsections of that theme. The entire first theme can be outlined as shown below.

Bars	Phrase	Division	Tonal Structure	Design
38–42	Phrase 1	Subsection 1: introduction	I → V₇–I	—
42–70	Phrases 2-5	Subsection 2: double period	I → V₇–I	AB
70–89	Phrases 6, 7	Subsection 3: period	I → V₇–I	A'

It will be observed that Ex. 11-2, though comprising only the first theme of a sonata-form exposition and therefore not a part in itself, nonetheless concludes with a perfect authentic cadence. The strength of this cadence has been emphasized and it has been presented as capable of dividing a composition into parts. But it is not rare for longer works, in which the parts are further divided into sections and subsections, to use the perfect authentic cadence as a means of marking the end of a section or subsection as well as the end of a part. In our example, and in similar cases, the rhythmic motion of the accompaniment helps to drive through the cadence. Moreover, compared to those at the end of the exposition, the cadence is not of divisive strength. The first movement of Schubert's "Unfinished Symphony" is similar in this respect to the first movement of Brahms' *Symphony No. 1*.

Although the tonal structure of Ex. 11-2 divides the first theme into two unequal subsections plus introduction, the melodic arrangement imposes on the section a ternary design: AB-A'. It is doubtful whether musical literature has another principal theme constructed quite like this one. Examination of the first theme of Ex. 11-3 will show it to be very different. There the single melody is presented without introduction and as a symmetrical period. This period is then repeated in a varied version. Actually, sonata form first themes have been constructed in any of innumerable different ways. In Mozart's little *Sonata in C Major, K. 545*, it consists of a single four-bar phrase, while the first theme of his *Symphony No. 38* ("Prague") is a section of thirty-five bars in two distinct subsections, each of which can be further subdivided, and the whole containing no less than seven different melodic ideas.

Although in a lengthy movement the first theme may contain within itself several subsections exhibiting a number of themes, it is usually not difficult to determine how far the first theme extends, for the whole section will express the tonic key. There may be temporary secondary tonics, but as long as a return to the original tonic is effected, the various subsections are considered part of the first theme.

EXERCISE

1. Each of the following passages is the first theme of a sonata-form movement. Identify and compare their formal characteristics.

A	B
a. Beethoven: *Op. 2, No. 1,* First Movement, mm. 1–8.	a. Mozart: *Sonata, K. 333,* Second Movement, mm. 1–8
b. Beethoven: *Op. 2, No. 3,* First Movement, mm. 1–12.	b. Beethoven: *Sonata, Op. 2, No. 1,* First Movement, mm. 1–8
c. Beethoven: *Op. 14, No. 1,* First Movement, mm. 1–12	c. Hindemith: *Piano Sonata No. 2,* First Movement, mm. 1–26

11-3. THE TRANSITION

Example 11-3 illustrates the first theme and transition from the exposition of the first movement of one of Haydn's piano sonatas.

Ex. 11-3. HAYDN: *Sonata in C Major, No. 35, First Movement*

The first theme (mm. 1–16) consists of the statement and varied repetition of an eight-bar symmetrical period, closing with a perfect authentic cadence on I. This I is sustained in order that the transition may begin immediately with no break in the flow of the music. The transition theme is clearly related to the first theme in that it is built entirely out of the latter's chief motives.

Modulatory aspect of the transition

From m. 16 to m. 22 the main tonality of C is expressed. With the last beat of m. 23, however, the note $f''\sharp$ is introduced and maintained from then on. No other chromatic alteration is made until m. 31, when the note $c'\sharp$ appears in the bass, passing between a c' and a d'. The harmonies of mm. 23–35 express the key of G major, the dominant aspect of the main tonality of C. When the note $f''\sharp$ is first introduced in m. 23, the listener does not know whether it presages a real change of key or whether it acts as a mere secondary dominant of V. But as it continues to appear throughout a number of bars, the listener's bearings begin to change, and the original tonality recedes in his mind. With the note $c'\sharp$ in m. 31 the D major chord (V in the key of G) that begins m. 32 is made a secondary tonic. When a dominant chord in the new key is preceded by its own (secondary) dominant, the home key sinks below the level of the hearer's consciousness, and the modulation is complete.

On the basis of first one and then another chromatic alteration, we can divide the modulatory aspect of the transition into three phases.

1. Phase 1 is that part before the modulation begins to set in (mm. 16–22).
2. Phase 2 contains the deflection away from the tonic key by the introduction of the leading tone, in this case the note $f''\sharp$ of the new key (mm. 23–31).
3. Phase 3 begins with V/V of the new key, in our example the appearance of the note $c'\sharp$, and continues to the end of the transition and the beginning of the second theme (mm. 31–35).

Locating the beginning of each phase can be simplified by looking for the chromatic alteration which appears at the point where the new phase begins. If the modulation is to be from I to V, the point at which the second phase begins will be marked by a raising of the fourth degree of the scale, and the third phase will be marked by a raising of the first degree. In other words, in a piece in F major, the beginning of phase 2 will contain a B♮ somewhere in the texture, the third phase will contain an F♯. In order not to be misled, however, one must make sure that these chromatic alterations actually reflect an essential modulatory change and are not merely passing secondary dominants or chromatic ornamentation of some kind (for instance, the B♭ in mm. 16 and 18 of Ex. 11-3).

Since the modulation is often not to V but to III or even VI, the preceding observations about chromatic alteration will not always apply. If, however, the following facts are kept in mind, the student should have no trouble in recognizing the various phases of modulation in a transition:

1. The beginning of phase 2 is marked by the appearance of the leading tone of the new key; this leading tone usually appears as an element of V in the new key, sometimes of VII.

2. The beginning of phase 3 is marked by the V/V or VII/V of the new key.
   Note: In the minor mode, phase 2 of a modulation from I to III does not
   necessitate a chromatic alteration for, in the natural minor, VII is
   also V/III.

Dependent and independent transitions

The transition in Ex. 11-3 begins in m. 16 immediately after the final
phrase of the first theme has come to its cadence.[1] It therefore has a clear beginning of its own and is spoken of as an independent transition.

Ex. 11-4.   MOZART: *Sonata, K. 333,* First Movement

The transition of Ex. 11-4 is different in that its beginning is not clearly
set off in the mind of the listener. He hears the beginning of the first theme
transposed to the lower octave and might well assume that this is to be a

---

[1] Another plausible reading would place the beginning of the transition at m. 20,
the preceding four bars being a *codetta* to the first theme. Such a view does not in-
validate the essential observations concerning this transition.

varied repetition of the exposition's initial section. Instead, the presumed first theme is soon deflected in its course and takes on the aspect of a transition. The process of deflection is known as dissolution for it involves the gradual disappearance of the first theme. Such a transition is considered dependent in that its transitory aspect emerges only gradually from what the listener supposes to be a restatement of the first theme.

Both dependent and independent transitions are frequently to be found in the music of the classical and romantic composers.

The function of the transition

Modulation is only one of the functions that a transition can perform. Consideration of other aspects will reveal a variety of uses to which it can be put. In Ex. 11-3, for instance, the transition's first and third phrases are based on motive a' from the first theme, while the second phrase is devoted to motive b. The transition here has provided thematic development, quite apart from the actual development section which will appear later. In addition, the progressive harmony combines with the melodic ascent throughout mm. 20–32 to produce a certain amount of tension. It can be maintained, then, that the transition of Ex. 11-3 achieves at least three things: (1) modulation to the new key; (2) development of motives of the first theme; and (3) emotional contrast.

Being a dependent transition, Ex. 11-4 recalls the initial notes of the first theme. Aside from this, there are certain motivic references to the first theme, but these do not assert themselves as a characteristic of the transition. This is, rather, an example of a transition that introduces new material.

The transition that connects the first and second themes of Brahms' *Symphony No. 1* is an independent transition, a phrase group of four phrases, consisting partly of new and partly of previously heard material. The illustration in Ex. 11-5 begins at the point where Ex. 11-2 left off.

Ex. 11-5. BRAHMS: *Symphony No. 1*

There are two features of this transition which should be especially noted. The first is that, although it is to lead to the major mode of III (that is, E♭), the transition emphasizes the minor mode of that key. Emphasis in the transition on the opposite mode is a useful device, for the listener does not tire of the new key's harmonies before the second theme begins. The classical composers also used this practice to good advantage.

The second feature to be noted is the length of this transition. From the modulatory standpoint it need not have been so long since it attains its objective, the establishment of the key of E♭ by means of V/V of that key in the eighth bar. Yet it continues for twenty-four more bars. There are two reasons for the length of this transition. The first is a matter of proportion. The first theme (Ex. 11-2) is quite long in itself, as are the second and closing themes (see Ex. 11-8), and it is reasonable that the size of the transition that connects them be in keeping with their length. Perhaps more important in this case, however, is the other reason. The first theme is of a violent and stormy nature, the second theme is quiet and restrained. Brahms has calculated that it will take some time to effect this emotional change, for the listener must be psychologically prepared if the mood of the second theme is to be convincing. A hearing of the exposition of this remarkable movement will demonstrate the gradual change from one quality to another which takes place during the transition.

On the basis of our examination of Ex. 11-5 we can deduce that an additional function of a transition may be to prepare the listener for the section that is to follow. Sometimes the transition goes further and actually anticipates the ensuing section by introducing a characteristic rhythm or motive (see Ex. 8-5). In these cases the transition can be compared to the montage, or fade-out, technique commonly employed in films.

To summarize, there are six common functions that a transition may perform.

1. Modulation to the new key
2. Development of a motive or motives from the first theme
3. Introduction of an emotional quality in contrast to that of both first and second themes
4. Introduction of new material which contrasts thematically with both first and second themes
5. Preparation of the listener for the second theme by gradual change from one emotional quality to another
6. Preparation of the listener for the second theme by anticipation of its characteristic rhythm or melodic motive

It is obvious that no single transition can perform all these functions since some are mutually exclusive (Nos. 3 and 5, for instance, or 4 and 6). Most transitions, however, are concerned with several of them. No one function is an indispensable feature of any transition, not even the first, as the following paragraphs will demonstrate.

The partially modulating transition

The three phases of modulation are to be found in the majority of transitions. The third phase, introducing V of the new key as a secondary tonic, obliterates the listener's sense of the original key as "home." These transitions can, then, be thought of as complete from the modulatory standpoint. Some, however, do not bring in phase 3. Instead, the secondary section enters in the new key after phase 2 has run its course. In other words, the transition prepares for the second theme by introducing the new key with its regular V, not a secondary tonic on V. Since the listener's feeling for the original key has not completely disappeared upon the entrance of the second theme, this type of transition will be called partially modulating. A number of piano sonatas by Mozart contain partially modulating transitions (K. 279, First Movement; K. 281, Second Movement; K. 309, First Movement), and such transitions occur from time to time in the works of most other composers as well. (For a partially modulating transition in a rondo see Ex. 9-3.)

The nonmodulating transition

Ex. 11-6.   HAYDN: *Sonata in D Major, No. 37,* First Movement

Example 11-6 illustrates a type of transition not infrequently found among eighteenth-century composers. In this type of transition no modulation takes place at all. Instead, the transition ends with a semicadence on V and the second theme follows immediately in the new key.

The nonmodulating transition seems to be found only in major mode sonata forms of which the second theme is in the dominant key.

Transition with deceptive modulation

In his *Trio, Op. 99,* for piano, violin, and cello, Schubert makes use of an interesting and effective modulatory device. The first movement, in Bb major, presents the first theme in I followed by a transition leading to III. Leaving Bb major in m. 35, the transition moves with apparent sureness of purpose to the key of D major. The listener, expecting the second theme in this key, is surprised to hear it enter instead in F major, the dominant. It is, of course, not possible to describe the particular effect of such deceptive modulations. They must be heard to be appreciated.

. The deceptive modulation appears in the music of most classical and romantic composers (for example, Beethoven's *Symphony No. 8,* Finale), but no one seems to have been quite so fond of it as Schubert, who used it often in his music.

Omission of the transition

Another device occurring several times in the music of Schubert, but rarely used by other composers, is the appearance of the second theme immediately after the first theme without an intervening transition. In this case, Schubert bridges over the gap by means of a short link, no more than a chord or two, or several unaccompanied tones. Well-known examples are to be found in the first movements of the "Unfinished Symphony" (mm. 38–41) and the *Symphony No. 9 in C Major* (mm. 132–133). The second movement of Mozart's piano *Sonata, K. 280,* provides neither transition nor link.

EXERCISE

2.   The following passages are the transitions from the expositions of the sonata forms dealt with in Exercise 1:

A	B
a. *Op. 14, No. 1,* mm. 13–22	a. Mozart: mm. 8–13
b. *Op. 2, No. 3,* mm. 13–26	b. Beethoven: mm. 8–20
c. *Op. 2, No. 1,* mm. 8–20	c. Hindemith: mm. 26–40

(1) Considering these transitions in the above order, locate the beginning of phase 2 and of phase 3, if present, of the modulations: First, look ahead to discover the key of the second theme; then locate the first appearance of V of the new key; finally, locate the first appearance of V/V, if any, of the new key.

(2) Which are "dependent" and which "independent" transitions?

(3) Describe the functions performed by each.

11-4. THE SECOND THEME

Relationship of first and second themes   Like the first theme, the second theme consists, in shorter movements, of a single section; in long movements it will probably comprise a group of subsections. Often the second theme is of a contrasting character to the first theme; sometimes it is not. In monothematic first movements, common in the works of the classical composers, the second theme is either identical with or closely related to the first theme. In longer works where the second theme forms a group of subsections, at least one or two of these will probably contrast with the first. But there is no standard practice in this regard. The sole feature that invariably distinguishes the second theme from the first is the change of key.

Except in the late romantic period, the tempo and meter of the first theme is shared by the second.[2] But toward the end of the century, composers sometimes used tempo and meter changes in imbuing the second theme with an

---

[2] It is, in fact, unusual for these to change anywhere in the movement until the coda is reached. Indeed, the very meaning of "movement" is very close to "tempo."

entirely new character. In Tchaikovsky's symphonies and overtures such far-reaching contrasts are the rule.

Key of secondary theme

Previous to Beethoven, the second theme very rarely expressed a key other than III for sonatas in the minor mode or V for sonatas in either major or minor mode. In the *Sonata, Op. 31, No. 1*, and in the *Sonata, Op. 53* ("Waldstein"), the second and closing themes of the first movements express III although both these sonatas are in the major mode.

In his later works Beethoven frequently substituted VI as the key of the secondary and closing themes (for instance, the first movements of *Symphony No. 9, Quartets Op. 95, Op. 130, Op. 132,* and *Piano Sonata, Op. 106*). Schubert did the same in the first movement of his "Unfinished Symphony."

By the use of mode mixture, the keys of III or VI often occur in a higher or lower position than might be expected. For instance, the Finale of Beethoven's *Symphony No. 8* in F major uses the key of A♭ major for the beginning of the second theme: III of F minor rather than F major. In Mahler's *Symphony No. 2* in C minor, the second theme is in E major: III of the major, rather than the minor, mode of C. The use of mode mixture in the selection of related keys is very common.

Occasionally the second theme does not express a single key but progresses from one to another. In the Finale of Beethoven's *Symphony No. 8* and the first movements of Schubert's *Quintet in C Major* and the *Quartet in D Minor* ("Death and the Maiden"), the second theme begins with III, then moves to V. In the first movement of Beethoven's *Symphony No. 8*, the progression is from VI to V.

The second theme often comes to a close with an authentic cadence in the new key. At other times the final phrase of the second theme leads by means of the elided cadence into the first phrase of the closing theme. From time to time, of course, exceptions occur. Example 11-7 is a case where the second theme comes to a semicadence (V_7), after which the closing section commences on I.

Ex. 11-7.   BRUCKNER: *Symphony No. 7*

EXERCISE

3. The following passages are the second themes from the expositions of the sonata forms dealt with in Exercises 1 and 2:

A	**B**
a. *Op. 14, No. 1,* mm. 22–46	a. Mozart: mm. 14–21
b. *Op. 2, No. 1,* mm. 20–41	b. Beethoven: mm. 20–41
c. *Op. 2, No. 3,* mm. 27–46	c. Hindemith: mm. 41–63

(1) Considering these second themes in the order above, identify the type of larger unit displayed (period, phrase chain, phrase group), if any.
(2) Divide each second theme into its subsections.
(3) Note which subsections rely mainly on melodies, which are basically motivic, which consist chiefly of figuration, and so on.
(4) Does each second theme express a single key and mode or does progressive harmonic movement and/or change of mode take place?
(5) Observe the type of cadence with which each second theme closes. Is there room for disagreement as to the point at which it ends and the closing theme begins?

11-5. THE CLOSING THEME

Reference to mm. 28–36 of Ex. 11-1 will reveal that the closing theme continues in the key (though not necessarily the mode) of the second theme. It does not, then, perform a tonal function of its own but rather reinforces and confirms that of the second theme. The closing section, for this reason, is not an indispensable feature of sonata form, and its omission from time to time is not particularly remarkable. In Haydn's *Symphony No. 103,* for example, its place is taken by a brief codetta.

Nevertheless, the majority of sonata forms include a closing theme, often of considerable length and importance. Example 11-8 presents the essentials of the closing theme from the first movement of the Brahms' *Symphony No. 1,* with whose first theme and transition we have already become acquainted.

Ex. 11-8. BRAHMS: *Symphony No. 1*

The four phrases of this closing theme are in reality only two, for the second is a varied repetition of the first, the fourth of the third. The theme is a period with a varied repetition of both the antecedent and the consequent in the key of E♭ minor—identical to the key but not the mode of the second theme. The minor mode of E♭, however, was prominent in the transition which led to the second theme (see Ex. 11-5). We find an almost identical tonal structure in the first movement of Beethoven's *Sonata, Op. 57* ("Appassionata").

The first eight bars of Ex. 11-8 (mm. 161–168 in the score) present a theme basically in two-part counterpoint. The upper voice is new, with a distinctly energetic character of its own, contrasting with that of the previous themes. The lower voice, however, begins as an inversion of the first theme (compare Ex. 11-2) and continues by a sequential repetition of the second phrase member of that theme. Measures 169–176 present the same two-part contrapuntal texture in exchanged positions: The upper voice is now in the lower position and vice versa, a technique known as double counterpoint (see Section 14-4). Phrase 3, and its varied repetition (mm. 177–185) have a new upper voice supported by motives from the previous phrases.

Upon concluding the closing theme Brahms introduces a single phrase as a bridge which leads either back to the beginning of the exposition or on to the development. This phrase is based on a motive of the first theme.

From this example, and from closing themes in the sonata forms of other composers, the following general observations are especially to be noted:

1. The closing theme usually has a character of its own, different from and contrasting to that of the first and second themes.

2. Nevertheless, *motivically* the closing theme is often related to one or more of the previous themes. In Schubert's sonata forms the closing theme is customarily based on the second theme; other composers frequently prefer it to be based on the first theme.

3. The closing theme is clear and emphatic in its delineation of key, consisting of one or more complete harmonic movements in the key of (usually) III or V and closing with a perfect authentic cadence.

4. A codetta often follows the closing theme. Not infrequently this codetta makes reference to the first theme, preparing the ear for its return in the repetition of the exposition and its appearance, when such is the case, at the beginning of the development section.

5. The closing theme or codetta, when present, often leads to a transition serving to introduce first the return of the exposition and, after its repetition, the development. This transition may refer to the first theme, as in the last

twelve bars of the exposition in the first movement of Beethoven's *Sonata Pathétique, Op. 13.*

EXERCISES

4. Examine the closing themes of the expositions of the sonata forms of the preceding exercises and comment on their characteristics. Is there a codetta? (Note: Hindemith's *Piano Sonata No. 2,* First Movement, has no closing theme.
5. Analyze the entire exposition of:

A	B
a. MF, Overture	a. Beethoven: *Sonata, Op. 53,* First Movement

11-6. THE DEVELOPMENT SECTION

General characteristics There is no standard design for the development section of the sonata form as there is for the exposition. Rather, each composition of the great composers is unique in this regard. The development can normally be divided into a series of subsections, each consisting of a single phrase, a phrase chain, phrase group, or period.

The material of the development consists of anything that the judgment of the composer deems appropriate. It might be based on one or more of the chief themes from the exposition, or it might use only motives from the transition. A favorite device of Mozart and Haydn is to base the initial subsection of the development on a seemingly unimportant fragment of the closing theme or codetta which concluded the exposition. Sometimes this little fragment appears throughout the development so that what at first seems trivial takes on great importance as the movement progresses. Usually the methods of motivic construction discussed in Chapter 3 play an important part. In addition, new material may be introduced, either as melody or figuration. Any of these possibilities might appear in combination with any others. One reason for the intense interest that many developments arouse is the fact that the listener cannot possibly guess in advance what is in store for him.

The short development: tonal structure and design

To illustrate a short development section, Ex. 11-9 presents that from Haydn's *Sonata in C Major, No. 35,* (see Ex. 11-3 for the first theme and transition in this sonata).

Ex. 11-9. HAYDN: *Sonata in C Major, No. 35*

The opening phrase, taken from the first theme, is clearly introductory. It ends with a semicadence (V/VI) leading the listener to expect the next phrase to begin on VI. Phrases 2 and 3, however, offer a surprise in that they bring in the first theme not in VI but IV. (This theme, stated as it was in the exposition, is not reproduced in our example.) From m. 79 on, the development is nonmelodic, expressing its harmonies through figuration which is a continuation of the triplet arpeggio characterizing most of the exposition. We conclude, then, that this development comprises three subsections.

Bars	Subsection	Material
67–71	1. Introduction (phrase 1)	Consequent of PT
72–79	2. Period (phrases 2 and 3)	PT
79–103	3. Figuration (phrase 4)	New, but using triplet figure from exposition

The tonal structure of this development section, as that of the *departure* of Ex. 10-3, involves a succession within a succession. First the cadential V of the exposition moves down a third to V/VI. By chord succession this V/VI is prolonged (mm. 71–98), after which it moves by descending fifths to the interrupting V_7 (mm. 98–103). Example 11-10 is a harmonic outline of the development showing its basic tonal structure.

Ex. 11-10.   Harmonic outline of Ex. 11-9

Example 11-10 shows how logical the tonal structure of a development section can be. When one hears of the "constantly shifting tonalities" and the "modulations to remote keys" which are commonly supposed to be characteristic of the development sections of this or that composer, it is easy to conclude that these "remote keys" are chosen almost at random. The whim of the composer leads him into strange realms from which somehow he must find his way back. Careful consideration of the tonal structures of the development sections of the great composers will, however, generally show that the various secondary tonics and modulations employed are only elaborate ways of stating a chord succession or progression which, whether simple or complex, is fundamentally reasonable and straightforward.

The lengthy development: design

Subsections 1 and 2 of the development discussed above (Ex. 11-9), though different from each other, are related in that they both make use of

the first theme, the former of the consequent only, the latter of both antecedent and consequent. The grouping together by means of thematic relationships of the various subsections becomes an important method of attaining
unity in a long development section. Beethoven in particular, in lengthy
sonata forms, does so systematically. A survey of the development section to
the first movement of his *Symphony No. 9* in D minor will illustrate both
this procedure and some other of Beethoven's developmental methods.

Themes from the first movement's exposition which are used in the
development section are shown in Ex. 11-11. The exposition begins strikingly.
Tiny motivic fragments hint at the principal theme (PT), finally gathering
themselves together for the initial unison statement. Particular note should be
taken of motives a, b, and c of the principal theme. The second theme (ST)
consists of a number of subsections, ST_1 through ST_5, and is followed by a
closing theme (CT) made up of CT_1 and a codetta, CT_2. ST_5 is a melodic
and rhythmic variant of motive c.

Ex. 11-11.   BEETHOVEN: *Symphony No. 9*

The development begins with a subsection presenting the fragments of
the principal theme as at the beginning of the movement. This passage can be
considered the introduction to the development, just as formerly it served as
introduction to the exposition. The development proper begins with three
contrasting phrases (subsections 2, 3, and 4; mm. 179–197). The first phrase
presents the first theme as a dialogue between winds and strings, the second
restates the codetta (CT_2), and the third builds a melodic phrase for woodwinds out of motive b of the first theme (see Ex. 11-12).

Measures 198–218 also consist of three phrases (subsections 5, 6, and 7)
which closely correspond to the preceding three, subsection 5 with subsection
2, 6 with 3, and 7 with 4. By this grouping Beethoven achieves a degree of

Ex. 11-12. BEETHOVEN: *Symphony No. 9*

unity, for the six subsections are felt as being two large groups of three subsections each.

It may be noticed that while each phrase has a clear cadence, that cadence always connects by elision with the beginning of the next phrase. The elision of phrase cadences is characteristic of developments for this is the section in which, more than any other, a sense of urgency and movement is customarily maintained.

Subsection 7 similarly overlaps with the beginning of subsection 8 (m. 218). This section uses a developmental technique of which Beethoven, in his later years, was particularly fond: fugal treatment (see Chapter 14).

Ex. 11-13. BEETHOVEN: *Symphony No. 9*

The theme of this fugal subsection appears in the bass and is constructed by using motives b and c, continuing with an expansion of c in the rhythmic guise in which it appeared as ST_5. It is marked by the Roman numeral I. The theme is accompanied throughout by two new themes (II and III) in the manner of a triple fugue (see Section 14-7).

Subsection 8, the fugue, as the lengthiest division of the development, can be considered equivalent to a group in itself. Subsection 9 uses motive b in the melody and accompanies it with a variation of ST_5—the same two motives of which the fugue theme consists. Here, however, they are not juxtaposed but are sounded simultaneously. Subsection 10 (mm. 275–286) brings in, for the first time, the initial melody of the second theme, ST_1. Subsection 11 (mm. 287–296) corresponds to subsection 9. Thus the last three subsections group themselves together in the mind of the hearer as a kind of ternary form and comprise a larger unit within the development section, just

Development of the First Movement of Beethoven's Symphony No. 9 from the Point of View of Design

Bars	Division	Material	Description
160–178	Subsection 1 (introduction)	Motive a	Fragments of PT as at beginning of movement
179–197	Group I		
179–188	Subsection 2	Motive a	Dialogue between strings and winds
188–192	Subsection 3	CT_2	Full orchestral statement
192–197	Subsection 4	Motive b	Motivic phrase
198–218	Group II		
198–206	Subsection 5 (= Subs. 2)	Motive a	Group II similar to
206–210	Subsection 6 (= Subs. 3)	CT_2	Group I, varied and transposed
210–218	Subsection 7 (= Subs. 4)	Motive b	
218–259	"Group" III: Subsection 8	Motive b, ST_5 (= motive c), also new material	Triple fugue; Subject I built of two motives from exposition; Subjects II and III new
259–297	Group IV		
259–275	Subsection 9 (like Subs. 4)	Motive b, ST_5	Motive b accompanied by ST_5 in a *cantabile* dialogue
275–286	Subsection 10	ST_1	As in exposition
287–296	Subsection 11 (= 9)	Motive b, ST_5	Transposed restatement of Subsection 9
297–300	Subsection 12 (retransition)	Motive b	Tutti unison cascade built from single motive

as subsections 2, 3, and 4 and subsections 5, 6, and 7 did. Measures 297–300, a furious cascade in the strings and woodwinds, based on motive b, punctuated by sharp outbursts in the brass and timpani, act as retransition and usher in the tonic chord (now altered to its major form) which begins the introduction to the recapitulation.

Although this development section is a long one of 140 bars, its design is easily comprehensible to the alert listener, for Beethoven has not presented an array of small subsections with little or no clear relationship. Instead, he has gathered the various small divisions into four large groups flanked by the introduction and the retransition.

The lengthy development: tonal structure

Consideration of the tonal structure of this development section reveals an unusual feature at its inception. It will be remembered that normally a sonata form in which the secondary and closing sections of the exposition are in a nondominant key has a development section which progresses from that key to the interrupting V ushering in the recapitulation. In this symphony, the exposition ends with a perfect authentic cadence in VI, that is, B♭ major (mm. 149–150) after which the codetta continues to sound this VI chord. Rather than beginning the development from there, however, and progressing gradually to the V, Beethoven drops without modulation from VI to V. From the point of view of the tonal structure, the development is an enormous chord succession prolonging this V and connecting it with the interrupting V immediately preceding the recapitulation. The harmonic outline of the development section in Ex. 11-14 shows its essential tonal structure.

Ex. 11-14. BEETHOVEN: *Symphony No. 9* (harmonic outline of development in first movement)

After the exposition has come to its close on VI, the development moves abruptly to V and thence to IV, through V₆/IV. Group I (subsections 2, 3, 4) all express the subdominant key, but with the appearance of group II this IV becomes, by means of a chromatic change, the dominant of VII. The fugue begins on VII and progresses by means of descending fifths and chromatic passing tones in the bass to V/V, expressed in subsection 9. Subsection 10 brings the return of V, pianissimo in trumpets and kettledrums, this V very gradually growing in strength throughout subsection 11. (An unusual feature here is that the low stringed instruments sometimes drop below the recurring V of trumpets and drums, so that there are moments when V is not in fundamental position.)

The significance of the key relationships in this development is shown by the summary bass outline in Ex. 11-15. The Roman numerals above the notes indicate the real scale steps expressed, while those below the notes show the function of these scale steps.

Ex. 11-15. BEETHOVEN: *Symphony No. 9* (key relationships in development of first movement)

A consideration of the function of the various keys which participate in a development section will point up the significance of each key chosen. As in this instance, the great composers follow an essentially straightforward tonal plan in spite of surface complications.

Variations of usual tonal structure

Sonata forms based on the usual tonal structure reach, during the last bars of the development section, the V (or V_7), following which the harmonic movement begins again with the recapitulation. Occasionally another chord serves for this interrupting V. In the first movement of Haydn's "Farewell Symphony," for instance, the VII, sounding much like the V_7, appears in its place.

In the second movement of his *Sonata, Op. 109,* Beethoven's intention at the opening of the recapitulation is apparently to startle the listener. He accomplishes his purpose in two ways. Most of the development is to be played *piano,* the last part *una corda* and *pianissimo,* with interspersed periods of silence. Suddenly the first theme bursts in, opening the recapitulation *fortissimo.* The dynamic surprise here is paralleled by the tonal structure. The V at the end of the usual development section leads predictably into the recapitulation. Here the substitute chord (V/V) does not "lead" into it at all. The effect of the recapitulation's opening is thus doubly abrupt.[3] Here is an outline of the tonal structure.

Part One	Part Two	
(Exposition)	(Development)	(Recapitulation)
I → V	IV V V → $\underbrace{}_{\text{of V}}$ (= II ♯ 3)	I → V I

EXERCISES

6. Study the development sections of the first movements of the sonata forms under examination.

a. Find the point at which the recapitulation begins and locate the V pedal point preceding this, if one is present. How far back does this V extend?

b. Note which chord closes the exposition. Does it relate with the V that closes the development by chord succession or does it progress to that V?

c. Analyze the development section to discover its design.

(1) Note whether and how it divides into subsections.
(2) Identify the material on which each subsection is based.
(3) Relate the subsections to each other. Do any group themselves together?
(4) Which subsection acts as retransition?

d. Follow the progress of the bass line from the end of the exposition to the first appearance of the V pedal point.

e. Make a summary harmonic outline of the tonal structure.

7. Analyze in a similar manner the development section of:

A	B
a. *MF*, Overture	a. Beethoven: *Sonata, Op. 53*, First Movement

11-7. THE RECAPITULATION

The purpose of the recapitulation   The recapitulations of a large number of sonata forms restate in the tonic key all the themes of the exposition in the same order in which they were first heard. This fact has caused many to believe that the purpose of the recapitulation is to provide balance through

---

[3] Two discussions of this singular passage are to be found in recent periodical literature: Edward T. Cone, "Analysis Today," *Musical Quarterly*, Vol. XLVI, No. 2 (April 1960), p. 172; and Robert Smith, "This Sorry Scheme of Things . . . ," *Music Review*, Vol. XXII, No. 3 (August 1961), pp. 212–213.

symmetry—the recapitulation is a counterpart to the exposition, just as part three of the sectional ternary form is a counterpart to part one. There is no question that there is some truth in this supposition, yet it falls far short of revealing the essence of the recapitulation. If the purpose of the recapitulation were to create a symmetrical balance with the exposition, then it follows that those sonata forms of the great composers which do no such thing must be considered defective to the extent that the recapitulation is altered, a conclusion that would eliminate from the rank of "perfect" works most of the great sonata forms of the classical composers. Nor is there justification for believing that the recapitulation that reproduces the exposition (partially transposed) is "normal" and others "exceptional." From the earliest examples of sonata form, deviations from this mythical "norm" have been too frequent to warrant considering them exceptional cases.

The real purpose of the recapitulation becomes clear when the tonal structure of the sonata form as a whole is considered. It will be remembered that a complete harmonic movement involves a move away from I with a return to I, while a progressive harmonic movement is to a different tonal area without a return (see Section 5-5). The exposition, moving from I of the first theme to III, V, or VI of the second and closing themes is a progressive movement and therefore incomplete. The development does nothing to alleviate this condition; on the contrary, it prolongs it. With the appearance of the recapitulation, however, the situation changes. Beginning the harmonic movement again, it presents the material of the exposition not as a progressive movement from I to some other key, but as a complete harmonic movement within the original tonality.

> The most basic function of the recapitulation is to complete a harmonic movement previously left incomplete.

Since this function can be performed perfectly well without an exact restatement of themes, we find composers often vary them in the recapitulation. Since it can be performed without a restatement of all the themes, not infrequently certain themes or even whole sections are omitted. Nor is there any absolute necessity for restating the whole of any one theme.

Differences in design between exposition and recapitulation

Summarized under the six headings below are common means by which recapitulations are made to differ from expositions.

CONDENSATION The recapitulation can be altered by shortening one or more of its divisions, especially the first theme. This device gives to the recapitulation all the themes of the exposition, but with one or more of them in condensed form (see Mozart's "Prague Symphony," First Movement).

ABBREVIATION The elimination of one or more sections results in the abbreviated recapitulation. Sometimes it is the transition that is eliminated. In monothematic sonata forms the secondary section might be omitted. In a monothematic movement the chief difference in the exposition between the first and second themes is their keys. Since the recapitulation presents the two in the same key, a restatement of both could be redundant. Haydn, who particularly favored monothematic movements, furnishes many examples of the abbreviated recapitulation, a famous one being the first movement of his *Symphony No. 103.*

VARIATION A varied form of one or more subjects in the recapitulation is rather common. In the last movement of his *Sonata, K. 279,* Mozart varies the first theme of the recapitulation by giving the melody to the left hand and the accompaniment to the right hand, the reverse manner of its appearance in the exposition. Beethoven sometimes lets the reappearance of the first theme be elaborately ornamented, as in the *Adagio sostenuto* of the *Sonata, Op. 106* ("Hammerklavier"). The original theme is given as Ex. 4-3, the ornamentation as Ex. 11-16. There is seemingly no limit to the possibilities for variation of any of the themes in the recapitulation.

Ex. 11-16. BEETHOVEN: *Sonata, Op. 106*

Special mention should be made of the recapitulation of a minor-mode movement. If in the exposition the second and closing themes were in a major mode, the composer often recapitulates them in the major mode of the tonic key, the parallel major. But, since the movement is itself in the minor mode, he may decide to alter the mode of these themes as well as their key, restating them in the tonic minor. A change of mode from major to minor drastically alters the character of most melodies, shedding on them a new and different light.[4] Mozart was fond of taking advantage of this fact in his minor-mode compositions. By changing the secondary theme from the major mode of the

---

[4] It used to be the common practice of film composers to herald an impending marital disaster by sounding in the minor mode the opening of Wagner's *Bridal Chorus* from *Lohengrin.*

exposition to the minor mode, he was able to endow his recapitulation with a dramatic significance. The effect is as if the theme, through the struggles and conflicts of the development, had become somehow altered, just as the character of, say, Hamlet, alters during the course of the play. In the Finale of his *Symphony No. 40 in G Minor*, Mozart goes even further, for in changing its mode the melodic contour itself is completely transformed.

REARRANGEMENT   The various parts of the exposition are sometimes recapitulated in a different order. Occasionally the order of first and second themes is reversed. An extremely interesting rearrangement is found in the first movement of Mozart's *Sonata in C Major, K. 279*: Part of the first theme is omitted in the recapitulation and inserted later in the middle of the secondary theme! This gives the impression that somehow the phrase was forgotten and the pianist must interrupt the second theme to run back and fetch it.

EXPANSION   Both the first and second themes normally being recapitulated in the main tonality, the composer runs the risk of monotony from overuse of a single key. Often he likes to utilize the intervening transition to provide key contrast. In its wanderings away from and back to the original key, this transition is sometimes lengthened.

A less common but more startling expansion of the recapitulation can occur from further motivic development of one of the themes during the course of the recapitulation. Mozart interrupts the closing section to insert a short development of part of the second theme in the Finale to his *Sonata, K. 279,* and Haydn, in his *Symphony No. 101* ("Clock"), interrupts the recapitulation of his second theme to introduce a lengthy development of its initial motive similar to the first portion of his development section.

VARIANTS USED IN COMBINATION   A single recapitulation may make use of more than one of the preceding methods of alteration. A movement that expands one portion will be likely to condense or omit another in order that some proportion between the large sections may be maintained. In the first movement of the "Clock Symphony," for instance, Haydn makes up for the enormous expansion of the second theme, referred to above, by greatly reducing the size of the preceding transition. Furthermore he omits the original closing theme entirely and substitutes for it a transitionlike passage leading into the coda which concludes the movement.

We have been dealing with differences between an exposition and its recapitulation from the point of view of design. It also happens that some recapitulations exhibit tonal structures which call for special comment.

Irregular tonal structures in the recapitulation

APPEARANCE OF RECAPITULATION BEFORE COMPLETION OF INTERRUPTING V_7 The first theme of Haydn's "Surprise Symphony" does not begin with tonic harmony but with a secondary tonic on II (V/II–II) which then moves to V–I. In this case Haydn does not follow the usual practice of closing his development section on an interrupting V_7. Instead, he ushers in the recapitulation with VI which, in its major form, is identical with V/II.

Ex. 11-17.   HAYDN: *Symphony No. 94* ("Surprise")

The first movement of the "Oxford Symphony" of Haydn is similar. Here the first theme begins on V_7 and is ushered in by a VII^6_5/V. In both these symphonies Haydn has incorporated the V_7–I progression within the opening bars of the recapitulation due to the very nature of the first themes. In Ex. 11-18 the first theme begins with tonic harmony and therefore a variant from the normal tonal structure is not strictly necessary. Nonetheless, the composer has chosen to begin the recapitulation without waiting for the completion of the interrupting V_7 chord. The result is an exceptional tonal structure corresponding to that with which we have already become familiar in ternary form (see Ex. 8-6).

Ex. 11-18.   MENDELSSOHN: *Symphony No. 4* ("Italian")

The example shows the final retransition measures of the development and the beginning of the recapitulation in the first movement of Mendelssohn's "Italian Symphony." The restatement of the first theme begins in the upper strings just as the cellos and winds reach the interrupting V in the following version:

Thus, the recapitulation begins four bars before the harmonic movement of the development has completed its course. The conflict produced between design and tonal structure at this point results in a tight dovetailing of the development and recapitulation sections.

Ex. 11-19.   MENDELSSOHN: *Symphony No. 4,* First Movement (bass outline)

A similar variant of the normal relationship between design and tonal structure is to be found in the first movement of Tchaikovsky's *Symphony No. 5 in E Minor.*

COMMENCEMENT OF RECAPITULATION IN NONTONIC KEY   The characteristic progression in the exposition of most major-mode sonata forms is from I to V, that is, upwards a fifth. Occasionally, particularly in works by Mozart, Clementi, and Schubert, this progression up a fifth finds reflection in the recapitulation. In this case, the first theme of the recapitulation does not express the main tonality of the piece but appears in the subdominant key. It then progresses up a fifth to the tonic for the secondary and closing sections. The development section thus becomes a progressive harmonic movement from V to I♭7 (that is, V_7/IV).

Part One	Part Two	
(Exposition)	(Development)	(Recapitulation)
$I \rightarrow V$ ——	———————$\rightarrow I\flat_7$ $(= V_7/IV)$	$IV \rightarrow I$

This tonal scheme results in a kind of display of equilibrium, for the tonic key is nicely balanced between its upper fifth (last part of exposition, V) and lower fifth (first part of recapitulation, IV). Some examples of its use are to be found in the First Movements of Mozart's *Sonata in C Major, K. 545,* and Schubert's *Symphony No. 5,* as well as in the last movement of Schubert's *Sonata, Op. 120,* ("Little A Major").

From time to time the composer, especially the romantic composer, elects some other nontonic key for the beginning of the recapitulation. In the Finale of Schubert's *Symphony No. 9 in C Major,* the recapitulation commences with E♭ major, III by mode mixture of the main tonality. The entrance of the first theme in this key is particularly surprising because the retransition of the development emphasizes the V and thus seems to be preparing for tonic harmony. Another exceptional case is the first movement of Tchaikovsky's *Symphony No. 4 in F Minor,* in which both first and second themes appear in D minor, VI by mode mixture.

EXERCISE

8. Make a detailed comparison of the recapitulations of the sonata forms of the preceding exercises with their respective expositions.

11-8. SUMMARY

The sonata form, like the continuous binary forms from which it evolved, is in its very nature rooted in tonality. Tension set up by sharply defined key centers is possible only to tonal music and it is this tension that constitutes the foundation of sonata form. A key center is established (first theme), undermined (transition), and a new key center set up (second and closing themes). The establishment of a second key center causes a tense situation demanding a reconciliation, which comes about after a period of harmonic fluidity (development) when the original key center dominates (recapitulation). More briefly, the tonal structure of the normal sonata form can be explained as a progressive harmonic movement (exposition) that is prolonged (development) and finally begun again and completed (recapitulation).

The specific design that provides flesh and blood for this tonal skeleton is constantly varied. The monothematic sonata form has but one tune which serves as both first and second themes. The two themes of the bi-thematic sonata form are often contrasting in character (one dramatic, the other lyric, and so on). In either of these cases the closing theme, unless it is absent entirely, may introduce still a third idea. Sonata-form expositions which include five or six themes are not rare. The development is even less susceptible to summary description for here there is no standard subdivision. The material on which subsections of the development are based may include anything from the exposition, even that which had seemed trivial. And not infrequently new material is introduced. Again, the recapitulation, especially in the works of Haydn, Mozart, and Brahms, is not predictable, often differing considerably from the design of the exposition.

When analyzing a sonata form, then, the student can avoid a good deal of trouble and misunderstanding by attempting to rid himself of *a priori* requirements. Rather than constantly referring the work under examination to his notions about what it "should" or "should not" do, the student should observe uncritically what the composer has done.

The most important features of the main sections of the sonata form have been discussed in this chapter. Optional sections (introductions, codas) and modifications of sonata form will be dealt with in the next. The description of many of the features of sonata form's main sections holds true when they occur in other forms as well. For instance, the development section of the first movement of a sonata rondo (Chapter 12) or a concerto (Chapter 13) is constructed along identical lines to those set forth here. The same is true of transitions. A thorough acquaintance with the principal sections that make up the sonata form will enable the student not only to understand works in this form but, by noting their appearance elsewhere, to be immensely aided in his understanding of other forms, both standard and unique.

EXERCISE

9. Analyze several first movements from the piano sonatas, chamber music, or symphonies of Haydn, Mozart, Beethoven, Schubert, Mendelssohn, or Brahms.

12

Further Aspects
of Sonata Form

12-1. THE INTRODUCTION

The symphonies and overtures of the classical and romantic composers often
open with a solemn introduction in slow tempo which leads into the sonata
form of the first movement. Example 12-1 is a reduction of the introduction
to the first movement of Mozart's *Symphony No. 36 in C Major*.

Ex. 12-1. MOZART: *Symphony No. 36 in C Major* ("Linz")

The first three bars present a strong unison statement followed by power-ful chords. They might be said to herald the opening of a solemn event and have been labeled here the heraldic section. The next four bars consist of a lyric melody with a quiet accompaniment, called the melodic section. The following seven bars present a one-bar motive stated seven times by imitation and sequence, the motivic section. The last five bars, the cadential section, bring the introduction to a close by dwelling on V, treated as a secondary tonic. The entire introduction expresses the key of C; the first two sections are in the major mode, the last two in the minor.

Design of the introduction

The heraldic, melodic, motivic, and cadential sections which comprise this introduction are the chief section types to be found in the introductions of most of the great composers of the tonal era. Not every introduction, how-ever, includes all four types and some introductions bring in others. Only infrequently does the introduction to a work for a small group of instruments contain a heraldic section. Few things are more absurd than an unsuccessful attempt at grandeur, and a handful of stringed instruments or a piano and violin are simply incapable of mustering the solemn dignity that a full orchestra has at its command. Introductions to chamber-music works can be expected to consist mainly of melodic and motivic types. In orchestral works, however, the heraldic opening is common. Sometimes it is very short. In Haydn's *Symphony No. 103*, a single roll on the kettledrum suffices to produce one of the most impressive openings in symphonic literature. On the other hand, the heraldic opening of Mozart's *Symphony No. 39* comprises six very slow measures for full orchestra. Tchaikovsky, in his *Symphony No. 4*, seems to think almost literally of a herald, for the work opens with a great summoning call in the wind instruments (see also, Schumann, *Symphony No. 1*).

Not infrequently an introduction opens with a short heraldic fragment, continues with a melodic phrase, and then returns to the heraldic opening.

Ex. 12-2.   HAYDN: *Symphony No. 102*

At times the introduction does not come to a cadence but leads directly into the first theme of the first movement. In that case, the cadential section is replaced by the transitional section. Usually the transitional section anticipates the opening motive of the first theme.

Ex. 12-3.   SCHUBERT: *Symphony No. 9*

Since the introduction does not form a complete movement in itself a conscious symmetry of parts is less usual than in a movement that stands alone. Few introductions, for instance, show a binary or ternary form. Rather, they are laid out as a series of sections, a phrase chain or phrase group. Sometimes there are rhythmic or melodic relationships between the various sections; often, as in Ex. 12-1, there are not.

Tonal structure of the introduction

The introduction does not necessarily share the mode of the movement proper. That to Haydn's "Clock Symphony" in D major is in the minor mode. Many introductions, like Ex. 12-1, begin in the major mode, then about half-way through change to the minor. Still others constantly fluctuate between major and minor.

In essence, the basic tonal structure of most introductions is a progressive harmonic movement from I to V, V often being treated as a secondary tonic. An outline of the basic harmonic movement of Ex. 12-1, for instance, shows a chord succession on I in which the bass descends an octave, with a change from major to minor en route, followed by a move to V.

Ex. 12-4.   Harmonic outline of Ex. 12-1

When the introduction does not begin on I the progressive harmonic movement to V is no less likely. The tonality of Tchaikovsky's *Symphony No. 6* is B minor, but the introduction begins in the subdominant key,

E minor. By means of a bass line that descends stepwise from the note E to A′♯ the essential harmonic move is from IV to V_6 in B minor, at which point the movement proper begins. Tchaikovsky has here devised his introduction so that the listener assumes the symphony is in the key of E, realizing later that this is only the subdominant aspect of the real key. Beethoven attempted something quite different in the introduction to his *Quartet, Op. 59, No. 3,* a harmonic outline of which is offered in Ex. 12-5.

Ex. 12-5. BEETHOVEN: *Quartet, Op. 59, No. 3* (harmonic outline of introduction)

This introduction might be called atonal in that no key is established by the chord series until the last is reached. The harmonic scheme can be understood without initial reference to a key by the purposeful stepwise descent of the bass line from the note *f*♯ an octave and a half to B′ (presumably the upper B is used here only because the range of the cello would not permit the use of the lower). Enclosing a series of chords is the bass-soprano framework which gradually spreads outward from the opening chord until, as the cello reaches its B, the upper instruments supply the remaining tones of a diminished seventh chord on that note. This chord is then repeated in close position, the note A♭ moves to G, and we hear V_5^6 in the key of C. Only at this point, just before the movement proper begins, is the listener given an inkling of this quartet's tonality.

On those rare occasions when the introduction does not end on V, the reason is likely to be that the first theme of the exposition does not begin on I but on some other chord. Examination of the first theme of the opening movement of Haydn's *Symphony No. 92* ("Oxford") shows that it begins with four bars of the V_7 chord. It is therefore incumbent on the introduction to progress to a chord that will lead into this V_7. Although the harmonic sequence of the introduction does reach the V (mm. 12–15, not quoted), this V is not prolonged to the beginning of the movement. It progresses instead to the chord of the augmented sixth on its own leading tone (VII_5^6 of V), hovering there in mid-air until its resolution to the V_7 opens the exposition.

Ex. 12-6.   HAYDN: *Symphony No. 92* ("Oxford")

Thematic relationships between the sonata form and its introduction

In a number of works there is a definite thematic relationship between the movement and the introduction preceding it. Sometimes this relationship is only a slight one—a similarity of melodic curve or a single motivic resemblance, as in Berlioz' *Symphonie Fantastique*. At other times some melody of the introduction may definitely anticipate a theme of the movement proper. Example 12-7 shows the close resemblance between the opening melody of the introduction and the first theme of the movement in one of Haydn's symphonies (see also Brahms' *Symphony No. 1,* first and last movements).

Ex. 12-7.   HAYDN: *Symphony No. 100* ("Military")

There may be no clear resemblance between the themes and still a relationship between the introduction and the movement may exist, for a part of the introduction sometimes returns once or twice during the course of the movement (Mozart, *The Magic Flute,* Overture; Beethoven, *Sonata, Op. 13*). Or a theme from the introduction might take part in the development section (Beethoven, *Sonata, Op. 13,* First Movement; Brahms, *Symphony No. 1,* Finale; Hindemith, *Organ Sonata No. 1,* First Movement).

EXERCISE

1. Consider the introductions to the following compositions. Note first the tonal structure, then the various section types employed (heraldic, melodic, motivic, cadential). Be sure to compare the mode (or modes) of the introduction with that of the ensuing sonata form.

A

a. MF Overture

b. Beethoven: *Op. 13*, First Movement

B

a. Beethoven: *Quartet, Op. 135*, Finale

12-2. THE CODA

Many sonata forms either possess no coda or a brief one. As far as the short coda goes, nothing need be added here to the discussion of the coda under ternary forms (Section 8-5). But sometimes composers have provided their sonata forms with lengthy codas so full of significance that they are heard as equaling in importance any of the preceding sections.

The after-development

Beginning with the Finale from Mozart's *Symphony No. 41* ("Jupiter") and continuing with the symphonies and chamber music of Beethoven, the coda to the sonata form frequently takes on immense significance, serving not merely as an appendage to the movement proper, but as a section with developmental properties of its own. In addition, it sometimes adds a new dimension to the tonal structure. As we are already familiar with the development section of the first movement to Beethoven's *Symphony No. 9* (Section 11-6), it will be convenient to examine the coda of that movement in illustration of the "after-development," as this type of coda is sometimes called.

There is no counterpart in the coda to the introductory section of the development, subsection 1 of the coda corresponding to subsection 2 of the development. Both are dialogues between the strings and winds on the first theme, but formerly only the initial motive, a, was involved while now motive b is added to the portion of the dialogue allotted to the strings (Ex. 12-8a).

Ex. 12-8.   BEETHOVEN: *Symphony No. 9*

The second subsection of the coda is concerned with ST_2, a theme that had not participated in the development (Ex. 12-8b). A subsection making use of a variation of CT_2 (Ex. 11-11d) then appears corresponding to subsection 3 of the development. This leads into the fourth subsection based on the fugue theme of the development. Subsection 5 takes up ST_2 again which leads into subsection 6, corresponding to subsection 4 of the development. The seventh subsection is made up of new material. Over an *ostinato* figure in the strings, possibly derived by diminution from ST_2, the wind instruments sound a new melodic motive which gradually builds up to a tremendous climax leading into the final subsection. This consists of the principal theme, expanded in the middle, sounding in a fortissimo unison by the full orchestra.

In design, half of the coda is based on the development section, the other half divided between restatement of material from the exposition and the newly invented *ostinato*.

Outline Summary of Beethoven's Symphony No. 9, First Movement, Coda, from the Point of View of Design

Bars	Sub-section	Material	Corresponding Subsection of Development	Description
427–453	1	Motives (a), (b)	2	Dialogue between strings and winds
453–463	2	ST_2	—	Statement, as in exposition
463–469	3	CT_2	3	Melodically altered
469–494	4	Motive a; ST_5 (= motive c)	8	Fugue theme; accompanied first by motive b, then by countersubject from development
494–505	5	ST_2	—	Statement; repetition with imitation
505–512	6	Motive b	4	Motivic phrase, as in development
513–538	7	New	—	Melodic motive repeated and developed over *ostinato* figure
538–547	8	Motives a, b, c	—	Unison statement with 4-bar expansion between motives a and b

From the examination of the outline summary we can draw the following conclusions regarding the design of the after-development, conclusions which are verified by reference to other codas of the same type (for instance, Beethoven, *Symphonies No. 2*, first and last movements; *No. 4*, Finale; *No. 5*, Finale; *No. 6*, First Movement; *No. 8*, Finale).

1. The coda divides itself into subsections on the basis of material employed.

2. New as well as previously heard material may appear.

3. Previously heard material may (a) be restated without change (other than transposition) from the exposition, (b) be restated without change (other than transposition) from the development, or (c) undergo new development.

✗ 4. Material from the exposition that had been neglected by the development section is apt to be restated or developed in the coda.

5. Many of the subsections of the coda, particularly the first, correspond closely to subsections within the development. This correspondence sets up a definite relationship between the coda and the development analogous to that between the exposition and recapitulation.

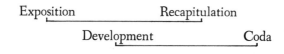

The epilogue — new material (extra)

Short codas not infrequently are based largely or entirely on new material. Occasionally large codas, too, show little or no specific thematic relationship with the movement to which they are appended. Though universally referred to as codas, many such movements would seem better served by the term "epilogue." The long *Adagio* closing Haydn's "Farewell Symphony" is, of course, a special case.[1] But the coda of the first movement of Tchaikovsky's *Pathétique* is no less an epilogue. In both these instances the slower tempo and the change of mode from minor to major combine with the nature of the new material to produce a subdued, consoling quality in contrast to that which dominates the movement itself. Beethoven's Overture to *Egmont* and the Finale to his *Quartet, Op. 95*, are alike in that both are in the key of F minor and both end with long epilogues in F major made up entirely of new material. Unlike the Haydn and Tchaikovsky examples mentioned before, these epilogues have a faster tempo than the movement and end on a note of triumph. Brahms' *Academic Festival Overture* ends with a joyous setting of the student song *Gaudeamus Igitur*. In this century epilogues have appeared in such works as the Finales to Ralph Vaughan Williams' *Symphony No. 6* and Schoenberg's *Chamber Symphony No. 2*.

Types of tonal structure in the coda

In our previous discussion of the coda (Section 8-5), it was pointed

---

[1] Written with gradually reduced instrumentation so that each player, upon finishing his part, snuffs out his candle and leaves the stage. The movement closes with two violinists playing alone in the dim candlelight.

out that there are three distinct types of tonal structures. Sonata-form codas, too, group themselves according to these three types of tonal structure.

1. Codas that prolong the final I by chord succession. This type is very common (for example, the first movements of all Beethoven's symphonies).

2. Codas that prolong the final I by a tonic pedal point. Though common in short compositions, especially ternary forms, this type appears infrequently as the tonal structure of a sonata-form coda. A rare case is the coda, all but a few bars, of the first movement of Brahms' *Violin Sonata No. 3.*

3. Codas that delay the final I by means of a deceptive cadence. With sonata forms this type of coda occurs rather frequently (for instance, Haydn, *Symphony No. 100,* First Movement, and *Symphony No. 104,* Finale).

Appended harmonic motion — *emphasis of foreign key*

Often the coda prolongs the final tonic by remaining almost entirely within the area of the home key. Except for brief secondary tonics it does not venture into the realm of foreign keys. This is the case with the coda to the first movement of Beethoven's *Symphony No. 9:* Each of its eight subsections expresses the key of D minor.

It is not infrequent, however, that the coda begins with a surprise jump into another key where it remains for a phrase or more. This sudden change of key is as apt to happen with codas that prolong the final I (type 1) as with those that delay the final I by deceptive cadence (type 3).

Ex. 12-9. BRAHMS: *Clarinet Sonata, Op. 120, No. 2*

In Ex. 12-9 the coda begins with a deceptive cadence from V_7 to V_7/IV. Rather than resolving to IV, however, it moves in another deceptive resolution to ♭II (expressed enharmonically as E major rather than F♭ major). The key of E major (♭II) is maintained for two phrases (eight bars) before returning to the home key of E♭.

When a foreign key is thus emphasized, the coda may be accurately thought of as supplying appended harmonic motion rather than merely as prolonging the final I. Appended harmonic motion often involves a move to IV, VI, ♭VI, or ♭II, and occasionally to some other key.

EXERCISES

2. In the sonata forms under consideration in the exercises of the preceding chapter, examine the point at which the recapitulation seems to end, then consider the music that lies beyond this point.

a. Do all have codas?
b. On what material is each coda based?
c. Does any coda consist of a number of subsections? Which? How many?
d. Does any coda act as an "after-development"?
e. What type of tonal structure does each exhibit?
f. Does any coda supply appended harmonic motion?

3. Do the same for other sonata-form codas.

12-3. MODIFICATIONS OF SONATA FORM

The sonatina form   The term "sonatina" originally referred to sonatas which were shorter, lighter, and easier than usual and is still used in this sense today. The sonatina form, however, is not inevitably associated with the sonatina. Some sonatinas include movements in sonata form (Kuhlau, Sonatinas, Op. 20, Nos. 1 and 3) and some sonata movements are in sonatina form. From the point of view of musical structure, the sonatina form is a sonata form without a development section. In its place is a link or transition leading to the recapitulation.

The sonatina form has found a place in the sonatas, chamber music, and symphonies of the classical and romantic composers, not as first but as second movements (Mozart, Sonata, K. 332, Quartet, K. 465; Beethoven, Symphony No. 8; Schubert, "Unfinished Symphony"; Brahms, Violin Sonata No. 3). The sonatina form is also common in the overtures of the classical period (Mozart, Marriage of Figaro; Beethoven, Prometheus; Rossini, Barber of Seville).

EXERCISES

4. Contrast:

a. Sonatina and sonatina form
b. Sonata form and sonatina form

5. Analyze:

A	B
a. Beethoven: *Op. 10, No. 1,* Second Movement	a. Beethoven: *Sonata, Op. 10, No. 1,* Second Movement

The enlarged sonatina form

The Finale of Beethoven's *String Quartet in F Minor, Op. 95,* offers an illustration of an interesting modification of sonata form. After a slow introduction, the exposition progresses from I to V (F minor to C minor). Immediately following the second theme (there is in this case no closing section) the first theme is restated in an abbreviated version in the tonic key. It is then developed motivically, passing from I through VI to IV. From here the harmony moves to V and at this point the transition is restated, now leading back to I for the restatement of the secondary section. A lengthy coda follows. Example 12-10, which omits the introduction and coda, shows the essential features of the tonal structure of the movement.

Ex. 12-10. BEETHOVEN: *String Quartet in F Minor, Op. 95* (harmonic outline of Finale).

The phenomenon which has occurred here is an actual fusion of the recapitulation and development sections, for part two contains both, as in the normal sonata form, but delays the development, inserting it in the middle of the recapitulation. Looked at another way, the form is a mixture of the sonatina and the sonata forms. Like the sonatina, part two begins with the restatement of part one. Yet it does not give up the sonata form's development section. For this reason the scheme is sometimes referred to as the enlarged sonatina. Beethoven used it again for the second movement of his great *Quartet in C sharp Minor, Op. 131.* Brahms was particularly partial to the form and employed it several times, famous cases being the Finales of *Symphonies No. 1* and *No. 3* and the *Tragic Overture.*

The sonata rondo

The sonata rondo is a hybrid, combining the rondo and the sonata form. The typical classical rondo bears a certain resemblance to sonata form in that part one (refrain, episode, refrain) is restated, partially transposed, as part three (see outline in Section 9-2), just as the recapitulation of a sonata form is a partially transposed restatement of the exposition. In sonata rondo another resemblance is brought about by substituting a development section for the second episode C (part two), the result being:

Part One (Quasi-exposition)	Part Two (Development)	Part Three (Quasi-recapitulation)
A-B A I V I (III)	$x\,x\,x\,x$ V_7	A-B A I I I

Not infrequently, one of the refrains in part three is omitted. Applied to the small rondo design, sonata rondo is A B A Dev. A, as in Beethoven's monumental *Marcia Funebre* from the "Eroica Symphony."

The sonata rondo, representing a compromise between the sonata form and the ordinary rondo, gains a development section but loses an independent second episode. To this extent it might be considered "less of a rondo" than a simple rondo. When occasion demands, as in Mozart's *Sonata, K. 333,* the contrasting second episode is included but, instead of being followed immediately by the refrain, it leads into a development section. Part three picks up from there.

The classical composers used the sonata rondo almost exclusively for finales and labeled it simply "rondo" without differentiating it from the simple rondo. Most of Brahms' rondos are of the sonata-rondo type, as is the *Scherzo* from Mendelssohn's *Midsummer Night's Dream.* More recent uses include Debussy's *Reflections on the Water* and Prokofiev's *Sonata No. 5,* Third Movement.

EXERCISES

6. Contrast:

a. Sonata form and sonata rondo
b. Sonata rondo and the typical classical rondo

7. Analyze:

A	B
a. Beethoven: *Op. 22*, Fourth Movement	a. Mozart: *Sonata, K. 333*, Third Movement

Other modifications

We have by no means exhausted the possibilities for modification of the standard sonata form. For instance, in the first movement of his *Quartet, Op. 77, No. 1*, Haydn fuses the development and recapitulation sections of his sonata form differently from the enlarged sonatina. He begins his development section like a normal sonata form, inserts the recapitulation of the second theme (tonic key) into the development, and later recapitulates the other themes in rearranged order. To take another example, in Beethoven's *Leonore Overture No. 2* and the Finale to Mendelssohn's "Italian Symphony," the recapitulations are omitted completely, the developments leading straight into the codas.

The interested student will not find it difficult to discover still other special sonata-form procedures which imaginative composers, particularly Haydn and the late Beethoven, have created and found useful (for instance, Beethoven, *Quartet, Op. 132*, First Movement; *Quartet, Op. 135*, Finale; Haydn, "Surprise Symphony," First Movement).

12-4. SUMMARY

This chapter has dealt with optional aspects and modifications of sonata form. The introduction is a section, normally in slow tempo, which opens most overtures, many symphonies, and some piano sonatas and chamber music. Occasionally finales are also preceded by introductions. Introductions usually subdivide into a number of distinct sections, some short solemn bids for attention, some stating a clear melody, others based on motivic interplay. Designed to lead into the first theme of the ensuing sonata form, the introduction ordinarily involves a progressive harmonic movement from I to a secondary tonic on V.

The majority of sonata forms end with a coda, some short, others quite long. The long coda, in addition to its role in prolonging the tonic chord and appending a new harmonic motion to the close of the movement, is often given over to thematic development. Less commonly, a coda will be devoted largely or entirely to new material. In either case it is possible for the coda to act not as a mere appendage, but as the culmination of the entire movement (Mozart, "Jupiter Symphony," Finale; Brahms, *Symphony No. 1*, Finale).

A common modification of sonata form is the sonatina form, which omits the development section. The sonatina form may be enlarged by inserting a development between the first and second themes of the recapitulation. The sonata rondo incorporates the sonata form's development section within the framework of the typical classical rondo, substituting it for the second episode. Special modifications occurring in isolated works are very frequent.

13

first movements of all

The Concerto

Historical Note on the Baroque Concerto The practice of alternating sonorities of different timbre and dynamics is a very old one. In the phenomenon of the echo we have in nature a prototype of this principle. The antiphonal psalm singing of the ancient Jews, the alternating choruses of Greek tragedy, the dialogue between priest and choir in the liturgical worship of the Christian church exemplify the principle of contrast in sounding bodies. In folk song we hear a solo singer or leader answered by the group. In instrumental music the principle of alternating sonorities on which the concerto is based is developed in the rich sounds of the *canzone* and *ricercari* written by the Gabrielis in Venice in the late sixteenth century, works which themselves grew out of the polychoral music of the same composers. The rapid development of instrumental technique and the rise of a school of violin virtuosos led to an exploitation of several genres, particularly the concerto. By the end of the seventeenth century Corelli, Torelli, Albinoni, and others had established the concerto as an important medium without crystallizing any particular scheme of movements. This was left for Antonio Vivaldi, whose three-movement plan of fast-slow-fast was used by J. S. Bach and is still considered the norm. It is interesting to observe that Handel, on the other hand, does not follow the three-movement plan, but uses varying movement schemes in the manner of Corelli.

The impact of the Vivaldian concerto on J. S. Bach was so far reaching that we find him composing works of quite different genres along the lines of a baroque concerto. Several of the longer organ preludes, for instance, such as those in E minor and B minor, are constructed like typical concertos of the period. The same is true of the first movements of the *Organ Sonatas II* and *VI* and the Prelude to the *English Suite in G Minor, No. 3* for harpsichord.

In postbaroque times the usual concerto was written for one soloist and orchestra. During the baroque era, however, the concerto for more than one soloist

226

was fully as common as the solo concerto. If there are several soloists, perhaps two violins and a cello, or two trumpets, these as a group are referred to as the *concertino* and the orchestra is called the *concerto grosso, tutti* ("all"), or *ripieno* ("full"). The composition itself is also often called a *concerto grosso*. During the first half of the eighteenth century, the ripieno consisted not of the orchestra as we know it today, but usually of no more than a group of stringed instruments and an accompanying (and improvising) harpsichord.

13-1. OUTER MOVEMENTS OF THE BAROQUE CONCERTO: CONCERTO GROSSO MOVEMENT

Procedure in the baroque concerto   In discussing the *da capo* aria (Section 8-9), we observed that a distinctive feature of the baroque aria was the use of orchestral ritornellos. These passages, preceding, interrupting, and following the vocalist's part, act as contrast to it. There is an antiphonal give-and-take between two different bodies of sound: the full orchestra on the one hand, and on the other a soloist with a portion of the orchestra lending support.

In the concerto a similar principle is at work except that both opposing bodies of sound are made up entirely of instruments. The forms that are associated with the concerto are a structural result of this opposition. The specific way by which the principle of alternation operates in a given piece of music can be thought of as the procedure of the work. To analyze and discover the form of a concerto movement, it is necessary to consider the procedure as well as the design and tonal structure.[1]

As far as the formal procedure of the late baroque concerto is concerned, it makes little difference whether there is one soloist or several to be pitted against the orchestra. In either case the basic idea of contrasting the two bodies of sound gives rise to a scheme of alternation. Just as in the baroque aria the orchestral ritornello alternates with the solo voice (Section 8-9), so here the tutti sections, which are in effect ritornellos, alternate with the soloist or with the *concertino*. The result is like a debate or struggle, the tutti at times gaining the upper hand and at others giving way to the soloist or *concertino*. Not until the romantic era were concertos written which could be considered works for a single instrument with orchestral accompaniment. In the concertos of the baroque era (and also in the classical, as we shall see) the main function of the orchestra was not so much to furnish an accompaniment to the soloist as to act as a sparring partner on an equal basis.

---

[1] Those works of Vivaldi and his contemporaries which are "orchestral concertos" (see Bukofzer, *op. cit.*, p. 226) are not being spoken of here. Nor do many movements of the *concerti grossi* of Handel's *Op.* 6 belong to this category.

Form of the concerto grosso movement

The slow movements of Vivaldi's concertos exhibit various forms but need not occupy us here as they present little in the way of structure that is exclusively an aspect of concerto writing. It is to the two outer movements— those in fast tempo—that we must turn our attention. These generally proceed by alternation between the *concertino* and the tutti, as mentioned before, but the precise form thus achieved varies from concerto to concerto. Examination of one of Vivaldi's better-known concerto movements—chosen for an organ transcription by J. S. Bach—will provide an illustration of one *concerto grosso* movement.[2]

Ex. 13-1.   VIVALDI: *Concerto in A Minor, Op. III, No. 8*

[2] Reproduced in *HAM, No. 270.*

The concerto opens with a sixteen-bar asymmetrical period made up of five phrases. Though the first three phrases contain motivic resemblances to a certain extent, they are not clearly thematically related as are the last two. The phrases are marked a, b, c, d, and d'. The first perfect authentic cadence is found in m. 13. It is on I and thus phrase d, the fourth, completes a harmonic movement. The fifth phrase acts as codetta, prolonging the final I until m. 16. At this point most of the orchestral players drop out and the soloists, who are also expected to play during the tutti, are left virtually alone, their sound greatly contrasting with that of the full body of strings. For six bars the soloists play without referring, except in the vaguest way, to any of the motives previously stated by the tutti. In m. 22 an imperfect cadence is reached and the tutti begins again, this time performing only the codetta phrase, d'. Another passage is then given to the soloists. This begins like the former solo passages except that the first and second violinists have exchanged parts. The accompaniment, which had been provided by the violas, is soon taken over by the bass instruments and harpsichord while the first violin has a solo of figuration. This solo leads from I to a perfect authentic cadence on III (mm. 36–37), whereupon the figuration is taken up by the tutti in a prolongation of this III (mm. 37–39). Continuing with material first introduced in the opening ritornello, it is interrupted several times by short interjections from the soloists. During its course it progresses from III to a perfect authentic cadence on IV (m. 48), at which point the next solo section begins. This section continues to express IV. The tutti then sounds a transposition to IV of phrase a (mm. 51–55). The ensuing solo section combines the figuration of the second solo section with motivic treatment based on phrase b, ending with the following semicadence:

$$\underbrace{\text{IV-V}}$$
$$\text{of IV}$$

The tutti enters with phrase d which brings a permanent return to I (mm. 62–65). A three-bar passage for solos recalls the first two solo sections. Measures 68–71, ending with a semicadence, bring in phrase a. After the next solo section, the tutti performs phrases b, c, and d', having this time skipped over phrase d. Another solo section intervenes before the final tutti plays phrase d'. All in all, the tutti has been entrusted with eight sections in this movement, and the soloists with the seven intervening ones. In addition, the soloists "invaded" the third tutti section several times.

The procedure can be represented graphically by assigning appropriate letters and numbers to the various sections. Thus, R1 stands for the first ritornello or tutti section, S1 for the first solo section, and so on. The design of the movement can be indicated by the use of the letters assigned to the various phrases of the opening ritornello and other letters representing the themes of the solo sections. Beneath the representation of the procedure and the design, a summary of the basic tonal structure can be indicated. In this way we shall have conveniently before us the necessary data for drawing a conclusion regarding the form of this movement.

Measures	1–16	16–22	22–25	25–37	37–48	48–51
Procedure	R1	S1	R2	S2	R3 (solo interjections)	S3
Design	abcdd'	ef	d'	egh	hcai	{ b h
Tonal Structure	I → V	I ——→ V		I → V-I of III	——→ V-I of IV	
		I		I ——→ III ——→ IV——→		

Measures	51–55	55–62	62–65	65–68	68–71	71–78	78–86	86–90	90–93
Procedure	R4	S4	R5	S5	R6	S6	R7	S7	R8
Design	a	{ b h	d	e	a	{ b h	bcd'	b	d'
Tonal Structure	(IV) ——→ V$_7$ ——→ V$_7$			I ——→ V-I ——→ V-I		I			

Although the movement contains a number of perfect authentic cadences, none of these have a strongly divisive effect due to the fact that in every case, except of course the last, these perfect authentic cadences are elided, occurring simultaneously with the beginning of the next section. In spite of the contrast in sound between the concertino and the ripieno, the work is characterized by a striking continuity of movement. It would seem, then, that these perfect authentic cadences do not possess a divisive quality strong enough to act as a basis for analysis into parts.

Reference to the tonal structure line of our graphic representation shows that the first twenty-five bars are essentially concerned with expressing I. Measures 25–65 show a progressive harmonic movement from I to III to IV and from there to V$_7$, which resolves in m. 65 on I. This I is then retained for the remainder of the piece.

As the perfect authentic cadences are nondivisive and no other aspect of design—such as far-reaching contrasts in quality—creates a divisive force, our conclusions regarding form must be based on tonal structure alone. The movement consists of three parts, the two outer parts expressing I, the middle part a move from I through III and IV and thence back through V_7 to I. Certain aspects of design combine to confirm this three-part analysis. Part one introduces all the important themes (f, g, and i are not striking, they occupy inconspicuous places, and, once stated, are never referred to again; h plays an important role, but it is not a theme, only violinistic figuration). Five of these are stated by the *concerto grosso*, one by the *concertino*. Part two takes up these themes, adding figuration h, detaches them one from another, and treats their motives separately. At the conclusion of part two, phrase d is restated exactly and is therefore the only important theme omitted from restatement in part three. Restatement here is particularly interesting in that the order of themes is entirely rearranged, though d', because of its singular codettalike quality, continues to close the sections. On the whole, the design might be summarily described as A-BA' and the form of this particular movement considered closely allied to the sectional ternary. Certain aspects foreshadowing sonata form will not, however, be lost on the discerning student.

Many of Vivaldi's concertos are much simpler to analyze—as they are simpler to play—than his *Op. III, No. 8*. The final movement of the *Concerto in C Major for Violoncello* (F. III No. 6—Tomo 211° in the Ricordi edition) for example, comprises only four ritornellos with three intervening solo sections. The first ritornello is a three-phrase period, each phrase repeated. The solo sections introduce no new themes, but instead restrict themselves to variants of the tutti's themes, slight development of some of their motives, and cellistic figuration. The tonal structure is also simple: A complete movement expressing I, a progression from I through V to VI, and an abrupt return to I which runs through two complete harmonic movements.

Procedure	R1	S1	R2	S2	R3	S3	R4
Design	abc	a'b'c'	ab	c'	a	d(fig.)	abc
Tonal Structure	$I \to V\text{-}I$	$I \longrightarrow$	V-I $V \to$ of VI	V-I $VI \to$ of VI	$I \longrightarrow$	V-I	$I \to V\text{-}I$
Form	One	Two		Three	Four		Five (= One)

The perfect authentic cadences indicated in the outline are definitely divisive. The resulting form is five part.

The observations listed below are the result of examination of a quantity of Vivaldi's concerto movements.

Regarding tonal structure

1. First and last ritornellos are always in the tonic key. The penultimate ritornello is very often in the tonic key.

2. The second ritornello begins by expressing III or V; it may remain here or it may make a progressive movement to IV or VI.

Regarding design of ritornelli

3. The phrases of the ritornello are detachable. Any phrase theme can be used separately or omitted, or the phrases can be arranged in a different order.

4. Only occasionally does any ritornello present material not included in the first ritornello. (The very term "ritornello" implies a "return" of previously heard material.)

5. The final ritornello is often an exact restatement of the first, the intervening ones being shorter. The penultimate ritornello is generally the shortest of all.

Regarding design of solo sections

6. Soloist(s) may present a harmonic progression as a figuration of some kind idiomatic to the instrument employed. When this occurs, the accompaniment often includes some melodic motive derived from the opening ritornello.

7. Solo instrument may play one or more of the ritornello's themes. Often the solo begins with a theme from the ritornello, varies it, then gradually moves into a figuration of some kind.

8. The solo instrument may be given a new melody of its own.

Regarding procedure

9. The movement invariably ends with a ritornello and usually begins with one; initial solo sections are not rare enough, however, to be considered really exceptional.

10. The soloists of a baroque concerto, unlike their counterparts in the classical and romantic concerto, play during the tutti sections, their part consisting merely of a doubling of the orchestral voices. Occasionally, however, in a tutti section the soloist is given brief passages of his own. Conversely, the orchestra sometimes invades the solo passages with short outbursts.

EXERCISE

1. Make a summary outline similar to the preceding, showing the procedure, design, tonal structure, and form of the following:

A	B
a. *VC*, First Movement	a. Handel: *Concerto Grosso, Op. 6, No. 12,* Second Movement

Historical Note on the Classical Concerto

Emulating the form and style of Vivaldi's concertos during the first half of the eighteenth century were a number of Italian composers who, like Vivaldi, were either Venetians or were living in the immediate vicinity of Venice. In other parts of Italy, however, the tendency of the younger generation was away from the sweeping drive and fiery energy of the baroque concerto and toward a more vocally conceived melodic style that led finally to the concertos of the classical composers of Vienna. The desire was for more melodious themes, greater rhythmic variety, and fewer alternations of the tutti and solo sections. Often the finales were no longer constructed according to the same principles as the opening movements, but were dancelike pieces in binary form. The concertos of Locatelli, Tartini, Padre Martini, Leo, Pergolesi, Durante, and Hasse show the early stages of the new type of concerto. A further stage in its development can be clearly followed in the concertos of J. S. Bach's youngest son, Johann Christian Bach, and others.

As a very young boy, Mozart came under the influence of J. C. Bach, going so far as to convert, in 1765, three of the older composer's sonatas into piano concertos. Mozart's concertos, of which there are about fifty, exhibit in their first movements the same basic structural plan found in those of J. C. Bach. Although Mozart's greater genius produced concertos which far outshine the pleasantries of his model, he did not deviate from his adherence to this standard procedure in the first movements. The first movements of the concertos of Haydn and Beethoven are laid out according to the same pattern. This pattern will be examined in the discussion to follow.

The concertos of Mozart, Haydn, and Beethoven regularly follow the standard movement scheme of the Vivaldian concerto: two fast movements surrounding a slow one. Many of J. C. Bach's concertos, on the other hand, have only two, rather than three, movements.

13-2. FIRST MOVEMENTS OF THE CLASSICAL CONCERTO: CONCERTO-SONATA FORM

Procedure in the preclassical concerto By the middle of the eighteenth century the structural pattern of the first movement of a concerto had become fairly well standardized. It usually consisted of four ritornellos, of which the penultimate was still the shortest, with three intervening solo sections. The usual tonal structure was:

	R1	S1	R2	S2	R3	S3	R4
Major Mode:	I	*x*	V	*x*	VI or I	*x*	I
Minor Mode:	I	*x*	III	*x*	V or I	*x*	I

The solo and tutti sections did not, as a rule, exhibit any melodic resemblances. The tutti parts tended to have themes of their own not shared by the soloist, and vice versa.

The first movements of the concertos of J. C. Bach composed in Berlin while he was still in his teens follow the general outline given above. However, after his move to Italy and thence to London, his concertos show important changes from his earlier essays in this genre. The basic outline of four ritornellos alternating with three solo sections remains the same. But R3, the short ritornello, is now usually, rather than sometimes, in the tonic key. Moreover, in design the solo sections have taken on characteristics of sonata form. S1, for instance, is patterned after the exposition of a sonata form. Its themes may or may not have been previously presented in R1. S2 prolongs the V and corresponds to the development section of the sonata form. The brief third ritornello, R3, is either omitted or merges with S3 to form a single section that recapitulates S1, now entirely in the tonic key. In all, then, there are six discernible sections in the first movements of the majority of J. C. Bach's London concertos (1763–1777)[3]:

Section 1. R1	Orchestral ritornello	I
Section 2. S1	Solo and orchestral exposition	$I \rightarrow V$ (III)
Section 3. R2	Orchestral ritornello	V(III)
Section 4. S2	Solo and orchestral development	$V(III) \rightarrow V_7$
Section 5. R3–S3	Solo and orchestral recapitulation	I
Section 6. R4	Orchestral ritornello	I

A cadenza improvised by the soloist was sometimes inserted between S3 and R4. In later classical concertos, however, the cadenza is an interruption of R4.

The regular appearance of these six sections as the chief structural principle of the first movements of the classical concerto is enough to warrant considering these movements a standard form. Because of the resemblance of sections 2, 4, and 5 to the exposition, development, and recapitulation, respectively, of the sonata form, the first movement of the classical concerto can be labeled the concerto-sonata form. Within the broad outlines of the six sections of the concerto-sonata form there is room for much variety. It is doubtful whether any two first movements of classical concertos are patterned just alike. Moreover, the grouping of the sections into parts is not the same in every case. Our approach, then, must be to select certain movements for examination, with the warning that identical designs are not likely to be found elsewhere. We shall concern ourselves with two of the greatest piano concertos, Mozart's in C minor, K. 491, and Beethoven's in E♭ major, Op. 78. The former will be discussed in some detail, the latter briefly.

Mozart's Concerto in C Minor, First Movement

The opening ritornello for orchestra comprises a complete harmonic

---

[3] The first movements of Leo's *Violoncello Concertos* in D major and A major (1737) show an almost identical procedure more than a generation earlier. The concertos of J. C. Bach's contemporary Luigi Boccherini are also the same in this regard.

movement, interrupted by the V at mm. 58–62, and closing with the authentic cadence on I at mm. 90–91, prolonged until m. 99. It can be labeled R1 and makes up part one of the concerto movement.

This great ritornello divides itself into five sections and presents altogether six distinct melodic ideas. The first of these contains three different motives, marked a, b, and c, from which spring many of the themes or accompanimental figures appearing later in the movement.

In Burkhart

Ex. 13-2. MOZART: *Concerto, K. 491,* ritornello themes

Section 1 (mm. 1–34), a phrase group of three phrases, deals with theme A, and carries the harmonic movement to a semicadence $(I \rightarrow VII/V–V)$. Section 2 (mm. 35–62) is a chain of three phrases, Ex. 13-2 quoting the first of these (B_1). The place of this phrase chain in the tonal structure is to prolong the V with which section 1 ended. This V acts to interrupt the harmonic movement that begins again with the presentation of A as section 3 (mm. 63–73), concluding with a deceptive cadence (V–VI in m. 73). Section 4 (mm. 73–91), an extended phrase (C_1), completes the harmonic movement with an authentic cadence on I (mm. 90–91) and this I is prolonged by section 5 (mm. 91–99), serving as codetta to the ritornello (D).

The bass outline in Ex. 13-3 shows how the whole ritornello is, in effect, a balanced period, magnified to immense proportions, which is based on the principle of interruption.

The opening ritornello is followed by the first solo section, S1, designed as a sonata-form exposition. Each division of this exposition except the transi-

Ex. 13-3. MOZART: *Concerto, K. 491,* bass outline of opening ritornello

tion presents not a single theme, but a group of themes entailing its division
into subsections. The solo piano introduces the exposition with a new theme
of its own, E (Ex. 13-4a), after which the orchestra and solo combine to
present theme A. A transition (mm. 135–147) leads to V/III and the second
theme group begins on III, maintained to the end of the closing section, a
modulation to the mediant key of E♭, the relative major. The second theme
group (mm. 147–220) divides itself into three subsections, the new theme
F presented in the first (Ex. 13-4b). The second subsection G, is built from
motives b and c, a fragment of D, and introduces the new bass motive d (Ex.
13-4c). The third subsection (mm. 201–220) presents a new theme, H (Ex.
13-4d).

Ex. 13-4. MOZART: *Concerto, K. 491,* exposition themes

The closing theme consists first of an extended phrase based on A (mm.
220–241) followed by an eight-bar codetta, with its varied repetition and
eight-bar extension. Immediately R2 (mm. 265–282) bursts in, its first chord
coinciding with the last of S1. It begins with a melody made up of motives
b and c and concludes with the final bars of D. In the tonal structure, R2
has done no more than extend the final chord of S1 and repeat the authentic
cadence on III (that is, E♭ major) with which S1 had ended. S1 and R2
group themselves together to become part two of this concerto movement.

The second solo section, S2, is designed like the development of a sonata form. On the basis of its material and phrase organization, it falls into five subsections. Subsection 1 (mm. 283–301) deals with theme E. Starting on III it progresses to IV, the chord that opens subsection 2 (mm. 302–329). Here the orchestra is given over to the sounding of A with particular stress on motives b and c, while the piano furnishes brilliant scales and figuration. Subsection 2 moves from V back to III, then to V_7/V, but the cadence resolves deceptively to a V^6_5 (m. 330), which opens subsection 3. Subsection 3 deals with a rhythmic variation of motive d, first heard as the bass of G in the secondary section of the exposition. This version of motive d is so disposed as to prolong the V^6_5 for four bars, then repeats sequentially three times, each time prolonging a $^6_5$ chord in descending fifths (mm. 330–345) until subsection 4 begins in m. 346 on III (Eb). This is the chord that closed the exposition and opened the development. So far, then, the tonal structure of the development has consisted of movement within an area, a great chord succession prolonging III. A harmonic outline of the development section shows that the long chord succession on III is in essence a move to the chord whose root is a second above III, then to the chord whose root is a second below III, then, through the series of $^6_5$ chords in descending fifths, back to the beginning III. The succession is a gigantic slow turn around the note Eb.

Ex. 13-5. MOZART: *Concerto, K. 491*, development of first movement (harmonic outline)

The development continues with subsection 4, thematically based on motive a which appears in diminution in the bass. In mm. 352–354 the III that had been prolonged by succession from the beginning of the development, finally moves to V which is itself prolonged by means of pedal point throughout subsection 5, the retransition (mm. 355–361). Here the woodwind parts are particularly interesting. They play the descending broken triad derived from H, but by preceding this motive with a sixteenth note, and indicating that it is to be played staccato, Mozart contrives to give it the aspect of motive b'.

It has been observed that the penultimate ritornello, even in baroque times, was customarily much shorter than the others and that in the preclassical concerto it shrank still further. The same holds true during the classical period, so it should afford us no surprise that R3 in this concerto consists of no more than a six-bar presentation of A. There is not even a cadence, for R3 merges immediately into S3 (m. 367), and the two together become the fifth section, the recapitulation.

The recapitulation of Mozart's *Concerto in C Minor* is quite different from the exposition, in design as well as in tonal structure. Theme A (mm. 363–387) begins as it did in R1, continues as in S1, and concludes as in R1. The transition to the second theme group, no longer necessary for modulatory purposes, is reduced to a mere four bars. The second theme is reduced to two subsections and entirely rearranged, beginning with H and closing with F— the reverse order of their original appearances—G being omitted completely. Moreover, theme F is altered considerably and incorporates in its final bars a motive from C_2. The closing theme is entirely different from that of the

Outline Summary of Mozart's Piano Concerto, K. 491, First Movement

Bars	1–99	100–265				265–282
Procedure	R1	S1 (exposition)				R2
Design	AB ‖ AC-D	PT (EA)	tr.	ST (FGH)	CT (A)	bcD
Tonal Structure	I (I → V ‖ I → VI)	I ⎯⎯→ of III	I → VI	III		III
Form	Part One	Part Two				

Bars	283–361	362–473	473–509	509–523
Procedure	S2 (development)	R3–S3 (recapitulation)	R4	Coda
Design	E A G A H (bc) (d) (a) (b″)	PT (A) ST (HF) CT (bB)	A Cad. C D	H b″
Tonal Structure	III ⎯⎯⎯→ V_7	I	I	I
Form	Part Three			

exposition for it opens with a new section, based on a rising octave derived from motive b″, and continues with the three phrases of B, taken from R1. The third phrase is especially to be noted, for this time it is presented in canonic imitation. The whole recapitulation has been concerned only with the tonic key and has completed the harmonic movement I V I. This final tonic chord coincides with the opening chord of the last ritornello, R4. It begins as a phrase stating theme A, but halts on a I_4^6 for an improvised cadenza. The piano soloist is expected to close his cadenza with the V or V_7, foreshadowed by the orchestral I_4^6 with which it began. The ritornello then continues, taking its material from R2 and themes C and D. The tonal structure of R4 has re-emphasized the tonic key. A coda, which corresponds thematically to subsection 5 or the development, prolongs the I by means of pedal point. S2, R3–S3, and R4 (with cadenza) group themselves together as part three of the concerto.

The problem of the double exposition

The initial ritornello of Mozart's *Concerto in C Minor* presents a half-dozen melodic ideas, and the exposition several more. While the exposition included some of the themes from R1, it by no means stated all of them. Yet these other themes, "exposed" only in the orchestral ritornello, are certainly an integral part of the work. Theorists often speak of a "double exposition" in the concerto-sonata form—the opening ritornello being considered exposition one, the first solo section exposition two. The pros and cons of this view of R1 have been much debated with no universal agreement. But whether or not one applies the term "exposition" to both the first and second sections of the movement, it can hardly be denied that the recapitulation, R3–S3, is usually based on both of them and can be thought of as a synthesis of the two. The fact that R1 is used along with S1 as material on which to base the recapitulation would seem to lend weight to the argument in favor of considering it an exposition.

The parts of a concerto-sonata form

In the *Concerto in C Minor*, Mozart employs R2 as a means of prolonging the final chord of S1. These two sections, then, group themselves into a single part, part two, in the mind of the listener (see the foregoing outline summary). In some concertos, however, R2 does not merely prolong the final chord of S1, but leads instead directly into the beginning chord, whatever it may be, of the development section, S2. J. C. Bach's *Concerto, Op. 13, No. 2*, and Mozart's *Sinfonia Concertante for Violin and Viola, K. 364*, both contain this type of R2. Except for the first two piano concertos, all of Beethoven's works in the genre follow this procedure in their first movements.

The result is a different grouping of sections into parts than was the case in the Mozart *Concerto in C Minor*. For if R2 should conclude its connective motion with a semicadence, it will inevitably be grouped with the part that follows, rather than with the part that precedes. There are concertos, then, in which part two is made up of S1 alone, part three consisting of the final four sections.

Beethoven's Concerto in E flat Major, First Movement

The first movements of Beethoven's concertos exhibit the same six sections as do Mozart's, disposed as orchestral ritornellos with intervening exposition, development, and recapitulation for soloist with orchestra. They differ from most of Mozart's in having fewer themes, for Beethoven sought to be economical in the use of his melodies. In all but the first two of Beethoven's concertos, the exposition consists entirely of material heard in the opening ritornello, and usually in approximately the same order.

In Mozart's early *Concerto in E flat Major, K. 271*, he brought in the solo piano at the very beginning, letting it help state the first theme of the opening ritornello. Mozart never did this again, but Beethoven took up the idea in *Concerto No. 4 in G Major*. In his *Concerto No. 5 in E flat Major*, after a single chord from the orchestra, he allows the piano to enter not with a theme, but with an introductory flourish. Another orchestral chord and the piano sets off again with a brilliant cadenza which, subsiding, leads into the opening ritornello for orchestra above. This is a gigantic affair in eight subsections, ABCA'DEF, concluding with the codetta, G. The third subsection, C, is a remarkable melody, always appearing first in the minor mode, then in the major.

Ex.13-6.   BEETHOVEN: *Concerto, Op. 73*, ritornello themes

The piano re-enters for the exposition before the orchestra has quite finished the ritornello, a device that had appeared in several of Mozart's concertos and that Beethoven had previously used in the *Piano Concerto No. 4*. The exposition uses most of the themes presented in the opening ritornello, but transposes to V those serving the secondary and closing sections. In this connection, Beethoven achieves a striking effect in his presentation of C as secondary theme. It appears first not in V (B♭ major), but in the minor mode of ♭VI (C♭ equals B), moves into the major mode in which it appears in a varied version, and finally bursts out in the orchestra in its proper key. This use of a progressive harmonic movement in the secondary section is occasionally to be found in sonata-form expositions as well, as was pointed out in Chapter 11 (see p. 191).

At the end of the development the repetition of the introductory piano flourishes leads into the recapitulation. The themes here are presented in the

Outline Summary of Beethoven's Concerto, Op. 73, First Movement

Bars	1–11	11–111	111–224	224–268	268–362
Procedure	Intro.	R1	S1 (exposition)	R2	S2 (development)
Design	Quasi-cadenza	ABCA'-DEFG	PT tr. ST tr. CT (A) (B) (C) (B') (A'DG')	AA'DFG	AGBFA'GA'
Tonal Structure	I–I V–V$_7$	I → V$_7$ I	I → ♭VI–V → V$_7$/V	V → III	III → V
Form	Part One		Part Two	Part Three	

Bars	362–373	373–485		485–562	562–582
Procedure	Intro.	R3-S3 (recapitulation)		R4	Coda
Design	Quasi-cadenza	PT tr. ST tr. CT A A' CA'EFG (A) (B) (C) (B') (A'DG') (quasi-cadenza)			G
Tonal Structure	I–IV–V$_7$	I → ♭VII–I → V$_7$		I I$^6_4$: V$_7$ I	I
Form	(Part Three continued)				

same order as in the exposition, but Beethoven is again unorthodox regarding the key of the secondary section. In the exposition it appeared first in a key a half tone higher than that for which it was ultimately destined. Now it appears first a whole step lower (D♭ major), but with its orchestral statement it settles into the tonic key.

The fourth ritornello enters normally and comes to the usual halt on I_4^6, preparatory to the cadenza, which begins accordingly. But after a few bars the listener is astonished to find the orchestra accompanying the pianist and realizes that this is not an improvised cadenza after all but a composed cadenza and only the beginning of one at that. It leads into a final restatement of all but D of the ritornello themes. This is the only concerto in which Beethoven eschewed the improvised cadenza in the first movement, though for his own use he composed cadenzas to his other concertos.

EXERCISE

2. Make an outline summary similar to those in the text.

A	B
a. The first movement of a concerto by Mozart, Beethoven, or Brahms	a. Brahms: *Violin Concerto,* First Movement

13-3. THIRD MOVEMENTS OF THE CLASSICAL CONCERTO: CONCERTO-RONDO FORM

A few classical concertos end with a set of variations on a theme. The finales of the others are rondos (see Chapter 9), a custom that was largely continued throughout the nineteenth century. The rondos that conclude the concertos of romantic composers do not differ substantially in form from the ordinary rondo or sonata rondo already discussed. The rondos of many classical concertos, too, are essentially the same. But there is a special type of rondo first developed by Mozart in certain early concertos and used with some consistency in his later ones, which, being especially designed for use in the concerto, we shall call the concerto-rondo form.

The finales of Beethoven's first four piano concertos are ordinary rondos as is that of the *Triple Concerto, Op. 56.* But in his last two concertos, the one for violin, *Op. 61,* and the *Piano Concerto in E flat Major, Op. 73,* he followed Mozart's concerto-rondo form.

The form bears many resemblances to the concerto sonata and may be considered an application of that form to the rondo. It proceeds as follows.

Refrain 1. In the concerto rondo the refrain plays approximately the same role as did the ritornello in the concerto-sonata form, with two differences: (1) The refrain of the concerto rondo usually begins with the solo instrument rather than with the orchestra, and (2) the refrain always recurs in the tonic key. Like the ritornello, it consists of several detachable parts.

Episode 1. The first episode is constructed along identical lines to the exposition in a concerto-sonata form except that normally no theme from the refrain appears in this exposition. There are a few exceptions to this general observation, an example being Mozart's K. 466, in which the refrain melody makes up the second half of the exposition's first theme. The first, second, and closing themes are presented as in any sonata form, after which a retransition leads back to the refrain.

Refrain 2. The return of the refrain is sometimes shortened. Normally, the solo instrument states it first, as in refrain 1, then the orchestra takes over. Progressive harmonic movement to the initial chord of episode 2 may occur during the orchestral statement of the refrain (compare similar treatment of R2 in concerto-sonata form, Section 13-3).

Episode 2. In some concertos this episode consists of new material, like the second episode of any typical classical rondo. In that case it is likely to express IV or VI. In many concertos, however, this episode is replaced by a development, as in the sonata-rondo form. Mozart's *Clarinet Concerto, K. 622,* includes both: an episode of new material expressing VI followed by a development (compare similar treatment in sonata rondo, Section 12-3).

Refrain 3. Like R3 of concerto-sonata form, the third refrain of the concerto rondo is frequently omitted.

Episode 3. This episode comprises the recapitulation section of the movement and hence is normally a restatement, entirely in the tonic, of episode 1. Often it is highly abridged. If, for instance, episode 2 was a development including treatment of the first theme of episode 1, that theme is likely to be absent here. If there is to be a cadenza, the closing theme will lead to a halt on the I^6_4 and the improvisation will begin at that point.

Outline of the Concerto-Rondo Form
(Frequent omissions are indicated by enclosure in brackets)

Refrain 1	Episode 1	Refrain 2	Episode 2	[Refrain 3]	Episode 3	Refrain 4 and Coda
Solo, orch.	Exposition PT tr. ST CT	Solo, orch.	New or development	Solo or orch.	Recapitulation [PT] tr. ST CT [Cadenza]	Orch., solo
I	I V(III)	I*	IV (VI)**	I	I	I

* Or progressive movement to beginning of episode 2.

** Or, when episode 2 is a development, progressive movement to V_7.

Refrain 4. The final appearance of the refrain is generally shortened and sometimes merges with the coda.

The chief distinction between the ordinary rondo with which many concertos end and the concerto-rondo form lies in the sonata-form construction of the first episode. In the usual rondo, it will be remembered, the first refrain is followed by a modulating transition leading to the key of episode 1 (III or V). In the concerto rondo, the refrain is concluded on I by the orchestra, and the solo instrument enters not with a modulating transition but with a new theme also expressing I. Thus the first episode does not begin on III or V but on I. After the first theme of the exposition episode has been stated, a transition leads to the related key for the statement of the second and closing themes. This difference has caused a great deal of confusion among annotators of phonograph record jackets, a confusion which has, no doubt, been passed on to their readers.

Outline summaries of two of Mozart's concerto rondos are given.

Outline Summary of Mozart's Concerto, K. 466, Finale

Bars	1–63	64–161	161–167	167–195
Procedure	Refrain 1	Episode 1 (exposition)		Refrain 2
Design	A-AA'BC	PT tr. ST CT (DA) (EF) (G)	retrans.	A-A'
Tonal Structure	$I \to VI$	$I \to \underset{\text{of III}}{II_6 V}$ $III\flat$-$\natural$	$III \to V_5^6$	I–$I \to \underset{\text{of V}}{VII_7/V\text{-}V}$
Form	Part one (A)	Part Two (BA)		

Bars	196–240	240–345	346–353	354–428
Procedure	Episode 2 (development)	Episode 3 (recapitulation)	Refrain 4 (Refrain 3 omitted)	Coda
Design	DA	PT tr. ST CT + Codetta (D) (EF)(G) (FC and cadenza)	A (abbreviated)	GB'G'
Tonal Structure	$V \to \underset{\text{of IV}}{V_7 I} \to V_5^6$	I I I I	I	$I\sharp$
Form		Part Three (Dev.-C, B'A)		

Outline Summary of Mozart's Concerto, K. 488, Finale

Bars	1–61	62–193	193–202	202–229
Procedure	Refrain 1	Episode 1 (exposition)		Refrain 2
Design	A-ABCDE	PT tr. ST CT + Codetta (F) (G)(H) (J)	retrans.	A-AA'
Tonal Structure	I → V I	I → $\underbrace{\text{IV VI}}_{\text{of V}}$ V♭—♮	V—V₇	I–I → $\underbrace{\text{VII}_7\text{–I}}_{\text{of VI}}$
Form	Part One (A)	Part Two (BA)		

Bars	230–293	293–312	312–423	423–441	441–480	480–524
Procedure	Episode 2 (new)		Episode 3 (recapitulation)		Refrain 4 (Refrain 3 omitted)	Coda
Design	J K	retrans.	PT tr. ST CT + Codetta (F)(F')(G')(H) (J)		A-ABC	JDE
Tonal Structure	VI IV $\longrightarrow$ V₇		I I♭ I♭ I♮		I I $\longrightarrow$ V I	I
Form	Part Three (C)		Part Four (BA)			

EXERCISE

3. Make an outline summary, similar to the foregoing, of the third movement of one of Mozart's later piano concertos (K. 450 and upwards, except K. 453, K. 482, and K. 491) or of the *Clarinet Concerto*, K. 622.

13-4. SUMMARY

Throughout the baroque and classical periods the fundamental characteristic of the concerto, contrast between sounding bodies, was maintained, demanding the constant use of the device of the orchestral ritornello. The first and third movements of the typical late baroque three-movement concerto proceeded by alternation between the orchestra (*concerto grosso*) and the soloist or soloists (*concertino*). No standard "*concerto grosso* form" emerged from this systematized procedure, since the number of these alternations was not fixed and there was no typical tonal structure. The *concerto grosso* movement regularly has the following general features:

1. *Ritornellos.* The movement usually begins with an orchestral ritornello comprising several sections in the tonic key. It always ends with one in that key. During the course of the movement other ritornellos appear in related keys (III, IV, V, or VI), although the next-to-last ritornellos are often in the tonic key. The middle ritornellos are much abridged; the final one sometimes is.

Relationships Among the Concerto Forms

Concerto Section	1. Concerto Grosso	2. Concerto-Sonata Form	3. Concerto-Rondo Form	Rondo Section
Tutti R1	A B C . . . I	A B C . . . I	A A B C . . . I	Solo, tutti Refrain 1
Solo S1	D (or A′, B′ . . .) I → V(III)	Sonata-form exposition of new or partially new themes *PT tr. ST CT* I → V(III)	Sonata-form exposition of new themes *PT tr. ST CT* I → V(III)	Solo Episode 1
Tutti R2	A (B C . . .) V(III)	A (B C . . .) V(III)*	A (B C . . .) V(III)*	Solo, tutti Refrain 2
Solo S2	E (or A″, B″ . . .) V(III) → VI(IV)	Sonata-form development V(III) → V₇	Sonata-form development V(III) → V_7 *or* new material VI(IV)	Solo Episode 2
Tutti R3	(A B) C . . . VI, IV, or I	Sonata-form recapitulation A (short) I	Sonata-form recapitulation A (short) I	Solo, tutti Refrain 3 (perhaps omitted)
Solo S3	F (or A‴, B‴ . . .) VI(IV) → I or I	Recapitulation (continued) *PT tr. ST CT* I	Recapitulation (continued) *PT tr. ST CT* I	Solo Episode 3
Tutti R4**	(A) B C . . . I	(A) B C . . . (interrupted by solo cadenza) Plus coda	(A) B C . . . (possibly preceded by solo cadenza) Plus coda	Tutti Refrain 4

* Or progressive movement to initial chord of S2.
** The *concerto grosso* frequently has more than four ritornellos.

2. *Solo sections.* Between ritornellos the *concertino* performs with an accompaniment of a portion of the orchestra. These solo sections may include new themes or simply figuration of a nature idiomatic to the instrument. Occasionally the soloist presents a theme first heard in the ritornello. The solo sections generally modulate from the key of the preceding ritornello to that of the following.

Though musical style underwent a great change during the course of the eighteenth century, the structure of the ritornello itself remained much the same. The usual number of ritornellos, however, shrank to four, and of these the third was often extremely short. In certain concertos of the preclassical composers (Leo, Boccherini, J. C. Bach) the first solo section takes on the characteristics of the exposition of sonata form, the second solo those of the development, and the third, those of the recapitulation, resulting in what is now called the concerto-sonata form. It appears (much enlarged) as the first-movement structure of the concertos of Mozart, Haydn, and Beethoven. Though the ordinary rondo often served for the concerto finale, Mozart developed a special concerto-rondo form by combining features of the concerto-sonata with the recurring refrains in the tonic key, characteristic of the rondo. The outline on page 246 shows the relationship among the various types of concerto forms.

Historical Note on the Concerto after Beethoven   The shadow of Beethoven loomed so large over the musical world that for a number of years after his last concerto was written many composers dared not attempt anything structurally very different. Weber's and Chopin's piano concertos, for instance, are constructed along lines similar to Beethoven's. When Weber disregarded the principles of the classical concerto he called the result not a concerto, but *Konzertstücke,* that is, a piece in the style of a concerto. But the romantic spirit could not forever take on a classical body, and soon a new type of first movement began to appear. Mendelssohn, with two concertos for piano and the *Violin Concerto in E Minor,* ushered in the new romantic type. An essential characteristic of the concerto had, hitherto, been the contrast in sounding bodies, the opposition of soloist and orchestra. Now it became a different thing entirely—a brilliant piece of music for a virtuoso performer with an orchestral accompaniment. Mozart and Beethoven wrote concertos for piano and orchestra. It is significant that Schumann called his *Op. 129* a concerto for violoncello "with the accompaniment of an orchestra."

Since the idea was no longer the contrast between sounding bodies, the form was altered to eliminate the orchestral ritornellos. The result in some cases is an ordinary sonata form, each theme usually being presented by the soloist and immediately taken up by the orchestra, or vice versa. In some cases entirely unique forms were devised. The concertos of Liszt and Schumann are among the great products of the new concerto type.

Brahms, though progressive in some ways, was as a rule conservative in formal matters. In his four concertos (two for piano, one for violin, and one for violin and cello) he restored the six sections of the classical concerto-sonata form. Except in the *Piano Concerto in D Minor, Op. 15,* he followed Beethoven in using for the exposition only material that had been previously heard in the ritornello. The opening of the *Piano Concerto in B flat Major, Op. 83,* takes its cue from both Beethoven's *No. 4* and *No. 5,* for the piano is allowed to help with the first theme of the ritornello, as in Beethoven's G major Concerto. It then proceeds with a cadenzalike flourish similar to the E flat major Concerto, remaining silent throughout the rest of the first tutti section.

One constantly hears the statement that Brahms' *Piano Concerto No. 2 in B flat Major* is not a concerto at all but a symphony with piano obbligato. It is true that this piece, like most symphonies, has four movements while concertos ordinarily have only three, but in its treatment of the contrast between soloist and orchestra it is a concerto in the true and historic sense of the word. Indeed, it is one of the few nineteenth-century concertos about which this can be said.

After Brahms had re-established the classical concerto-sonata form, romantic composers had two choices open to them. They could continue along the path first opened by Mendelssohn and followed by Liszt and Schumann—to eliminate the tutti sections and concentrate on the soloist's part, providing it with an interesting and elaborate orchestral accompaniment—or they could retain the tutti sections and thus achieve the contrast between sounding bodies which had been in the past the concerto's most characteristic feature. The great majority disregarded Brahms and chose the former way—Grieg, Tchaikovsky, and Saint-Saëns, being outstanding among these. One of the few who chose the latter way was Dvořak, in his *Concerto for Violoncello in B Minor.*

The twentieth-century concerto generally continues to be essentially a work for a solo performer with accompaniment. In spite of highly elaborate orchestral writing, contrast between a large and a small sounding body is no longer in evidence as a structural principle, for in the modern concerto, as in that of the nineteenth century, the soloist is very prominent most of the time. The three-movement scheme, fast-slow-fast, continues to appear with regularity. Nevertheless, other movement schemes occur from time to time, as in Berg's *Violin Concerto* (four movements played as two) and Schoenberg's *Piano Concerto, Op. 42* (four movements played as one).

14

Fugue and Related Genres

Historical Note on the Fugue The fugue is properly considered to have emerged as a distinct genre in the seventeenth century, although its origins can be traced back several centuries in the imitative contrapuntal texture of polyphonic vocal music.

So far as is known, the term *fuga* was first used by Jacobus of Liège in his theoretical treatise *Speculum musicae* (c. 1330), where it is equivalent to *caccia*, a work in which two voices move by canonic imitation over a free third voice. In the latter part of the fourteenth century it was sometimes synonymous with *rondellus* or *rota*, a round. Fugal treatment was defined around 1475 by Tinctoris in his *Diffinitorium musicae* as "the identity of rhythmic and melodic writing in various parts of a composition," that is, equivalent to what we think of today as canonic writing. In the fifteenth and sixteenth centuries, composers frequently made great use of fugal procedures in both their sacred and secular vocal works— the masses and motets on the one hand, the *canzoni* or French chansons on the other—procedures which were sometimes reflected in the title: Dufay, Josquin des Prez, and Palestrina each composed a *Missa ad fugam*.

During the sixteenth century, the motet and the chanson or *canzona* became models for similar instrumental genres, the *ricercar* and the *canzon da sonar*, respectively, such as the organ *ricercari* of Cavazzoni. The style of the *ricercar*, derived as it was from the sacred motet, was generally of a solemn character, while that of the secularly inspired *canzona* was rhythmic and lively. The *canzona* differed further from the *ricercar* in being less rigidly contrapuntal and in introducing contrasting sections of a different nature. The two styles persisted in the fugal writing of the seventeenth and early eighteenth centuries and are exemplified in the first two Fugues of Bach's *WTC*, that in C Major being of the *ricercar* type, that in C Minor the *canzona*.

249

The early seventeenth century saw the organ *ricercar* and *canzona* established in Italy, chiefly by Frescobaldi. An important northern counterpart was the fantasia, a term referring in the late sixteenth and early seventeenth centuries to an instrumental piece in imitative counterpoint that often combined features of the *ricercar* and the *canzona*. The English fancy (or fantasia) for a consort of viols, such as those of Orlando Gibbons, the early works of John Jenkins, and, much later, Henry Purcell, foreshadowed fugal writing in many respects. The keyboard fantasias of Sweelinck in the Netherlands, however, came even closer to the fugue in that they were composed on a single theme throughout.

The most important organ fugues of the latter half of the seventeenth century occur as sections within the toccatas or "praeludia" (now often called preludes and fugues) of Buxtehude, though fugues as independent pieces were also being composed (Krieger, Pachelbel, J. K. F. Fischer). The evolution of the fugue reached its peak in the works of J. S. Bach—not only in the famous organ fugues and those of his *WTC*, but in the mighty fugal choruses from the sacred vocal music, although the best fugal choruses of Handel are equally impressive.

In Bach's time it was customary to precede the independent keyboard fugue with a composition of a less contrapuntal, or even of a completely homophonic, texture. The result is the two-movement prelude and fugue, toccata and fugue, or fantasy and fugue.

After Bach the majority of important fugal composition occurs in choral music. The masses and oratorios of Haydn, Mozart, Beethoven, Mendelssohn, Brahms, Verdi, and others are rich with *fugato* (that is, fuguelike) passages as well as entire fugal movements. Although most nineteenth-century composers wrote instrumental fugues, only Beethoven can be compared with Bach in this field. As he advanced in years, Beethoven came to rely more and more on the fugue as a means of artistic expression (*Quartets, Op. 131, Op. 133, Piano Sonatas, Op. 101, Op. 106, Op. 110,* the *Diabelli Variations, Op. 120,* and so on).

The fugue cannot be said to play an important role in twentieth-century music as compared with the late seventeenth and early eighteenth centuries. Nevertheless, certain important works with a fugal texture continue to appear from time to time (Hindemith, *Ludus Tonalis;* Schoenberg, *Variations on a Recitative,* Finale; Stravinsky, *Symphony of Psalms,* Second Movement; Bartók, *Music for Strings, Percussion, and Celesta,* First Movement).

14-1.　FUGUE AND FORM

The fugue is not a form. Two Bach fugues may have much in common, but the relationship between them is not of the same kind as the relationship between, say, two of Beethoven's sonata forms. Fugues are classed together in a single species not because of similarities of form, but because they exhibit in their texture similar contrapuntal procedures. From the point of view of form, each fugue is independent. It may show a binary or ternary form; it may exhibit resemblances to the rondo. The Finale from Brahms' *Violoncello*

Sonata in E Minor, Op. 38, is a fugue in sonata form. Frequently a particular fugue has a unique form of its own.

In this chapter, then, we shall be dealing not with standardized patterns of musical structure like the rounded binary form or the rondo, but with pieces in any form which are based on certain contrapuntal practices.

14-2. CHARACTERISTICS OF FUGUE

A fugue is a polyphonic composition with a texture made up of a constant number of melodic lines, usually three or four, occasionally five, rarely two or six. It is customary to refer to these melodic lines in vocal terminology, that is, the uppermost line is called the soprano voice, the lowest the bass. In a three-voice fugue the middle line is the alto, the fourth voice, when it exists, being the tenor. The fugue is based on a theme that begins in one voice, is imitated by another, again by a third, and so on, until each voice has stated it. The theme is called the subject, its imitation the answer. The subject then reappears at intervals throughout the piece. Imitation in fugal writing is generally of two types: real (or exact) imitation and what is known as "tonal imitation."

14-3. THE FUGUE SUBJECT AND ANSWER

The principle of tonal imitation

Ex. 14-1. HANDEL: *Messiah,* Part II

The familiar passage in Ex. 14-1 illustrates a procedure in imitative writing which is exceedingly important for the study of fugue. For convenience in explication, the system will be employed here whereby 1 stands for the tonic note, I for the tonic chord, 2 for the supertonic note, II for the supertonic chord, and so forth.

The subject as sung by the altos begins with three upward leaps of a perfect fourth each, separated by downward leaps of a sixth (5–1, 3–6, 1–4); then it descends to 1 by stepwise motion. When answered by the sopranos, however, it has a slightly different melodic contour. The soprano's answer is not a literal imitation of the subject, for the first upward leap is a fifth rather than a fourth (1–5). Except for this difference the remainder is an exact transposition of the subject a fifth higher. If Handel had allowed the sopranos to enter on the note e″ rather than on d″, the imitation would have been altogether exact. What is the purpose behind his alteration of the first note?

In the overtone series, the first and third overtones encompass the interval of an octave. The second overtone divides the octave into two unequal parts. The lower part comprises the interval of a fifth, the upper part is a fourth. The second overtone is related to the first and third overtones (and to the fundamental) as a dominant is to its tonic.

By taking the following steps, composers have quite commonly constructed their fugal answers in such a way that the octave's natural division by 5 is emphasized:

1. An implication of I is answered by an implication of V and, conversely, V by I.
2. A prominent 1 (that is, a 1 that is not merely passing or ornamental) is answered by 5, a prominent 5 by 1.

Such a procedure is known as tonal imitation because it results in the establishment by both subject and answer of a single tonality.

In Ex. 14-1 the subject begins by outlining I with its first three notes and continues until it settles on I at its conclusion (m. 48 third beat). According to the first principle, the sopranos answer with a transposition a fifth higher, implying dominant harmony, V. But for an exact transposition up a fifth the first note of the answer should have been e″. It is changed to d″ in accordance with the second principle—the note 5 is answered by the note 1. Due to this alteration of the first note, the initial melodic interval of the answer is an inexact imitation. Because the distance from 1 upward to 5 is greater than that from 5 upward to 1, the answer has a slightly different shape from that of the subject. But due to this change the first note of the answer can help to express the main tonality of D major rather than jumping too quickly into A major, the dominant key.

Tonal imitation in practice

The two general principles governing tonal imitation are simple enough, but in actual practice the situation is more complex, for a musically unsatisfactory answer may emerge if "rules" are followed slavishly. Great composers are never pedants. They strive for the best musical result in their fugues regardless of rules. An examination of one of Bach's well-known fugue subjects will illustrate this point. We shall observe what possibilities were open to him and then what he actually did.

The tones 1 and 5 appear prominently several times in the subject (Ex. 14-2a). Two 5s occurring toward the end of the second bar are short passing notes, not prominent enough to take into account for the purpose of tonal imitation.

Ex. 14-2. BACH: *WTC*, Vol. 1, *Fugue No. 2*

If Bach had transposed the subject to the upper fifth in an exact imitation, the answer would have been Ex. 14-2b. This answer takes into account the first rule but not the second. While 1 is answered with 5, 5 in this version is not answered with 1 but with 2. If, then, the prominent 5s are answered throughout with 1s, the result is Ex. 14-2c. A single playing will convince anyone that this version is unsatisfactory due to the change of the first note of the second bar from *d″* to *c″*. One of the intriguing elements in this seemingly innocent subject is what we might call an implied lower voice, consisting of a four-note descending scale fragment, one of whose notes falls on each strong beat. Thus in the subject, Ex. 14-2a, the *ab′* in the first bar moves down to *g′*, the first note of the second bar, and thence to *f′* on the third beat, and *eb′* on the next first beat. This pattern is an essential characteristic of the melody and should reappear in the answer as *eb″*, *d″*, *c″* and *bb′*. Bach therefore employs the tonal imitation only in the first part of the answer, where it destroys no essential characteristic of the subject, and continues with real imitation (Ex. 14-2d).

Sometimes a fugue subject is susceptible to more than one version of tonal imitation. The subject in Ex. 14-3 was answered by Buxtehude with a tonal imitation for the first note but a real imitation for the fourth. Bach, on the other hand, answers it tonally throughout.

Ex. 14-3. **a.** BUXTEHUDE: *Organ Fugue in E*
b. BACH: *Organ Fugue in E flat* (BWV 552)

The real answer

If the subject does not stress the 5, the answer is a real imitation at the upper fifth or, essentially the same thing, at the lower fourth.

Ex. 14-4. BACH: *WTC*, Vol. 1, *Fugue No. 1*

The subject with a leading tone

Special mention should be made of subjects which include a leading tone. The leading tone 7 can be understood as 3-of-V. Since V and I are complementary in tonal imitation, a logical answer to 3-of-V is 3-of-I. Consequently

Ex. 14-5. BACH: *WTC*, Vol. I, *Fugue No. 19*

many, but by no means all, fugue subjects displaying a conspicuous 7 are answered in a special way.

The first note of the subject, 1, is answered in a normal manner by 5. The second note, 7, is interpreted as the third of the dominant triad, 3-of-V; accordingly, Bach answers it by the third of the tonic triad, 3. The second note of the subject leaps up a perfect fourth to the third note. This perfect fourth, being a characteristic feature of the melody, must be preserved in the answer. Therefore the third note of the answer is 6, not 7. But the remainder of the subject can be answered satisfactorily at the normal interval of the upper fifth (expressed as a lower fourth).

Ex. 14-6. BUXTEHUDE: *Organ Fugue in E Minor*

In the minor mode, 7 is often raised to become the leading tone ♯7. In Ex. 14-6, the subject includes both the natural 7 and the raised ♯7. The corresponding notes of the answer, then, are 3 and ♯3. These notes govern the remainder of the subject so that the last note 4 is not a fifth but a fourth higher than the original (expressed as a fifth lower). Similarly, in Ex. 14-7, the ♯7 which appears as the second note of the subject is answered by ♯3, a fourth rather than a fifth higher, and the remainder of the answer follows suit.

Ex. 14-7. BEETHOVEN: *Quartet, Op. 131*

In spite of the cases cited above and a number of other similar ones, a prominent 7 or ♯7 in the subject is not necessarily answered by 3 or ♯3. In his "Hammerklavier Sonata," for instance, Beethoven's fugue subject opens with a situation similar to that of Ex. 14-7. Yet his answer is not as in that example, but appears at the perfect fifth above throughout with, of course, the one exception of the initial 5 answered by 1.

Subject with a secondary tonic

Ex. 14-8. BACH: *Magnificat, No. 11*

In this subject, V is stressed to a marked degree by the vigorous upward drive from 1 to 5 in the first two bars, by the threefold repetition of this 5, and by the expression of V as a secondary tonic in the fourth bar.[1] We can anticipate that the answer will reflect this emphasis of the dominant by a corresponding emphasis of the tonic. If Bach had answered the subject entirely at the upper fifth, as in Ex. 14-9a, the emphasized scale degree would not have been the tonic but the supertonic. This situation could have been rectified by a substitution of 1 for 2, as in Ex. 14-9b, but this spoils the effect of the eighth notes rising energetically to their goal. Bach's solution (Ex. 14-9c) transposes only the first note to the upper fifth. Thus the initial 1 is answered regularly by an initial 5. The remainder of the melody is transposed to the upper fourth. Though such a solution delays the beginning of the ascent, the vitality of the second bar is not impaired. The rise from 1 to 5 in the subject is answered by a rise from 5 to 1, this 1 is now repeated three times, and the implied authentic cadence on V is answered by a similar cadence on I.

Ex. 14-9. BACH: *Magnificat, No. 11*

---

[1] Many theorists call this secondary tonic on V a "modulation to V" and refer to this as a "modulating subject."

Some subjects seem to justify their answers from more than one point of view. In Ex. 14-10, for instance, the answer is, except for the first note, at the fourth above rather than the fifth. Is Bach's reason exclusively to answer the implied cadence of the secondary tonic on V ($\sharp$4–5) with a similar cadence on I (7–1)? Or is he also thinking of the second note of the subject as 3-of-V, calling for a corresponding 3-of-I in the answer?

Ex. 14-10.   BACH: *Organ Fugue in C Major* (BWV 547)

Method for answering a fugue subject

From the foregoing examination it is possible to arrive at a five-step method for constructing the answer to a fugue subject.

Step 1. Examine the subject and note whether it exhibits (a) a prominent 5, (b) use of V as a secondary tonic (that is, $\sharp$4–5), or (c) a conspicuous 7 or $\sharp$7.

Step 2. If none of these conditions exist, one has merely to answer with real imitation: Transpose the subject a perfect fifth higher (or perfect fourth lower). Even though condition (c) above should exist, real imitation is nevertheless possible (see Bach, *WTC*, Vol. 1, *Fugue No. 4*).

Step 3. If condition (c) exists but real imitation is not desired, or if conditions (a) and/or (b) are present, it is necessary to note further in the subject any characteristic feature displayed, a feature that must be maintained.

Step 4. (a) Subjects with a prominent 5: Transpose the subject a perfect fifth higher, substituting in the answer a 1 for each 5 prominently displayed in the subject. (b) Subjects with a secondary tonic on V: Do the same, but answer the $\sharp$4–5 in the subject with 7–1 (or $\sharp$7–1) in the answer. (c) Subjects with prominent 7 or $\sharp$7: If real imitation has not been employed, answer the 7 or $\sharp$7 of the subject with 3 or $\sharp$3 in the answer.

Step 5. Now play or sing the result, observing whether any characteristic feature noted under step 3 has been destroyed in the answer. If the subject was a satisfactory melody and the answer is not, one can be certain that an important melodic characteristic has been destroyed. The final step, then, is to adjust the melody to restore this characteristic. Usually a subject exhibiting only condition (a) can be restored simply by reverting at some inconspicuous point (for instance, a weak beat or fraction of a beat) to real imitation at the fifth above. The characteristic feature of subjects exhibiting condition (b) can usually be restored by preceding the implied authentic cadence of the answer (7–1) with transposition at the fourth above.

An application of the various steps of the method for answering a fugue subject is given in Ex. 14-11. The subject chosen is unusual in that conditions (a), (b), and (c) are all present.

Ex. 14-11.   BACH: *Mass in B Minor*

The lengthy subject

Tonal imitation often makes it possible for the composer to begin his answer with tonic harmony even when that answer will later stress the dominant (see Ex. 14-1, Ex. 14-3, Ex. 14-5). Thus too abrupt an establishment of a secondary tonic on V can be avoided. Very long fugue subjects, such as that of the "Little G Minor Fugue" for organ, are frequently answered by real rather than tonal imitation. In these cases since the answer does not enter until some time after the beginning of the piece, there is no necessity to postpone stress on dominant harmony.

EXERCISE

1. Copy all the fugue subjects from *WTC*, Vol. 1, without glancing ahead at the answers. Following the five-step method just presented, construct answers to these subjects. Compare with Bach's answers and explain any differences.

14-4. CONTRAPUNTAL DEVICES COMMONLY OCCURRING IN FUGUE

In fugue the composer often employs any or several of the technical devices with which we are already familiar: augmentation, diminution, inversion (rarely retrograde, though Beethoven makes use of it in the fugue of his "Hammerklavier Sonata"). In addition two other devices regularly appear.

Stretto

We speak of stretto when the subject is presented in one voice and imitated in one or more additional voices, the imitation beginning before the original statement has run its course. It is thus made to overlap itself. Here is a stretto that occurs in the fugue of Ex. 14-3b.

Ex. 14-12. BACH: *Organ Fugue in E flat Major* (BWV 552)

Sometimes the whole subject is used for stretto (*stretto maestrale*), sometimes only the first part. Stretto may occur at any time in the course of the fugue. It is particularly valuable, however, as a means of building up excitement and tension at some climactic point. The subject does not make its first appearance in stretto, although an exceptional case occurs in the *Fugue No. 4* of Bach's *WTC*, Vol. 2.

Multiple counterpoint

Most fugues employ to a great extent a device known as double counterpoint. This occurs when two melodic lines exchange places so that the line which first appears in the lower position is put in the upper.

Ex. 14-13. BEETHOVEN: *Grosse Fuge, Op. 133*

Triple counterpoint occurs when three different melodic lines exchange places. There are a few cases of quadruple and quintuple counterpoint, a famous example of the latter being in the Finale to Mozart's *Symphony No. 41.*

EXERCISE

2. Examine the following fugues for technical contrapuntal devices:

A

a. *WTC, No. 23.* Compare subject and answer as they appear in mm. 1–4 with their appearances in mm. 18–21.

b. *WTC, No. 22.* Copy out on five staves the stretto which begins in the ninth bar before the end.

B

a. *Art of Fugue, No. VII.* Examine mm. 1–13, locating and comparing all entrances of the theme.

b. *WTC, No. 16.* Copy out on four staves the stretto in mm. 28–29.

A and B

c. *WTC, No. 21.* Identify the type of relationship to be found among mm. 9–12, mm. 13–16, mm. 22–25, mm. 26–29, mm. 37–40, and mm. 41–44.

14-5. FUGAL PROCEDURE

Ex. 14-14. MARCHAND: *Organ Fugue in G Minor*

In Ex. 14-14, the four voices, making use of tonal imitation, enter singly in descending order: soprano, alto, tenor, bass (mm. 1–12). The original version of the subject alternates with that of the answer. As each completes its statement it continues with a counterpoint flowing against the new presentation of the theme. After the bass statement, the four voices continue for four bars (mm. 12–17), with no reference to the subject. The subject reappears in mm. 18–20 in the bass, and again in the tenor (mm. 21–24). Here the last three notes are augmented to cover two bars rather than a single one. The theme is absent from mm. 25–28, enters as answer in the soprano voice in mm. 29–31, and is absent from the final bars of the fugue. Twice it is shortened: In the first bass entrance the theme is diverted a half bar before its conclusion (m. 12), and in the final entrance it is diverted three quarters of a bar before (m. 31). It is to be noted that the passages in which the theme does not appear (mm. 12–17; mm. 25–28; mm. 31–37) are, by virtue of the chains of suspensions they contain, motivically related to each other but not to the theme. Having the nature of digressions from the subject, they are called episodes. Passages that present, or "expose," the theme are called expositions. Thus, in this fugue, the first exposition (mm. 1–12) comprises an entrance of the theme in each of the four voices (subject-answer-subject-answer). Relief from the theme is afforded by episode 1 (mm. 12–17) after which exposition II presents, in bass and tenor, two appearances of the theme, both subjects. Episode 2 (mm. 25–28), recalling episode 1, affords a few bars'

Ex. 14-15.   BACH: *WTC, Vol. 1, Fugue No. 16*

digression, following which is exposition III, a single entrance of the answer in the soprano. Episode 3 brings the fugue to a close.

Before attempting to draw any general conclusions from this single short composition, let us consider one of the fugues of J. S. Bach.

The theme of the fugue in Ex. 14-15 is clearly made up of two motives, marked a and b, which are separated by a rest. It appears as subject low in the alto voice and is imitated tonally by an answer in the soprano. During the soprano's statement, the alto continues with a counterpoint against it. This counterpoint is ingeniously devised from inversion of the two motives of the subject (Bach chooses the answer for the inversion), which are placed in reverse order. A perusal of the rest of the fugue will show that when the subject appears it is nearly always accompanied by this same counterpoint. The counterpoint, then, is spoken of as the countersubject of the fugue. Sometimes it appears beneath the subject, sometimes above it; that is, it is composed in double counterpoint.

One might expect the third entry of the subject to follow immediately after the entry of the answer in the soprano, but instead we find a one-bar episode treating motive b in sequence. Only in m. 5 is the subject heard in the bass, followed in mm. 6–7 by the tenor answer. Although an episode intervenes between the first pair of subject entries (subject and answer) and the second pair, the four first entries taken together are considered to comprise a single exposition. Later on in the fugue only those entries not separated by episodes group themselves into a single exposition. Exposition I leads into the second episode which, like episode 1, is based on motive b. This episode is much longer than the first, covering four bars (mm. 8–12) rather than a single one. Although motive b is derived from the subject, as used here it offers a certain amount of contrast by reason of the absence of motive a and the new countermelody in the uppermost voice. The episode leads to a cadence on the first beat of m. 12 at which point the alto begins a new exposition. This second exposition contains five entries of the theme, the last two occurring in stretto. Episode 3 (m. 19) is again based on motive b and like episode 1 is only a single bar in length. Exposition III (mm. 20–24) contains three entries of the subject. Episode 4 corresponds to episode 2 in length and in the use of the new countermelody against motive b. This melody is now used in both upper voices. Exposition IV is very short (mm. 28–29) but by means of stretto squeezes in two complete statements of the subject in the soprano and tenor, plus motive a in the bass. Episode 5 (mm. 29–31) uses only motive b. Exposition V (mm. 31–34) closes the fugue with two statements of the subject. In the last two bars the alto voice divides to provide a climactic close in five voices.

A comparison of this fugue with Ex. 14-14 will show some similarities and some differences (see table, p. 264).

These are, of course, only two examples chosen from the hundreds of tonal fugues in existence. An examination of a large number of them would certainly reveal the use of still other procedures. Generally speaking, however, the chief methods involved in the construction of a fugue are included in one

Comparative Observations

	Fugue in G Minor *by Marchand*	*Fugue in G Minor* *by Bach*
Exposition I	1. Order of entry: S-A-T-B. 2. Each entry follows immediately after previous entry. 3. Subject and answer versions of the theme alternate.	1. Order of entry: A-S-B-T. 2. Episode separates entries into two pairs. 3. Same.
Later expositions	4. No standard arrangement of subject and answer versions. 5. No fixed number of entries. 6. Sometimes entire theme is not stated, final notes being diverted.	4. Same. 5. Same. 6. Same. In addition, in m. 23 the first note of the subject is halved in its rhythmic value.
Episodes	7. Only new material is employed. 8. Episodes related to each other.	7. Without sacrificing their value as relief from the subject, episodes are motivically related to it. 8. Same.
Over all	9. Except for mm. 19–20, once the four voices have entered, they all continue steadfastly to the end. Final chord in five voices. 10. The piece consists of three expositions and three episodes, ending with an episode. 11. Virtually no use made of any special contrapuntal devices. 12. Each statement of theme accompanied by new and different counterpoint.	9. Only in a few passages do all four voices sound at once. Most of the time one of them is silent. Final entry (last two bars) in five voices. 10. The piece consists of five expositions and five episodes, ending with an exposition. 11. Relies heavily on inversion, double counterpoint, and stretto. 12. Theme regularly accompanied by the countersubject.

or the other of the two fugues we have examined. Nevertheless, the following comments on the table of Comparative Observations should be made.

1. Regarding No. 1, an examination of a great number of fugues reveals no preferred order of entry for the voices.
2. Regarding No. 3, exceptions occur from time to time (for example, *Nos. 1 and 14* in *WTC*).

3. Regarding No. 10, fugues have been written without episodes (for example, *No. 1* in *WTC*).

4. Regarding No. 11, some fugues use the additional devices of augmentation and/or diminution (*No. 8* in *WTC*). Not infrequently certain entries of the subject are inverted (*Nos. 8* and 23 in *WTC*).

EXERCISE

3. Make a summary outline of the procedure of the following fugues:

A	B
a. *WTC, Fugue No. 2*	a. *WTC, Fugue No. 13*

14-6. THE FORM OF A FUGUE

Our examination of the fugue has begun by investigation of the procedure customarily associated with the genre. This serves as an introduction to the study of the form of the fugue. Both tonal structure and design have to be taken into account before a conclusion regarding form can be reached. It is time to reconsider these fugues, first as tonal structures, then as designs.

Tonal structure

Very striking in the fugue of Ex. 14-14 is the absence, until the last bar, of any definite cadence. The final note of each phrase coincides by elided cadence with the first note of the next (first beats of mm. 4, 7, 10, 12, and so on) so that the piece seems to move with an uninterrupted flow. Expected cadences, as in m. 28, are diverted before being completed.

Each statement of the subject and answer expresses G minor by means of I and V. A possible exception is the tenor entrance in m. 21, which, by means of the B♮ in the bass, emphasizes IV in its opening bars. But it does not fail to make a quick return to I (mm. 24–25). Nor do the episodes provide relief from this insistence on the home key.

The tonal structure, with its alternations of I and V, devoid of obvious cadential goals, comprises an extended prolongation of I followed by the final full authentic cadence IV V I (mm. 34–37). This fugue, like most others prior to those of Bach and Handel, does not transpose the theme to other pitches than those used for the initial subject and answer.[2]

The tonal structure of the composition, then, is restricted to an essential alternation between I and V.

[2] See, for instance, the organ fugues of Buxtehude or those in the organ masses of François Couperin; also the fugue by J. C. F. Fischer in Schering's *Geschichte der Musik in Beispielen* (No. 265) and that by J. Christoph Bach in Karl Geiringer, *Music of the Bach Family*. Cambridge Mass.: Harvard University Press, 1955, pp. 34–35.

In Bach's fugue quite another situation prevails. Episode 2, following the prolonged I of the first exposition, moves into the region of the mediant key (III) and closes there with a perfect authentic cadence. Exposition II expresses III and V/III. The ensuing episode moves on to the subdominant and the first two entries of exposition III dwell on IV. The third entry of this exposition returns to I and comes to a perfect authentic cadence in m. 24 on I. The remainder of the fugue (episode 4, exposition IV, episode 5, and exposition V) maintains this I and closes with another full authentic cadence. The over-all harmonic movement can be summarized as:

$$\text{I} \rightarrow \overset{\displaystyle \overset{\text{II V I}}{\frown}}{\text{of III}} \rightarrow \text{IV} \rightarrow \text{II V I} \rightarrow \text{II V I}$$

EXERCISE

4. Examine the fugue of the preceding exercise from the harmonic point of view:

a. Consider the expositions and episodes individually, noting which chord (or chords) is essentially expressed by each.
b. Compare the relative strengths of the cadences, taking note of any strongly divisive (that is, masculine perfect authentic) cadence.
c. Note the point at which the final perfect authentic cadence takes place. Is there a coda?
d. Make a summary of the tonal structure.

Design

The episodes of Marchand's fugue cannot be said to afford any striking contrast to the expositions. In no fugue, for that matter, is any great contrast, such as often occurs between the first and second parts of a ternary form, to be looked for. The episode of a fugue rarely initiates a new mood or emotional quality, or still less a change of basic rhythmic structure or tempo. The contrast it provides is usually a lightening of the texture by restricting itself to fewer voices, and omission of references to the fugue theme or at least to its opening motive. Far-reaching contrasts are contrary to the continuously flowing, unified nature typical of fugal style.

It will be remembered that a composition divides itself into parts either by completion of more than one harmonic movement or by certain divisive factors in design, such as perfect authentic cadences, or strong contrasts in quality (see Chapter 6). Since most fugues do not exhibit contrasts in quality, the usual basis for division into parts would seem to be completion of more than one harmonic movement or the divisive effect of the perfect authentic cadence. Marchand's fugue, possessing neither of these criteria is, then, a one-part form with the design ABA′B′A″B″. In this scheme, A stands for the expositions, and B for the episodes.

Bach's fugue, on the other hand, is divisible on two accounts. First, two harmonic movements are completed during the course of the fugue, the first at the perfect authentic cadence on I in m. 24, the second at the end of the fugue. In addition, there is an emphatic perfect authentic cadence on III in mm. 11–12. The fugue, then, is in three parts, in an "arched" design.

Part One				Part Two			Part Three			
Ex. I	Ep. 1	Ex. I	Ep. 2	Ex. II	Ep. 3	Ex. III	Ep. 4	Ex. IV	Ep. 5	Ex. V
			(cont.)							
A	B	A	C	A′	B′	A″	C′	A′″	B″	A‴
			II V I of III	III ⟶ IV II V I			I ⟶ II V I			

Part One	Part Two	Part Three
I ⟶ (II V I) of III	III ⟶ IV II V I	I ⟶ II V I

The presence of the divisive authentic cadences does not necessarily inhibit the continuity which seems to be a genuine and regular feature of fugal style. Measure 12 of Ex. 11-22 reveals that the final chord of part one is not released before part two begins. The continuity is even more marked at the point where parts two and three meet.

Ex. 14-16.   BACH: *WTC*, Vol. 1, *Fugue No. 16*

g: V   I

EXERCISES

5. Examine the fugue of the preceding exercises from the point of view of design:

a. Compare and relate the expositions to each other.

b. Compare and relate the episodes to each other.

   c. Compare and relate the expositions with the episodes.

   d. By the use of letters, make a symbolic representation of the design.

6. Using information arrived at by the foregoing exercises, make a chart (similar to that in Section 14-7) representing the form, procedure, design, and tonal structure of the fugue presently under examination.

7. Make a complete analysis (procedure, tonal structure, design, form) of the following fugues:

A   B

a. *WTC, Nos. 21, 22,* or *23*   a. *WTC, No. 21*

14-7. SPECIAL TYPES OF FUGUE

Fugue in contrary motion Many fugues make use of the possibility of inversion at various desirable points in their course. A fugue that makes systematic use of inversion is referred to as a fugue in contrary motion. In this case the answer appears from the start as an inversion of the subject and this inversion recurs during the course of the fugue.

Ex. 14-17. BRAHMS: *Fugue in A flat Minor for Organ*

Double fugue

    Fugues based on two subjects which at some point appear simultaneously are called double fugues. There are two types of double fugue. In the ordinary type, the subjects are associated with each other throughout the fugue, appearing together from the start, and continuing together much as the subject of an ordinary fugue is often associated with its countersubject. Bach was not partial to this type of double fugue, though one of his most famous compositions, the *Passacaglia*, includes one in its final portion. It was used, however, a great deal during the eighteenth century by Italian composers, and also by Haydn and Mozart. The *Kyrie* of Mozart's *Requiem Mass in D Minor* is a famous example. The two subjects are always well contrasted in character and rarely begin exactly together. The theme that begins first is labeled subject I, the one entering later is called subject II.

Ex. 14-18. MOZART: *Fantasy for Mechanical Organ, K. 608*

The other type of double fugue presents the first subject alone before combining it with the second in a simultaneous statement. Thus the first section is a short fugue on subject I, with one or more expositions and episodes. A fugue on subject II follows which may combine the two subjects. Or this second section may be devoted exclusively to subject II in which case a third section presents the two subjects simultaneously.

This larger type of double fugue occurs in the works of certain of J. S. Bach's predecessors and contemporaries, such as Luigi Battiferri and Gottlieb Muffat. Nevertheless, it can be called the "Bachian type" in that examples by great composers other than J. S. Bach are rare. Exceptional cases are Schumann's *Op. 60, No. 6,* and Reger's *Op. 85, No. 4.* A few of Bach's numerous double fugues of this type are *No. 14* and *No. 18* in Vol. 2 of *WTC,* the *Toccata and Fugue in F Major* for organ, and the first part of the *Confiteor* from the *Mass in B Minor.* The organ "fughetta" *Allein Gott in der Höh'* is an interesting case in miniature.

Triple fugue

We have seen that Beethoven uses triple fugue in the development section of his *Symphony No. 9,* First Movement (Ex. 11-13) and it occurs in part two (mm. 146 ff) of the *Scherzo* of his *Quartet, Op. 18, No. 4.* Both of these illustrate the use of fugal procedures within a movement in sonata form. Triple fugues that comprise entire movements in themselves are so seldom found that we can scarcely speak of any preferred procedure. We are limited instead to description of a few specific cases.

Since the ordinary double fugue begins with a simultaneous statement of the two subjects, one might expect a triple fugue to begin with a combined statement of its three subjects. The portions cited from Beethoven's sonata forms begin in this way, and the triple fugue in the *Concerto for Four Violins* by Leonardo Leo follows a similar procedure. Yet a triple fugue of this type is not to be found among Bach's pieces expressly called fugues. Still, he did write one, and it occupies a place in the Vol. 1 of his *Well-Tempered Clavier*—not among the fugues but among the preludes! Prelude *No. 19* in A major turns out on examination to be a triple fugue with the three subjects stated together from the outset (the first note in the bass is to be disregarded).

Ex. 14-19.   BACH: *WTC, Prelude No. 19*

The procedure and form of this fugue can be outlined as follows:

Bars	1–12				12–14	14–24		
Proce-dure	Exp. I	Episode 1	Exp. I (cont.)	Episode 2	Exp. II	Episode 3	Exp. III	Episode 4
Design*	A	B	A	C	A	B C	A	C'
Tonal Structure	I			II V I of VI	I →II V I		→ I	→V I
Form	Part One				Part Two	Part Three		

* In the representation of the design, A indicates the whole complex of the three subjects.

Bach's *Art of the Fugue* contains two triple fugues, *Contrapunctus No. 8* in three voices and *Contrapunctus No. 11* in four. Both of these comprise several parts, and in each case part one presents the aspect of a complete simple fugue on a single subject, the other subjects being kept in reserve for later appearances. Aside from this initial similarity, the forms and procedures of the two fugues, *Nos. 8* and *11*, are very different. Part two of *No. 8* begins as a double fugue on subject I—the theme of part one—combined with a new theme, subject II (m. 39). After five expositions and four episodes this double fugue comes to a semicadence, and subject III (a rhythmic variant of the main theme that runs through the whole volume) enters with an exposition of its own (mm. 94–109). A rather long episode which makes use of fragments of subjects I and II brings part two to a close (m. 124). Thus in neither of the first two parts have the three themes been brought together, though subjects I and II have combined a number of times. Bach postpones the simultaneous presentation of the three subjects until he can do so as a kind of climax to the whole fugue. Even part three does not state them together at first. It begins with subjects I and II combined in a rhythmic position different from that in which they previously appeared together. After two expositions of these subjects and two episodes, the three subjects are combined (m. 147) and from this point on they keep constant company, even though the fugue contains four more expositions and three episodes. The effect of the three subjects is therefore cumulative: In part one of the fugue, subject I appears alone, but in part two it is joined by subject II, and the two themes are thereafter inseparable. Toward the end of part two, subject III (the main theme of the entire work) appears alone, and after observing, as it were, the other two themes from a distance, decides to join them.

In *Contrapunctus No. 11*, subjects I, II, and III are the inversions of subjects III, I, and II, respectively of *No. 8*. Part one is a simple fugue of two expositions and one episode (mm. 1–27). Part two (mm. 27–71) is another simple fugue on subject II which is here constantly accompanied by a fragment of a chromatic scale as countersubject. Part three (mm. 71–89) is comparatively short, comprising a single exposition (four entries) of the inversion of subject I (this inversion of an inversion returns the theme to the position it had in *Contrapunctus No. 8*). Part four (mm. 89–129) is made up of several entries of the three subjects. While II and III appear together, the combination of the three is reserved for part five, but as in *No. 8*, the combination does not appear until this part is well under way (m. 145). An episode based on subject III follows (mm. 150–158) after which Bach makes clear his reason for devoting part three to an exposition of the inversion of subject I. He was preparing the listener for the presentation of this theme simultaneously with its own inversion (mm. 158–162; mm. 164–168). After another episode, the final exposition of the fugue brings two more statements of the three combined subjects (mm. 174–184).

It would seem that the simultaneous presentation of the three subjects at some point in its course is requisite to the triple fugue. Certain theorists, at least, deny the label to Bach's *Organ Fugue in E flat Major* ("St. Ann") even though it possesses three subjects, each with expositions of its own. In part two, subject I appears with subject II, in part three with subject III, but all themes are never stated together. For this reason it has been suggested that this fugue be considered a "double fugue with three subjects."[3]

Fugues with uncertain classifications

Some fugues are difficult to classify with certainty. If a subject is accompanied throughout the fugue with a distinctive countersubject, might not that countersubject be considered in essence a second subject? Thus, in *Fugue No. 2* of *WTC*, Vol. 1, once the second voice has entered, the countersubject appears constantly in the company of the subject. According to some, then, this should be considered a kind of double fugue, and so should a number of other seemingly simple fugues. Similarly, some which might be classed as double fugues are considered by certain theorists, because of a recurring countersubject, to be triple fugues (for example, the final section of the organ *Passacaglia*).

It would seem best, however, not to regard a consistently recurring countersubject as a second or third subject. In a double fugue the listener is forcibly made aware of the presence of subject II—in the ordinary type because it appears from the beginning along with subject I, and in the Bachian type because it is first presented alone in a new fugal exposition. A countersubject, on the other hand, is first heard along with a later entry of the subject and is, for this reason, partially obscured. It is never given an exposition of its own. If the composer expects the listener to recognize a melody as the subject of a piece, he must present it in such a way that the alert listener cannot fail to grasp its significance.

Quadruple and quintuple fugues

Fugues using more than three subjects are almost nonexistent. The Finale of Haydn's *Quartet, Op. 20, No. 2*, is called *"Fuga a IV Soggetti"* but the four subjects never appear together. The final piece of the *Art of the Fugue* was to have been a quadruple fugue. Bach, however, did not live to complete it and the piece breaks off before the entry of the fourth subject.[4] A single example of quintuple fugue exists in the works of the great composers—this

---

[3] Kent Kennan, *Counterpoint.* Englewood Cliffs, N. J.: Prentice-Hall, 1959, p. 193.

[4] Several musicians, among whom are Riemann, Busoni, and Tovey, have ventured to finish it. Without doubt, it is Tovey's version which is the nearest approximation to what Bach must have intended.

is the celebrated fugal coda in the Finale of Mozart's *Symphony No. 41 in C Major.*

Other fugue types

Bach's last work, *The Art of the Fugue,* being a demonstration of the various forms and techniques of fugue writing, includes a number of fugue types that are very rarely met with in other musical literature. A statement in brief of the contents of this work will act as a summary of the fugue types described and add a few others not previously mentioned. It should, perhaps, be pointed out that Bach uses a single theme as the basis for all fourteen fugues of the work, this theme appearing in many interestingly varied forms.[5] He added new themes when necessary for those fugues based on more than one subject and some of these new themes appear in more than one fugue. All fugues except *Nos.* 8 and 12 are in four voices, but Bach made no indication as to instrumentation.

Group I. Simple Fugues.

1. Simple fugue with episodes making use of new material.
2. The same with dotted rhythms.
3. Simple fugue on the inversion of the subject.
4. Simple fugue on the inversion of the subject with episodes derived from the subject.

Group II. Fugues in Contrary Motion.

5. The answer is the inversion of the subject.
6. The answer is the inversion in diminution of the subject.
7. The subject is the diminution of the main subject of the whole work; the first answer is the inversion of the main subject; the second answer is the inversion in diminution; the third answer is the inversion in augmentation.

Group III. Multiple Fugues.

8. Triple fugue on main subject and two new subjects.
9. Double fugue on main subject in augmentation and a new subject.
10. Double fugue on main subject in inversion and a new subject.
11. Triple fugue on subjects of No. 8 in inversion.

Group IV. Invertible Fugues. (An invertible fugue is one which can be played either as written—"rectus"—or with all parts simultaneously exchanged and inverted—"inversus.")

12. Invertible fugue in three voices: in "inversus" the alto becomes the soprano, the bass becomes the alto, the soprano becomes the bass, and the whole is inverted.

[5] In addition to the fugues, Bach composed four canons based on variants of the main theme.

13. Invertible fugue in four voices: in "inversus" the bass becomes the soprano, the tenor becomes the alto, the alto becomes the tenor, the soprano becomes the bass, and the whole is inverted. The effect of this fugue is as if "inversus" were a reflection of "rectus" in a mirror. It is usually referred to as a mirror fugue.

Ex. 14-20.   BACH: *Art of the Fugue, Contrapunctus No. 18*

Group V. Quadruple Fugues.

14. Quadruple fugue on three new subjects, the third beginning B-A-C-H (that is, B♭, A, C, B♮ in German), and the main theme. Left unfinished by Bach at his death.

15. There is good reason to believe that Bach's original intention was to add still another fugue to the work. This was to be an invertible ("mirror") quadruple fugue. To prove the possibility of such a fugue, Tovey composed one using two new subjects, the main theme, and B-A-C-H.

EXERCISE

8. Examine:

A	**B**
a. *WTC, Fugue No. 4*	a. *Art of Fugue, No. 9*

14-8. THE VOCAL FUGUE

A fugue for voices is not basically different from an instrumental fugue in its structure. The great choral fugues which appear in the sacred works of the eighteenth and nineteenth centuries are, however, provided with a more or less independent orchestral accompaniment—more or less because usually a seemingly independent orchestral melody turns out on examination to be only an ornamented version of one of the vocal parts.

In the choral fugue, the orchestra often provides quite a full independent accompaniment in the beginning section of the fugue, where the choral texture contains first only one, then two, then three voices. After all the voices have entered and the choral texture accordingly becomes more complicated, the orchestral accompaniment tends to be less so, providing, say, an ornamented bass line and contenting itself otherwise with little more than a mere doubling of the voice parts.

Occasionally the initial statements of the fugue subject are accompanied not only by the orchestra but by outbursts from the other voices of the chorus (for example, *Patrem Omnipotentem* from *Mass in B Minor* of J. S. Bach).

14-9. THE INVENTION

The thirty short keyboard pieces of J. S. Bach which we refer to today as the *Two-* and *Three-Part Inventions*[6] are similar in some ways to the fugue.

1. Both are polyphonic compositions with a consistent number of "voices" or parts.
2. Both are based on a single theme, normally stated at the outset by each voice in succession,[7] and reappearing at intervals throughout the piece.
3. Both are founded on imitative counterpoint and frequently use tonal as well as real imitation.
4. Both make frequent use of contrapuntal devices such as inversion and double or triple counterpoint.
5. Both are contrapuntal procedures rather than forms.

The chief differences between the invention and the fugue are as follows.

1. The fugue subject is answered at the fifth above (or fourth below); the invention subject is answered either in this way or at the octave.
2. In fugue, the initial statements of the subject are normally unaccompanied;

[6] Bach called those in two parts *Praeambula* or *Invenzioni*; those in three parts *Fantasias* or *Sinfonie*.
[7] Exceptions are No. 2 and No. 5 of the *Three-Part Inventions*.

in the three-part inventions, and usually in the two-part inventions, these statements are accompanied by a counterpoint in the lowest voice.

3. Very short themes, hardly more than motives, are more common in the inventions than in fugues. These motivelike subjects are generally heard in almost every bar of the invention.

4. The fugue is an instrumental or vocal genre; the invention is for a keyboard instrument.

Bach used the idea of the invention for other compositions. The four duets from Part III of the *Clavierübung* and the *Prelude No. 13* from *WTC*, Vol. 1 are two-part inventions. The three movements of *Organ Sonata No. 1* are very much like three-part inventions.

EXERCISE

9.

<table>
<tr><th>A</th><th>B</th></tr>
<tr>
<td>a. Examine the *Two-* and *Three-Part Inventions* of J. S. Bach. Analyze one or more of them.</td>
<td>a. Analyze one or both: Bach: *Invention IV*. Bach: *WTC*, Vol. 2, *Prelude 20*.</td>
</tr>
</table>

14-10. THE FRENCH OVERTURE

During the seventeenth century the Venetian opera was distinguished by a certain type of overture consisting of two parts, a slow part followed by a fast one. This overture became the model on which Lully based the overtures to his operas written for the entertainment of the French royalty in the latter part of the seventeenth century, and it is therefore referred to as a French overture. In Lully's overtures, the slow part is characterized by dotted rhythms giving the effect of pompous solemnity. The fast part begins with imitation in the various voices, a partially fugal texture rather than a real fugue. Often this movement broadens out toward the end in an *allargando*.

Many eighteenth-century composers continued to write French overtures, both as introductions to their operas and oratorios and as the first movement of instrumental suites. Virtually all of Handel's operas and oratorios, for example, open with a French overture, that to *Messiah* being, no doubt, the most frequently performed. Bach, too, though he wrote no operas and no real oratorios, has composed French overtures, among which the opening of his *Suite in B Minor for Flute and Strings*[8] is a celebrated example.

[8] In eighteenth-century terminology, suites that begin with a French overture are called simply "overtures" though in reality they are overtures followed by a series of dances. Hence, Bach's title for his suite is *H moll Ouverture à 1 Flauto, 2 Violini, Viola e Basso*.

By the eighteenth century fugal procedures had reached a higher stage of development than in the seventeenth century, and we find the fast part of the French overture taking on more and more the appearance of a true fugue. The Overture to *Messiah,* for instance, contains a genuine Handelian fugue. He continues the seventeenth-century practice of broadening the final few bars to prepare the movement for its close. Some composers during the eighteenth century made this *allargando* at the end of the fugal portion much larger, producing the effect of a second slow movement. This practice has

Outline Summary of Bach's Suite No. 2, Overture, Fugal Movement

Bars	21–55	55–78	78–94	94–102	102–119
Procedure (concerto aspect)	RI	S1	R2	S2	R3
Procedure (fugal aspect)	Ex. I Ep. (4 entries) Ex. II Ep. (1 entry)	First solo episode	Ex. III Ep. (2 entries)	Second solo episode	Ex. IV (4 entries)
Design	A	B	A	C	A
Tonal Structure	I → V I	I → V_6 I of III	I → VI of III	III → V/IV	IV → I
Form	Part One	Part Two		Part Three	

Bars	119–143	143–151	151–174	175–198
Procedure (concerto aspect)	S3 (with tutti interjections at mm. 127 and 137)	R4	S4	R5
Procedure (fugal aspect)	Third solo episode (with tutti interjections at mm. 127 and 137)	Ex. V (1 entry, altered)	Fourth solo episode	Ex. VI Ep. (1 entry) Ex. VII Ep. (1 entry)
Design	B' (A)	A'	C	A
Tonal Structure	I → V/IV	IV → V	I → V^6_5 I	(deceptive cadence in m. 186) I → V_7 V^4_2/IV IV_6 → V I
Form	Part Three (cont.)			

given rise to the opinion that the French overture has three movements: slow, fast, slow. In actuality, this final slow part does not appear often enough to justify such a view, though Bach used the idea in his *Suite for Flute and Strings*.

The fugal portion of this suite deserves some discussion for it presents an interesting case of the form of a composition being influenced by its medium. The fact that Bach uses a single flute with a body of strings would suggest at once that he probably has designed it as a showpiece of some kind for the flute. The music bears out this contention. While the opening slow movement of the overture, a continuous binary form using Lully's dotted rhythms, lets the flute double the first violins, the fugal portion is constructed to show the flute off to best advantage. Naturally the weak tone of a flute could not hope to hold its own as one of the voices in a fugue against a body of strings. Therefore Bach designs this portion to be a cross between a fugue and a *concerto grosso*. The fugal expositions are entrusted to the orchestral ritornellos as are some of the episodes. Other episodes are given to the solo sections. The third solo section is twice interrupted by tutti interjections which refer to the fugue subject but do not present it in its entirety as full-fledged entries. These interjections may have been provided by Bach for physical as well as musical reasons, for they give the struggling flutist a sorely needed chance to breathe.

14-11. THE CHORALE PRELUDE

The chorale prelude is simply a sacred melody arranged to be played, usually on the organ, rather than to be sung. For Catholic services this tune is either a plainsong hymn or a segment of some other plainsong melody. For Protestant services it is a chorale, usually one of the German chorales of the Lutheran Church. Its place in the Protestant service was originally to precede the actual singing of the hymn, hence its familiar name chorale prelude, although it was sometimes also performed after the hymn or between stanzas. Today such compositions are performed independently of congregational singing.

The chorale prelude bears the following resemblances to the fugue:

1. It is normally a polyphonic composition with a consistent number of "voices," usually four, not infrequently two, three, or five, occasionally six.
2. Imitative counterpoint (real imitation, tonal imitation, canon) plays an important role.
3. It is not a form; any chorale prelude may exhibit one of the standard forms or have a unique form of its own.

The chief types of chorale prelude are listed below.

1. *Simple chorale prelude.* In this type of setting the chorale is presented

in one of the voices, not necessarily the soprano, and surrounded or supported by the others. These accompanying voices are almost always motivic, that is, based on one or two motives which recur by means of repetition, sequence, and imitation. The chief motive or motives on which the accompaniment is based may be either derived from the chorale or newly invented.

2. *Chorale prelude with ritornellos.* The idea of a regular recurring passage, familiar to us from the baroque aria and concerto, also found a place in the organ chorale prelude. The piece begins with a ritornello, either contrapuntal in texture or not, and the successive phrase or phrase members of the chorale are separated by its return. Very often the melody of the ritornello, or motives derived from it, appears as accompaniment against the chorale tune.

3. *Chorale prelude with prelude and interludes.* The various phrases of the chorale may be preceded and separated not by a recurrence of the same material, as in the ritornello, but with different material. In this case the intervening sections are almost sure to be derived in one way or another from the chorale melody. Brahms provides some interesting organ chorale preludes of this type (*Op. 122, Nos. 4, 7, 10, 11*).

4. *Chorale prelude with fugal expositions (the chorale motet).* The technique of this type is similar to the vocal motet technique of the sixteenth century, one of the forerunners of the fugue. The first phrase of the chorale serves as the subject for a short fugal exposition. Sometimes all voices participate in this exposition. Usually, however, one voice is reserved to present the phrase intact, as the last entrance. A second exposition, treating the second phrase similarly, follows, and so on through all phrases of the chorale. Often the theme of each fugal exposition is a variant rather than the original form of the chorale melody (for example, Brahms, *Op. 122, No. 1*).

5. *Chorale fugue.* Sometimes rather than using the whole melody, the opening notes of the chorale are chosen as the subject for a fugue or *fughetta* (a "little fugue").

6. *Chorale fantasia.* The chorale fantasia is a piece which is not a setting of a pre-existing melody but a free composition making use of portions of such a melody. The most famous example is undoubtedly Bach's *In Dir ist Freude* from the *Orgelbüchlein*.

7. *Groups of organ chorale preludes.* Not infrequently, two or three settings of a single chorale are grouped together, usually marked Verse 1, Verse 2, and so on. Often in these cases, each setting reflects the text of a particular stanza. When a larger number of settings of a single chorale are grouped together, they are generally entitled *chorale variations* or *chorale partita*. In this case, too, the suggestion for each successive variation normally comes from the text.

One of Bach's final works was a set of *Canonic Variations on a Christmas Song*. It consists of five chorale preludes on *Von Himmel Hoch*, each demonstrating a different type of canonic writing.

8. *The Vocal Chorale*. The technique of the organ chorale prelude also occurs in vocal music, especially in the great choruses of Bach's cantatas and passions. Sometimes while the chorale is sung by the chorus, either in unison or four parts, the orchestra is given an elaborate, independent accompaniment. A unique example of this type of vocal chorale prelude is found in the Finale to the Act II of Mozart's *Magic Flute*. Using an old German hymn tune, *Ach Gott, vom Himmel sieh' darein,* to which he added a final phrase, Mozart gives the tune to two men in armor who sing it (with new words) in octaves. Against this the orchestra plays an accompaniment based on two motives, also providing ritornellos between phrases. This type of vocal chorale is analogous to the organ chorale prelude with ritornellos.

EXERCISE

10.

<table>
<tr><td align="center">**A**</td><td align="center">**B**</td></tr>
<tr><td>Examine, classify, and analyze chorale preludes by Bach or any from the following collections:</td><td>Examine, classify, and analyze:</td></tr>
<tr><td>a. Couperin: *Messe Solemnelle* (first, second, and last *Kyrie*, first *Sanctus*, first *Agnus*)</td><td>a. Bach: *Wenn wir in höchsten*</td></tr>
<tr><td>b. Brahms: *Eleven Chorale Preludes, Op. 122*</td><td>b. Bach: *Vor deinen Thron*</td></tr>
<tr><td>c. Hindemith: *Organ Sonata No. 3,* each of the three movements</td><td>c. Bach: *Jesu meine Freude,* Fifth Movement</td></tr>
</table>

14-12. SUMMARY

Due to the variety of forms exhibited by the fugues of the great composers of the tonal era, the fugue cannot be considered a form at all. It is, rather, a musical genre for instruments, voices, or both, with the following characteristics:

1. It comprises a constant number of melodic lines, referred to as "voices" or "parts," which state and develop a theme by contrapuntal imitation.

2. The theme, or subject, is imitated either by real or by tonal imitation. The imitation, called the answer, has in the latter case a different melodic contour from the original subject, especially in the opening notes. Both versions of the theme are apt to be used throughout the fugue.

3. Often, particularly as the fugue is nearing its close, the imitating voices begin before the preceding statement of the theme has been completed. The result, an overlapping of the theme upon itself, is termed stretto. Other

contrapuntal devices frequently occurring are inversion, double, and triple counterpoint.

4. Occasionally fugues are written in which the theme is constantly sounding in at least one of the voices. But most fugues make use of episodes—passages from which the theme is absent.

Special types of fugue include (1) the fugue by contrary motion, (2) the double fugue, and (3) the triple fugue. Of these the double fugue is by far the most frequently found. Ordinarily Bach gives each of the two subjects of his double fugues an exposition of its own before combining them in a simultaneous statement. Other composers, such as Handel and Mozart, present the two subjects together from the start.

There are several musical genres that are more or less closely related to the fugue. The invention presents and develops a single subject by imitative counterpoint, often using tonal imitation. The French overture includes a fugal movement within its over-all movement scheme. The chorale prelude depends largely on imitative counterpoint, maintains a consistent number of melodic lines, and often includes fuguelike expositions by tonal imitation.

15

Unique Forms

Historical Note on Unique Forms Unique forms are commonly found in every era of music history. Baroque genres in which they frequently occur are the fantasias and toccatas for organ or harpsichord. During the rococo and classical periods they were particularly common in keyboard fantasias, such as those by C. P. E. Bach and Mozart. Much music of the nineteenth century displays nonstandard forms, including the many program symphonies, opera preludes, and symphonic poems that appear so regularly on our concert programs. For instance, each movement of Berlioz' *Symphonie Fantastique* except the second is unique in form. And opera, oratorio, and other vocal music abound in such unique forms. Of particular interest are the unique composite forms of the lengthy finales to the individual acts of a classical opera.

While many composers of the first half of this century have tended to rely heavily on standard forms of the past (Ravel, Hindemith, Berg, Bartók, Prokofiev) the trend in recent years, among composers of the greatest variance in styles, is toward the creation of compositions that display formal singularity.

15-1. STANDARD AND UNIQUE FORMS

In expressing his musical thoughts the composer is free to make use of pre-existing forms or to invent new ones. In addition, as we have seen, he can use established forms but modify them, adapting them to his needs. So far we have dealt, with the exception of the chapter on fugue, only with standard forms—those which are the common property of a number of composers and which with certain modifications recur again and again in their works.

In this chapter we shall concern ourselves with forms which occur in isolated cases, forms not regularly used which were created especially for par-
282

ticular compositions. Clearly a mere description of a unique form is applicable only to the single work in which the form appears and would in itself be of little use to us in this study. However, to consider the *causes* for the unique aspect shown by various special forms would be profitable.

We speak of a standard form when both design and tonal structure conform in their general outlines to a pattern that occurs often enough in music literature to receive recognition as established. But should one of these elements, say the design of a work, be constructed in a way essentially different from the norm, the piece will have a nonstandard form even if this design is applied to an established tonal structure. If, for instance, a three-part form has the design ABC (as in Schubert's *Winterreise No. 11*) it is not to be considered one of the standard ternaries whatever its tonal structure, for the standard ternaries are in design laid out as ABA. Conversely, some works bear frequently used designs but these are applied to a unique tonal structure. Here, too, the result will be a special form. There are in addition other procedures that result in nonstandard forms. In this chapter several compositions that illustrate these various methods will come under scrutiny.

15-2. COMBINATION OF STANDARD FORMS INTO A UNIQUE COMPOSITE FORM

Brahms' *Rhapsody, Op. 53,* is a setting of part of Goethe's *Harzreise im Winter* ("Winter Journey in the Harz") for contralto solo, men's chorus, and orchestra. Against the background of snowy desolate mountain scenery, the poem contrasts the natural happiness of a band of hunters with the bitter loneliness of the misanthrope. From this ode Brahms selected for musical treatment those stanzas which make up the chief picture of the misanthrope. Each of the three stanzas presents him from a different point of view. In the first he is seen from without, the second stanza reveals his inner self, and in the third he is the recipient of a prayer for grace.

> But who is it there apart?
> His way is lost in the thicket,
> Behind him the branches clash together,
> The grass rises again,
> The waste land devours him.
>
> Ah, who can heal his pain
> For whom balm has become poison,
> Who has drunk hatred of mankind
> From the fullness of love?

Once the scorned, now the scorner,
Unknowingly he consumes his own worth
Through insufficient self-concern.

If on Thy psalter, Father of Love,
There be one tone audible to his ear,
Revive his heart!
Open his darkened eyes
To the myriad springs
Beside the thirsty one in the desert.

Brahms has chosen to reflect these three aspects in the form of the music and the result is three relatively independent parts, unified only by general mood and by identity of key: C, minor mode, changing at stanza 3 to major.

Part one divides into two sections. The first is given to orchestra alone and seems to be a musical representation of the scene described in the first stanza. It is a phrase group that moves from I to a secondary tonic on V. The second section is given to the alto soloist who sings the words in an arioso style, while the orchestra sounds an expanded version of section 1. The basic tonal structure of both sections is the same, as is the basic design. Section 2, being a varied repetition of section 1, adds nothing essential to the form. The rhapsody, then, begins with a one-part form and its varied repetition.

The second stanza is treated by Brahms as a continuous ternary form (ABA'), the first section comprising the initial four lines, and the middle section the last three lines. The return to the opening section is accomplished by repeating the first four lines in the manner of a *da capo* aria. The repetition of these lines, far from making nonsense of the poem—as occasionally happens when careless composers attempt the trick—actually points up with increased clarity the connection between the second and third stanzas. The reiterated question "who can heal his pain . . . ?" leads with great plausibility into the third stanza's prayer.

Since part two is not to be the final part of the work, the harmonic movement does not complete itself as in an independent continuous ternary form. Rather, like part one, it moves from I to a secondary tonic on V. A short transition provides a bridge to the third and final part.

In the third stanza the men's chorus is heard for the first time. As in the second stanza, the opening lines are here repeated to make possible a ternary form, and by further repetitions of the line "revive his heart" Brahms manages to have words for a coda.

The first section of part three is a complete harmonic movement ending with a perfect authentic cadence on I. Section 2 leads by descending thirds through ♭III and VII to V, then to V_7 and back to I for the return of the opening as section 3. Part three, then, is a sectional ternary (A-BA). The coda uses material from both A and B.

Outline Summary of Brahms' Rhapsody, Op. 53

Bars	Division	Design	Tonal Structure
1–47	Part One: initial part (one-part form, repeated)	A	$I \rightarrow VII_7$ I $\underbrace{\quad}$ of V (Minor)
1–18	Section 1: orchestral statement	a	$I \rightarrow VII_7$ I $\underbrace{\quad}$ of V (Minor)
18–47	Section 2: solo statement, varied repetition	a	$I \rightarrow VII_7$ I $\underbrace{\quad}$ of V (Minor)
48–115	Part Two: middle part (continuous ternary form)	B	$I \rightarrow V_7$–I $\underbrace{\quad}$ of V
48–69	Section 1: part one	a	$I \rightarrow VI$
69–73	Section 2: transition		$VI \rightarrow VII_7/VI$
73–90	Section 3: part two	b	$VI \rightarrow V_7$
90–108	Section 4: part three	a'	$I \rightarrow V_7$ I $\underbrace{\quad}$ of V
108–115	Section 5: transition		$V–V_7–V^6_5$
116–175	Part Three: closing part (sectional ternary form)	C	$I \rightarrow V_7$ I (Major)
116–127	Section 1: part one	a	$I \rightarrow V_7$ I
128–141	Section 2: part two	b	V_7 I V_7 I V_7 I of ♭III of VII of V
141–145	Section 3: retransition		$V \rightarrow V_7$
146–156	Section 4 (= sec. 1): part three (= one)	a	$I \rightarrow V_7$ I
157–175	Coda	ba	$V_7/♭III \rightarrow IV$ I

Taken as a whole the tonal structure of the three parts can be succinctly expressed as I→ V, I →V, I → V-I, and the design as ABC. The rhapsody shows a composite continuous form in three parts, but since part three is not in any sense a restatement of part one, there is no analogy here with the standard continuous ternary form, or with any of the composite ternaries. Rather, the form is unique, having grown out of the particular situation for which it was created—the musical expression of the selected stanzas of Goethe's poem.

Another formal masterpiece achieved through a combination of various standard forms is the Finale to Act I of Rossini's *The Barber of Seville*. The form here grows out of the dramatic situation, and yet Rossini has so fashioned it that it is perfectly intelligible as pure music. The four large parts into which it divides itself correspond in quality but not in form to the usual four movements of a symphony. Unlike most symphonies, however, the Finale has transitions which connect these movements.

Part one: first movement, *marziale* (Count, "*Ehi di casa!*") I
    transition (Rosina, "*Ecco qua*") $I \rightarrow V_3^4/\flat III$
Part two: scherzo, *allegro* (Figaro, "*Che cosa accadde*") $\flat III \rightarrow V I$
    transition (chorus, "*Fermi tutti*") $I \rightarrow V$
Part three: slow movement, *largo* (Rosina, "*Freddo ed immo-* $\flat VI$
    bile")
    transition (orchestral, two bars) $\flat VI \rightarrow V_7$
Part four: finale, *allegro* I
    1. Introduction (recalling first movement)
    2. Movement proper (Sextet, "*Mi par d'esser*")

Taken as a whole, the tonal structure has involved a move from I up a third to $\flat III$, a return to I, a move down a third to $\flat VI$ and a return to I. The design, ignoring the transitions, is A-BC-D. Though the entire finale can be labeled a sectional composite four-part form, it has nothing to do with the standard four-part form which has an entirely different tonal structure and design (see Section 6-6).

15-3. DESIGN OF ONE STANDARD FORM COMBINED WITH TONAL STRUCTURE OF DIFFERENT STANDARD FORM

The Prelude to Handel's *Suite in E Major* for harpsichord is given as Ex. 15-1. The first two bars, virtually in one voice, are an introductory phrase. Beginning with the last quarter-note value of m. 2, the musical texture flows uninterruptedly, linking the phrases or avoiding an expected cadence in such a way that the entire piece shows a remarkable coherence. The endings of phrases 1 and 2 are obscured by the sixteenth-note movement in the alto voice, and the third phrase is extended to great length by avoiding the expected cadence in m. 16. The tonal structure is basically a move from I to a secondary tonic on V and a return to I with a brief secondary tonic on IV. Judging from the single harmonic movement and the absence of conclusive cadences within the composition, one would conclude that it is a normal one-part form. But a comparison of the thematic content of the four chief phrases of the piece shows that they are related in a way which recalls a different standard form. The second phrase is a transposed repetition of the first, while the others in spite of motivic resemblances differ from the previous two. The design, then, is AA′B, a clear reference to the design of the barform. The prelude cannot be considered a real barform which, being a type of sectional binary, has a different tonal structure (see Section 6-4). We have, rather, a unique form: one part, because of the tonal structure and absence of divisive cadences, but designed like the barform.

Ex. 15-1.   HANDEL: *Suite in E Major, Prelude*

15-4. STANDARD DESIGN APPLIED TO UNIQUE
TONAL STRUCTURE

Debussy's preludes contain a number of interesting and unusual forms.
Prelude No. 10 ("The Engulfed Cathedral") from the first volume is selected
here because it demonstrates the technique of providing a unique tonal
structure with a commonly used design. In this case the design is ABAB.

Ex. 15-2.   DEBUSSY: *Prelude No. 10* ("The Engulfed Cathedral"),
themes

Used with the authorization of Durand & Cie, Editeurs-
propriétaires, Paris, copyright owners; Elkan-Vogel Co.,
Inc., Philadelphia, Pa., agents.

The work opens with introductory chords using motive a. Then theme A,
a melody that includes three appearances of motive a in augmentation, is
stated. The introductory chords reappear to close the section, after which a
transition leads to the second section, a statement of theme B. The transition
uses motive a and anticipates theme B by emphasizing the descending scale
fragment, motive c. Theme A then returns with a short development of
motive a in its augmented version. Finally, theme B is restated and a short
coda, beginning with the introductory chords (motive a) and continuing
with motive b (from theme A) in the left hand, concludes the work. There is
nothing extraordinary in the design itself. It is only when the tonal structure

is viewed in conjunction with this design that the singularity of the form can be appreciated. Here is the harmonic outline.

Ex. 15-3. DEBUSSY: *Prelude No. 10* (harmonic outline)

The opening harmonies begin on V and move stepwise down to I. Halfway through this progression, on III, theme A is stated. The tonality of theme A is ambiguous. Taken alone it seems to imply the Dorian mode, transposed to C♯. As presented here, however, the theme is stated with an inner pedal point on E. The listener hears the theme as expressing the major mode of the mediant key, and the A♯'s are understood as implying V/V in that key. This E major is, of course, but a temporary secondary tonic on III and the movement continues down to I. The transition begins by dropping a half step to VII from which it leaps upward in two jumps of a major third each to V, soon expressed as a ninth chord with omitted third, in preparation for theme B which enters on I. At the conclusion of B a short transition follows in which the bass moves down two whole steps to ♭VI changing enharmonically from the note A♭ to G♯. This G♯ becomes a pedal point underlying the second presentation of theme A. The tonal ambiguity of this theme is again utilized, for without transposition of the theme itself, Debussy makes it sound as if it were expressing the key of G♯ minor, that is, the low submediant (by enharmonic change) of the tonality of the whole work. This ♭VI pedal point remains throughout the development of motive a, whereupon it moves to I. Theme B appears for the second time on I, closing the harmonic movement. The coda prolongs I.

Though unusual, the resulting form is entirely logical: sectional binary with the design AB-A′B. Theme A is first heard on III, that is, a major third above I; after B has expressed I, Theme A is heard again, untransposed but this time expressing ♭VI, a major third below I; the final return of B is again on I. The two statements of B are like a tonic pivot which balances the two statements of A presented at equidistant points above and below.

It may be pertinent here to point out the reason for the omission of any remarks regarding the shape of the prelude: How the various sonorities, motives, and themes gradually build so that. the listener seems to see the mysterious cathedral rising from the depths of the sea and sinking again beneath the waves. The shape of the prelude, the title, and the images evoked in the listener's mind by the knowledge of the legend behind the title, are not without significance to the musician as performer or listener. But these extra-musical factors are not in the province of the musician in his capacity as analyst. An understanding of the form of a textless piece of music comes about only by preoccupation with the music itself as the composer left it, not by speculation about what he was attempting to express through the music, valuable and interesting as that speculation may be.

The work to be discussed next is Richard Strauss' tone poem, *Don Juan,* *Op. 23,* the composition of which seems to have depended to a large extent on certain dramatic incidents and concepts of a psychological and philosophi-cal nature in Lenau's poem. But, as in the case of the Debussy prelude, in our rôle as analysts we must direct our attention solely to the music.

15-5. UNIQUE DESIGN APPLIED TO STANDARD TONAL STRUCTURE

Ex. 15-4. STRAUSS: *Don Juan* (themes and motives)

Richard Strauss' tone poem, *Don Juan*, contains a large number of themes and motives that are presented in Ex. 15-4. See the outline summary below.

Outline Summary of Strauss' Don Juan

Bars	Division	Function	Design	Tonal Structure
1–168	Part One	Exposition	Themes A, B, C, D	I → V–I of V → V_7
1–40	Sec. 1	PT	A B A' abcdef c" cf dec" ab	♭VI–V–I → V_7–I
40–89	Sec. 2	Transition	g (anticipatory), C, i, h (anticipatory), various motives from sec. 1	I → V/V
89–149	Sec. 3	ST	D hj	I → V_7 → IV♭ of V
149–168	Sec. 4	Transition	h, A	IV♭/V → V_7
168–196	Part Two	Development	B	♭VI → VII/♭III
197–314	Part Three	Episode	E, F	I → V_7 I of ♭ III
197–231	Sec. 1	Intro.	E with interjections of e and c	I → V_7 ‖ I → VII^4_3 I of ♭ III ♭
232–296	Sec. 2	Quasi-slow movement	F accompanied by k	I → V_7 ‖ I → V_7 ‖ I → V_7 I of ♭ III ♮
296–314	Sec. 3	Codetta and link	k	♭ III (= V/♭VI)
314–567	Part Four	Development and Recap.	G plus all previous themes except E	♭ VI → V_7 ‖ I → V_7 I

Outline Summary of Strauss' Don Juan (Continued)

Bars	Division	Design	Tonal Structure
314–350 Sec. 1	Development	G (derived from F?), F in diminution, A	♮VI → V/V
351–386 Sec. 2	Development (Scherzo)	i, G (free diminution), A	♮VII → V₇/VI
386–424 Sec. 3	Development	H (from d and c) with new motive n, in combination with G	VI → IV → V₇
424–473 Sec. 4	Retransition	Restatement of C, D, F; abc in combination with n	V → V₇ (pedal point on V)
474–567 Sec. 5	Recapitulation	A abbreviated to abc, B in combination with n, G developing and intertwining with l and m, A, B, final phrase like that of part one, section 1	♮VI–V–I → V₇ I
567–606 Coda	Coda	c′, new figuration, I	I → V₇ IV → I
566–585 Sec. 1		c′, new figuation	I → V₇
586–606 Sec. 2		New figuration, I related by inversion to k (also to D, F, and G?)	IV → I♭

For greater ease in comprehending the essential tonal structure of this complex work, a succinct harmonic outline is presented in Ex. 15-5.

Ex. 15-5. STRAUSS: *Don Juan* (harmonic outline)

The outline shows the establishment of I (E major) followed by a modulation to V (B major) succeeded by a V_7. This V_7 is prolonged by chord succession which, like Ex. 10-3 (see also Ex. 10-4), shows a succession within a succession: a prolongation of $\flat$VI (C major) by means of its V (G minor-major). Following the V_7 is a return to the beginning and a complete harmonic movement on I. The basic tonal structure, then, is that of the standard sonata form: I → V–V_7 ‖ I → V_7 I. But in design the work is quite different. The first part, corresponding to the exposition of a sonata form is, it is true, similar in most respects to the exposition of many sonata forms, nor is the insertion of new material into the development section in itself enough to disqualify it from being considered a sonata-form development. But the great length of the G minor-major episode, its complete harmonic movement, its perfect authentic cadences, and its codetta, combine to stamp it clearly upon the listener's mind as a part in itself, not a subsection within a sonata-form development. Another difference in design is the fact that the recapitulation completes the interrupted harmonic movement with a theme (G) which made its first appearance not in the exposition but in the development, while no theme of the exposition other than A and B is to be heard during the recapitulation.

The tone poem is a continuous four-part form with coda having the over-all design AA′BA″ arrived at by the grouping:

A	A′	B	A″
(Part One)	(Part Two)	(Part Three)	(Part Four)
A, B, C, D	B	E, F	G, H, C, D, F, A, B, G–(I)

The work can also be conceived, though not with strict accuracy, as a gigantic sonata form in which a lengthy episode has been inserted into the development section and which, in the secondary section of the recapitulation, substitutes for the original secondary theme a new theme first heard in the development. This conception of the work brings up a perplexing question. When a form bears certain strong resemblances to a standard form but also differs from the norm in important ways, is it to be considered a unique form with certain characteristics of the standard form, or should it be thought of as a modified version of that standard form? Only the pedant would insist on a cut-and-dried rule regarding this question for if the design and tonal structure of the music are understood, it is of no great import what formal label is given the piece. Nevertheless, if a decision is desired, it would seem best to consider whether the form in question is of the same general type as the standard form which it resembles. For instance, we have said that Strauss' *Don Juan* cannot "with strict accuracy" be considered a modified version of sonata form. The reasoning behind this statement is that the standard sonata form is a type of continuous binary. Since the G minor-major episode in *Don Juan* has all the characteristics of a part in itself, the work is not in two parts but four. This

fact makes it impossible to consider it a real sonata form, even a highly modified one, in spite of its other similarities. Another example is the first movement of Mahler's *Symphony No. 4*, which has all the earmarks of sonata
form except the essential one of being a continuous binary. Since the exposition makes a complete harmonic movement, closing on I (mm. 97–101),
the form is an immense sectional binary, and therefore unique, not a modified
version of sonata form.

15-6. DESIGN AND TONAL STRUCTURE BOTH UNIQUE

Ex. 15-6. CHOPIN: *Ballade in G Minor, Op.* 23 (themes)

Chopin's well-known *Ballade in G Minor* makes use of neither a standard
tonal structure nor a standard design. Below is an outline summary of the form
and Ex. 15-7 is a harmonic outline of the basic tonal structure.

Outline Summary of Chopin's Ballade, Op. 23

Bars	Division	Design	Tonal Structure
1–7	Introduction	Independent phrase	$\flat$II → V
8–56	Part One	A, B, and codetta	V_7 I → V_7 I

Outline Summary of Chopin's Ballade, Op. 23 (Continued)

Bars	Division	Design	Tonal Structure
8–36	Sec. 1	A (motive a)	V_7 I → IV_6 V_7 I
36–44	Sec. 2	B	I → V_7 I
44–56	Sec. 3	Codetta	I–IV–I
56–67	Transition	anticipates C	I → V/V $\underbrace{\quad}$ of VI
68–90	Part Two	C, D	V_9 I → V_7 I $\underbrace{\qquad}$ of VI
68–82	Sec. 1	C	V_9 I → V_7 I $\underbrace{\qquad}$ of VI
82–90	Sec. 2 (codetta)	D (motive a)	I–$IV^{6\flat}_{4}$–I $\underbrace{\qquad}$ of VI
90–94	Transition	motive a	VI → V/II
94–165	Part Three (Quasi-development)	A', C, E	V_7 I V_7 I → V^4_3/V $\underbrace{\quad}$ of II → $\underbrace{\quad}$ of VI
94–105	Sec. 1	A'	V_7/II
106–125	Sec. 2	C	V_7 I $\underbrace{\quad}$ of II → II_7/VI
126–137	Sec. 3	New (quasi-cadenza)	V_7/VI
138–165	Sec. 4	E (accompaniment begins like that of B)	I → V^4_3/V $\underbrace{\quad}$ of VI
166–188	Part Four	Varied repetition of part two	(Same as that of part two)
166–180	Sec. 1	C	(Same as that of part two)
180–188	Sec. 2 (codetta)	D (motive a)	(Same as that of part two)
188–194	Transition	motive a (like transition mm. 90–94)	VI → V
194–208	Part Five	A' (like part three, sec. 1)	V_7 → I
208–262	Coda	New material, motive a	I → V_7 I
208–248	Sec. 1	F	I → V_7 I
248–262	Sec. 2	Motive a, scales	I

Ex. 15-7. CHOPIN: *Ballade in G Minor, Op. 23* (harmonic outline)

This *Ballade* is a unique type of sectional five-part form. Its over-all design [A-B-Dev. B-A'—(C)] is arrived at by the following grouping:

A	B	Development	B	A'	(C)
(Part	(Part	(Part	(Part	(Part	
One)	Two)	Three)	Four)	Five)	(Coda)
A, B	C, D	A', C, E	C, D	A'	F

At first glance this would seem to be somewhat like the "arch" design of Bach's *Fugue No. 16* in G minor from *WTC* (see Section 14-16); Chopin's *Waltz, Op. 34, No. 1*; and Brahms' *Rhapsody, Op. 119, No. 4* (see Section 8-8). This view of the design might be plausible if part five resembled part one to a greater extent. But although both are based on theme A there is little similarity between them. On the other hand, part five is an almost exact transposition of section 1 of part three. Such a close tie between the two re-statements of theme A, both standing in opposition to the original statement, effectively destroys any resemblance to an arch which the design might other-wise have displayed.

Part three, though labeled in the outline summary "quasi-development" has, except for section 1, nothing to do with the motivic development char-acteristic of many development sections of the classical composers. But, as we have seen, some developments of the classical composers are, like this one, occupied with presenting either new material or previously heard material transposed intact to a new key.

The unique aspect of the tonal structure of Chopin's *Ballade in G Minor* lies not in its initial delay of the tonic chord, but in the lengthy chord succes-sion which prolongs VI through parts two, three, and four. The harmony of part five, too, is remarkable, for in its essence it expresses no more than a drawn-out V_7 followed by I.

15-7. SUMMARY

The means of achieving a unique form are summarized as follows:

1. Standard design; standard tonal structure of different form
2. Standard design; unique tonal structure
3. Unique design; standard tonal structure
4. Unique design; unique tonal structure
5. Unique composite of standard forms

The student who makes the effort to discover for himself the characteristics of some of the unique forms will be richly rewarded, for he will gain an insight into the workings of the composer's mind which cannot be acquired by other means.

EXERCISE

1. Analyze some or all of the following music. If unique forms are discovered, indicate the specific factors that have brought about this unique quality.

A	B
a. *WJ, Nos. 5, 11, 16*	a. Wagner: Prelude to *Tristan*
b. *WTC, Preludes No. 9* and *21*	b. Wolf, *In dem Schatten meiner Locken*
c. Chopin: *Prelude No. 24*	c. Debussy: *L'après-midi d'un faune*
d. *MF, No. 3*	d. Mozart: *Fantasia, K. 475*
	e. Schubert: *Erlkönig*
	f. Brahms: *Intermezzo, Op. 119, No. 3*

16

Retrospection

The ancient principle of variety in unity emphasizes that a worthy work of art will inevitably contain a number of diverse elements which cohere to form a single impression in the mind of the beholder. "How all's to one thing wrought!" There can be little doubt about which single factor does most toward achieving unity in tonal music: It is the utilization of the twelve tones in such a way that a set of relationships emerges among them, relationships that point out to the listener a single tone as center.

From another point of view the action might be looked at the other way round: to see the composition as something which has developed from a single tone. A seed is, to all appearances, almost insignificant. Yet, over a period of time, it develops by the processes of nature into the complex organism we call a flower or tree. A single tone, too, may seem almost nothing compared to a symphony. But the great compositions of the recent past have, in the last analysis, "grown" from a single tone, the keynote.

A tone, because of the implication of its overtones, can give rise to a series of chords which are dependent on that tone and which group themselves about it as planets, to use a different analogy, do around a sun. By the phenomenon of secondary tonics and the process of modulation, a composer can focus interest on any of these "planets" in turn, making it act as a temporary "sun" surrounded by its own "planets." A series of chords, then, or what we call the harmonic movement, can either remain within the orbit of the original tonal center or appear to abandon the original and proceed to orbit around a secondary one. Except for special reasons, the composer does not let this secondary tonal center equal the first in importance, for to do so would contribute toward disunity, equivalent to having two suns in our musical solar system. Hence the second is allowed to have temporary significance only.

Harmonic movement which leaves one area to focus its attention on another is progressive. Harmonic movement which, after having left an area, returns to it again is complete.

Throughout this study of musical form one particular scheme of harmonic movement has appeared more often than any other. In this scheme a tonal center is first established (I), then a progressive harmonic movement sets in which establishes a second tonal center with a dominant relationship to the first (V). This V is extended in time by a series of harmonies which may focus temporary attention on other scale degrees but which returns to V. At the return, however, V no longer acts as a secondary tonal center, but as a chord dependent on and pointing to I, the original tonal center. Finally, then, a complete harmonic movement on I takes place.

Progressive harmonic movement	Extension of V	Complete harmonic movement
I ——→ V	x x x x x x V	I

$$\underbrace{\qquad\qquad\qquad\qquad\qquad}_{V}$$

A common variant of the harmonic scheme outlined above comes about when III rather than V is the immediate goal of the first phase of the harmonic movement, a situation not limited to but occurring most often in the minor mode. Located midway between I and V, III acts like a steppingstone between them.

Progressive harmonic movement	Continuation of the harmonic movement	Complete harmonic movement
I ——→ III	x x x x x x x x V	I

The fundamental harmonic movement underlying the surface of any composition is called its tonal structure. Comprehension of the tonal structure of a composition is of paramount importance in attempting to understand its musical form. Nevertheless, it is not the only factor to be considered, for music displays a number of other contributing elements. Chief among these are cadences and the various relationships (variation, contrast, restatement) discernible in melody, rhythm, and texture. The interaction of all these, grouped together as *design*, is crucial to the form. A cadence, if perceived as relatively stronger than its surrounding cadences, can divide a composition into separate parts regardless of the tonal structure. (In practice, such a cadence is normally the perfect authentic.) Strong rhythmic or melodic contrast is capable of setting off a passage of music as a part in itself. It is just because design plays such an important role in the final form which a composition assumes that the basic tonal structure and its variant, outlined above, can be utilized

again and again in works of differing forms. We have seen how it is able to
serve the one-part form (Ex. 6-13), the three types of continuous binary
(simple Ex. 10-1; rounded, Ex. 6-3 and Ex. 10-3; balanced, Section 10-1), the
continuous ternary (Ex. 6-11), the sonata form (Section 11-1), and unique
forms (Ex. 15-1, Ex. 15-5). Beethoven introduced a further variant of this
tonal structure by substituting VI for V or III as the first goal of the progressive harmonic movement. In this version, the tonal structure has been utilized
in sonata form (Ex. 11-15) and even theme and variations (bass outline of
tonal structure, Section 7-6). Bach anticipated Beethoven's use of VI in the
triple fugue outlined in Section 14-7.

These tonal structures are, of course, identical or similar only in their
broadest outlines. The precise route taken when moving from I to V, or the
particular sequence of harmonies which prolong the V will, to be sure, vary
greatly among the different compositions. But the fundamental outline of this
harmonic scheme is found frequently enough to stamp it as the chief tonal
structure of the continuous forms.

Like continuous forms, sectional forms begin by establishing a tonal center.
But instead of a progressive movement to a secondary tonal center they make
a complete harmonic movement on I. Only then does the question of a second
tonal center present itself. There is little uniformity among the sectional forms
concerning the particular relationship of the secondary tonal center to the
original. In the typical classical rondo, it will in all likelihood express III or
V, but in a sectional ternary IV or VI is preferred as often. Indeed, not infrequently the original key, with a change to the opposite mode, is retained.

In concluding this study, it would perhaps be well to re-emphasize an
observation made at several points along the way. We cannot assume that
any great composer, in creating a piece of music, has proceeded along pre-
scribed lines with the intention of producing a work that conforms to an
established standard or model. It follows that if we approach the first movement of a symphony or the last movement of a concerto with a firmly fixed
notion that the former will necessarily be a sonata form and the latter a rondo
we will risk missing the meaning of the work. What might well be worse, we
will also be imposing arbitrary restrictions on the composer who has never
been under any compulsion to accept them. It would be far better to reserve
opinion until the piece has been carefully examined, preferably following the
six-step method of analysis outlined in Section 6-8. Moreover, it is usually
not particularly revealing or interesting simply to place the label "rondo" or
"sonata form" on a piece of music. Should the analysis cease with the discovery that a certain composition falls into a particular category of standard
forms, the student's musical insight will have increased but little. Rather,
aspects of the structure which contribute to the individuality of the work
should be sought out and identified. An interesting variant of the usual tonal

structure, an ingenious rearrangement of subsections in a recapitulation, a particularly lengthy episode in a fugue—features like these, once noted, can do much toward spurring the mind to the pursuit of even further degrees of understanding. It is one thing to note a variant from a customary practice, but it is much more to understand the reasons behind that variant. When the student finds himself pondering the significance of the note g♭ ‴ in m. 71 of Schubert's *Impromptu, Op. 90, No. 2,* and postulating for it a reason which takes into account the whole composition, he will know he is progressing toward musical maturity.

Appendix

SCHEDULE 1

Week	Reading	Exercises
1	Preface, Chapter 1, Chapter 2	Nos. 1–5
2	Chapter 3	Nos. 1–5
	Chapter 4	No. 1
3	Chapter 5	Nos. 1–6
4	Chapter 6, sections 6-1–6-5	Nos. 1–7
5	Chapter 6, sections 6-6–6-10	No. 8
6	Chapter 7, sections 7-1–7-7	Nos. 1–4
7	Chapter 7, sections 7-8–7-10	Nos. 5–8
	Chapter 8, sections 8-1–8-2	Nos. 1–6
8	Chapter 8, sections 8-3–8-9	Nos. 7–12
9	Chapter 9	Nos. 1–5
10	Chapter 10	Nos. 1–4
	Chapter 11, sections 11-1–11-2	No. 1
11	Chapter 11, sections 11-3–11-7	Nos. 2–9
12	Chapter 12, section 12-3	Nos. 4–8
	Chapter 13, section 13-1	No. 1
13	Chapter 13, section 13-2	No. 2
	Chapter 15, Chapter 16	
14		No. 1 (Chapter 15)

SCHEDULE 2

Week	First Term Reading and Exercises	Week	Second Term Reading and Exercises
1	Preface, Chapter 1 Chapter 2, sections 2-1–2-4	1–2	Chapter 9
2	Chapter 2, sections 2-5–2-6	3	Chapter 10
3	Chapter 3	4–5	Chapter 11
4	Chapter 4	6	Chapter 12
5–6	Chapter 5	7–8	Chapter 13
7–9	Chapter 6	9–11	Chapter 14
10–11	Chapter 7	12–13	Chapter 15
12–13	Chapter 8	14	Chapter 16
14	Review Chapters 1–8		Review Chapters 1–15

INDEX OF COMPOSERS
AND COMPOSITIONS

307

SUBJECT INDEX

Boldface numbers indicate definitions or extended discussions.

315